James Webb is a business and orga   and researcher, having previously held senior management positions in the pharmaceutical and communications industries. He has worked in the field of business and personal performance for many years and has written and presented extensively on the subject. James has a particular interest in supporting managers in the practicalities of being more effective.

PUTTING
MANAGEMENT
BACK INTO
PERFORMANCE

a handbook for
managers and supervisors

JAMES WEBB

ALLEN&UNWIN

First published in 2003

83 Alexander Street,
Crows Nest NSW 2065 Australia
Phone: (61 2) 8425 0100
Fax: (61 2) 9906 2218
E-mail: info@allenandunwin.com
Web: www.allenandunwin.com

National Library of Australia
Cataloguing-in-Publication entry:

Webb, James, 1941- .
    Putting management back into performance : a handbook for
    managers and supervisors.

    Bibliography.
    Includes index.
    ISBN 1 86508 965 6.

    1. Performance - Management. 2. Personnel management.
    I. Title

658.312

Set in 11/14 pt Adobe Caslon by Midland Typesetters, Maryborough

10 9 8 7 6 5 4 3 2 1

Contents

Acknowledgments

The following individuals and organisations have been instrumental in the long development of the ideas presented in this book and to them I owe a debt of thanks.

Steve Harris provided me with an early, first-hand glimpse of what good performance management looks like; Wyndham & Associates introduced me to the benefits of behavioural rehearsal in the development of performance management skills; John O'Connell and Dr Paul Walsh respectively awakened and reinforced my interest in work process and measurement. Colleague and friend, Kerrie Murray, has been an inspiration in the interpersonal side of performance management; Cheryl Hannah has provided insights and ideas to challenge and extend my thinking. Ideas need to be tested in the workplace and I am grateful to all the organisations and their people who have shared their experiences and wisdom, particularly the management and staff of Coal & Allied Industries (part of Riotinto Coal) for allowing me to spend two years in the field refining many ideas and practices; and, finally, to those who have, over the years, allowed me to manage them and have been tolerant of my experimentation.

I am also grateful to my many consulting colleagues who have shared their ideas and experiences, which I hope have been treated well in this book. Tim Edwards of Business and Professional Publishing patiently encouraged my foray into business publishing and helped to focus my initial ideas. Ian Bowring, Emma Singer and Alex Nahlous of Allen & Unwin have had the unenviable task of taking over the manuscript at a late stage and have been sympathetic to my intentions and ideas while guiding me towards a book of wider appeal than the original. My wife, Nola Webb, has accepted my obsession, mental absences and occasional tantrums with serenity and helped me back from bouts of self-doubt.

Preface

I wrote this book for two main reasons, one to do with the performance of Australian enterprise and the other to do with the quality of work life for Australians.

First, despite continuing developments in technology, the principal wealth-creating component in enterprise is people-related, yet my observations led me to conclude that human potential is very often wasted and almost invariably underutilised. One of the most valuable points of leverage is each person's direct manager or supervisor and, by strengthening the effectiveness of this relationship, my desire has been to enable more successful, more sustainable enterprises and a greater return for all stakeholders.

Second, gains made in the quality of work life and in the quality of life generally are being reversed by an economic rationalism that, according to indicators, is eroding the health and welfare of the employed. Many of these social results run contrary to the values that have come to be the norm and which are still espoused by those in power. Although no more or less important than the rest, there is one group finding it particularly tough because they are at the interface of economic and social policy and the people affected. This group is management who, as well as being the 'meat in the sandwich', is confronted by a workplace that in many ways seems to be growing less and less manageable.

Managing the work performance of people is the work of managers and it is work that requires certain methods and skills. Some managers do it well while some do it less well. One of the internal resources available to support managers with the necessary methods and skills are the Organisation/Human Resources/Personnel specialists. Overwhelmingly, they have failed. These specialists have introduced performance management systems but these 'systems' have been, in the main, nothing more than a personnel process for remuneration decisions, an input to training needs and a panacea for dealing with difficult employees; they have not been a major contributor to individual and enterprise performance. Some have, commendably, included a planning component but it is usually far removed from the realities of business planning conducted by the enterprise.

This book is an attempt to acknowledge the role of managers and to provide some ideas, methods and tools to support them in the better management of their people towards meaningful results in a dynamic and ever-changing workplace. Some of the methods and skills are basic, some are more complex, but it is an attempt to treat performance management as a true system, linked to the performance of the enterprise and the well-being of the individual.

James Webb
Bungendore, May 2003

Introduction

This book sets out to develop the ability of managers like you to manage the performance of your people more effectively. To achieve this we follow three interwoven methods—knowledge and understanding, management processes and management skills.

Although 'doing' is the desired end point of your journey, if you have an *understanding* of the reasons behind a particular method you are better able to apply it, adapt it or devise your own. This enhances the 'doing'. Effective management is very much about what you do as well as how you do it, so all the management tasks are presented in a *step-by-step process* format. These processes apply to both business tasks and people-management tasks. By making use of the ideas and methods in this book you will become more *skilled* in your role of managing your people's performance.

Because managers like you are increasingly busy, it's hard to keep new management methods and techniques in your head as you work. For that reason we include *tools and templates* which you can use on the job to jog your memory, allowing you to concentrate on the content and the people.

Part I describes the changes in the working environment that affect the ability of managers to manage the performance of their people and then presents a blueprint for putting 'management' back into performance management. In particular we look at emerging forces that seem to have caught management in the cross-fire. On one hand, we have the growth of performance management 'systems' where the expectations of the system are frequently at odds with the demands of producing performance in the workplace; on the other, we have the old, dominant assumptions about work, workers and management which conflict significantly with today's 'new reality'. The blueprint for action is a series of seven strategies to ensure that gains made in one area are not lost in others. The execution of these strategies is dealt with in subsequent parts of the book.

Part II begins the process of on-the-job management of perform- ance, moving in logical fashion through the steps of assigning work, performance planning, employee development and using performance data, and finishing with the understanding and management of work as an 'open system'.

In Part III the focus is still on-the-job management but the emphasis shifts to the more intense interpersonal interactions involved in performance feedback, performance coaching and the management of difficult performers.

Part IV tackles the complex aspects of formal review processes, or 'appraisal'. The balance now shifts from a focus on achieving results to meeting the needs of various organisational systems, such as staff evalu- ations, remuneration and training and development. The formal review process requires from you a special set of skills, in addition to those already acquired.

Finally, Part V describes some of the more successful ways of ensuring that you take your newly developed knowledge, skills and management processes back to the job and *make them work* for you, for your people and for the enterprise.

The book takes you through a process of learning by way of discovery and refinement. This means that in each chapter you will discover further refinements of methods and skills introduced in earlier chapters. In this way you are not overloaded in any chapter and the refinements you encounter are in the context of the practical application.

To illustrate the application of the ideas presented, the book uses extensive examples of situations drawn from a composite of my organ- isational experiences. In some of these examples we present dialogue, which is intended to illustrate the principles in action, not to provide a script for you to use in similar circumstances. In several sections activi- ties are included. These are an opportunity for you to challenge your learning to date by relating your learning to your own workplace, or by resolving a sample problem.

Because the management of work performance touches all aspects of enterprise performance we have had to limit our coverage to our chosen topic, which is the management of performance through *people*. Thus, although we refer frequently to performance management systems, this book won't show you how to design an administrative system for performance management. Again, we talk about work design but we don't have the space to show you what changes to make to ineffective work design and processes. Nonetheless, as a result of putting some of the ideas into practice, you will be better placed to identify opportunities for work improvement.

Part I

Putting 'Management' Back into Performance

Part 1 sets up the premise for the rest of the book so the focus is more on understanding than doing. The areas of understanding addressed include the nature of the management environment and an overview of a broad-based approach to better performance management.

The environment in which managers like yourself manage is changing quite significantly and you will be better equipped if you know what those changes are, how they affect you and what you can do to work with them more effectively. Chapter 1 outlines the changes and their impact on performance management while Chapter 2 provides a blueprint for an overall approach for individual managers towards more effective management.

1 State of play

Why should you, as a manager, read this book? This chapter develops a range of answers to this question but two basic reasons stand out. First, 70–90 per cent of public and private sector enterprises have some form of centrally formalised system of performance management and most of these have at least one stakeholder group that is not happy with its performance management system. While managers may not be the architects of these performance management systems, they are at the front line in the management of people's performance and therefore affected by any centralised systematisation of the role.

Second, and more important perhaps, managers are under increasing pressure to achieve higher performance from fewer resources, in an increasingly dynamic and unpredictable operating environment, through a workforce that is becoming increasingly unmanageable! This means that, system or no system, any ways that help managers to be more effective and efficient should be of value.

An introduction to performance management

As we shall see, performance management covers a wide spectrum of ideas and we need to begin by establishing some common understanding. First, we offer a definition of the term, followed by a look at the extent to which the practice exists in Australia and what various groups of users think of it.

Performance management defined

In the literature, 'performance management' of individuals is referred to mostly as 'performance appraisal'—that is, formally *reviewing and evaluating or assessing* a subordinate, usually at the end of the planning year. It is common for a *skills development* component to be included to ensure that the employee can meet performance targets. Some include a *planning* component at the beginning of the period, where goals are agreed to and from which a skills-development plan may arise. Overall, it is a formalised or deliberate process mandated by executive management, and is a uniform practice throughout the organisation.

A broader and more useful approach is to treat performance management as the day-to-day management of the performance of an individual or a work group, by both the immediate manager and the individual employees themselves. This book is largely a result of the fact that this fundamental role of managers is, at best, downplayed and, at worst, ignored by many authors on the subject of performance management.

The state of performance management in Australia

By understanding how well performance management is practised we can get some idea of where improvements can be made, and this translates into strategies for individual managers who want to be more effective. We'll look at this from two perspectives: the extent of use of formalised performance management systems, and what users think about performance management in their organisation.

Use of formalised systems
A number of surveys have looked at the extent to which formalised performance management is used, in both private and public sector organisations. In 1986, 46 per cent of large companies had a formal appraisal scheme and by 1999 this had risen to 90 per cent of large private and public enterprises. Along with the increase in the number of organisations using systems, the span of their usage has widened to include management and non-management staff and professional, technical and clerical employees.

What users think
Studies that look at manager and employee views on performance management deal mostly with formal performance systems and the subject of

appraisal. Over a period of five years (1994 to 1998) a colleague and I interviewed, observed and/or surveyed managers and employees from thirty public and private sector Australian organisations, ranging in size from 100 to 10 000 employees, in relation to performance management, both formal and on the job.[1] The results indicate that different groups within an organisation have different views of what performance management is and what it should achieve. Inevitably, this leads to some degree of un-met expectations by all, including those most directly involved—managers and their employees.

Table 1.1 is a summary of some of the key points from our research, the results of which have been consistently reinforced in my work with organisations, right up to the present time, and are also in line with other published research. What the summary shows, and what is quite palpable in the majority of workplaces, is a tension between performance management systems and the needs of day-to-day performance management. In the main, systems do not greatly help performance but at the same time require compliance. Increased reliance on performance management systems, at the expense of attention and resources given to on-the-job management, means that good management has been progressively taken out of the management of performance.

Emergence of the 'unmanageable' workplace

Compounding the systemic dilution of on-the-job performance management skills and processes is the impact of the social and business evolution of work and workplace. Society's expectations of work are changing and there have been significant shifts in the contract between society and employers and in the make-up of the workforce. This is the *social evolution*. Globalisation and advances in communications technology have had a profound impact on business and consumer expectations, all of which have affected the nature of work. This is the *business evolution*. The events of social and business evolution have created a workforce whose motivation and commitment vary widely, and some have come to regard this workforce as less 'manageable'. In one study, only one in five of 350 top executives worldwide felt prepared to manage tomorrow's organisations.[2]

A significant influence on the ability of managers to manage performance is the extent to which they are caught between the 'old

Table 1.1 The state of performance management in Australian organisations: predominant views of managers and staff

Formalised systems

The views of managers

Positive views	Negative views
• provides a structure for individual performance planning • provides targets against which to assess people • provides hard evidence to act against poor performers	• is an administrative impost; time-consuming • has little impact on work performance over the year • is rigid, not responsive to day-to-day realities of the workplace • is interpersonally challenging—formalised assessments, ratings, performance counselling (discipline)

The views of employees

• provides some role or goal clarity • links individuals to the bigger picture • provides a planning framework • ensures at least a minimum of feedback	• mistrust the intentions of (senior) management • system itself is not always valid or reliable • is rigid, not responsive to day-to-day realities of the workplace • own manager is incapable of administering the system effectively • open to unfair treatment • formal assessment is an intimidating experience

Day-to-day performance management

The views of managers

• mostly clear about their own roles and goals • have reasonable degree of control over at least some areas of performance	• not adequately skilled in business planning • not adequately skilled in understanding and responding to performance data • work becoming more complex, harder to manage • performance interactions can be difficult (ranging from dealing with difficult performers to giving positive feedback)

The views of employees	
Positive views	Negative views
• mostly clear about their own roles and goals	• work processes often rigid and not responsive to needs of the work
• believe they are making a difference 'out in the market or community'	• little recognition from own manager; feel undervalued
• when allowed to do their best, work is very motivating	• little on-the-job feedback from own manager
• confident in own abilities	• not enough on-the-job performance support from own manager (e.g. coaching)
	• not kept up to date with enterprise plans and performance

assumptions'—about work, workers and management—and the 'new reality'. The decisions that we make about how to manage the enterprise and the performance of our people are based on assumptions about the way things supposedly are. These assumptions are often based on a reality that did once exist but has either ceased to exist or is in the process of disappearing. Two common examples of the tensions brought on by social and business evolution are:

1. We plan for a stable, predictable environment with controllable outcomes when we work in a dynamic, less predictable environment with emergent outcomes.
2. We manage our people, assuming that they are company-loyal and desire a long career with the company when they are self-loyal and plan to develop their own careers through many companies.

The longer the management model—that is, the way managers manage their people, their management practices and their organisational systems—is based on a workplace that doesn't exist, the more under pressure managers will be in trying to meet performance expectations.

References
1. J. Webb & K. Murray. *Performance Management—Culture and Counter-culture*. Presented at the Australian Human Resources Institute, Human Resources Week Conference, Canberra, August 1999.
2. Andersen Consulting, *Vision 2010: Designing tomorrow's organisation* at <www.ac.com>.

2 Putting 'management' back into performance

Each chapter in this book deals with specific aspects of management development and performance management practices. Before going any further, however, we need to position your development process in an integrated approach to ensure that the knowledge, skills and methods that you develop can be put into practice. The following seven strategies represent a useful and achievable way for you to put 'management' back into performance management.

- Strategy 1 Assume the performance management role
- Strategy 2 Strengthen your management capability
- Strategy 3 Establish effective on-the-job performance management systems and processes
- Strategy 4 Establish an effective approach to performance interactions
- Strategy 5 Manage the 'unmanageable'
- Strategy 6 Create a performance management culture
- Strategy 7 Manage the change to a high-performance workplace

Strategy 1 Assume the performance management role

It seems redundant to say that you should assume the performance management role because, after all, that's your job, isn't it? But it is common enough for some managers to take this part of their responsibility pretty lightly and therefore its importance needs to be stressed.

Common reasons for not fully assuming the responsibility of day-to-day management include:

- 'That's what we have a performance management system for.'
- 'That's the role of Human Resources/Personnel.'
- 'People know their job and don't need my help.'
- 'Nothing's changed since last year so everyone just keeps doing the same.'
- 'I'm busy enough doing my own work.'

No matter how sophisticated a system is introduced or how well your people know their work, your role as manager is fundamental to facilitating optimum work performance and work fulfilment of individuals and groups. What may vary is the nature of the support that you bring, according to the performance level of each individual.

Strategy 2 Strengthen your management capability

To manage your people's performance effectively you need to have knowledge and skills in two areas—business and people. This book will help you to develop your knowledge capability in these two areas but your skills capability can only be developed by *doing*. Important issues that need to be considered first are your level of *commitment*, your level of *effort* and the acquisition of *core people-management skills*.

Commitment

The starting point of becoming a more capable manager is that you must want to do it and you must be prepared for whatever it takes. Commitment requires (a) that you have a worthwhile reason and (b) that you acknowledge the risks. It has been claimed that the principal reason performance systems fail is *low management commitment*, but this is generally because systems are seen by managers to be of no help. Managers who believe they can make a difference are more likely to undertake personal development, which improves their work group's performance and strengthens their managers' commitment (see Figure 2.1). So, to start, you have to believe that you can achieve something more.

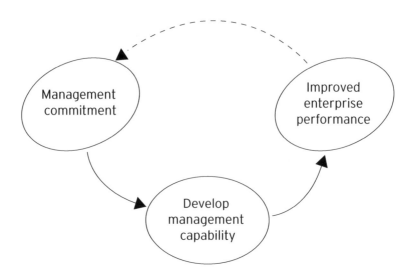

Figure 2.1 The commitment–capability cycle of managing performance

It is also important to acknowledge the potential risks; otherwise you are not truly committed. These might include taking personal risks with new behaviours, not getting the support of your own manager, needing extra time and the resistance of your staff.

Effort

You've seen that sign: 'Our new performance management scheme— do a good job and you get to keep it!' This always gets a smile but it is often a symbol of a management culture that believes that people are the 'performance problem' and it requires a 'stick and carrot' approach to bring them into line. Although people are the easier target, the more common problems are your management, your products, your service or your work practices and systems, and all of these take more effort than the 'stick and carrot' technique.

Managing your people's performance well takes effort and it's when we can't make the effort that we resort to positive ('carrot') and negative ('stick') sanctions. 'Stick' sanctions include ignoring, denigrating or humiliating an employee, disadvantaging by withholding high-value work or career opportunities and threatening to dismiss. 'Carrot' sanctions include reward incentive schemes, bonuses, annual pay increments linked to annual appraisal, hero/heroine status and favoured treatment. Both approaches have been shown to be short-term motivators only, at best.

Core people-management skills

There is a set of core people-management skills that underpins effective interactions with your staff and is critical to success in performance-related interactions. Because these basic skills are covered in a multitude of other books, we restrict ourselves in this book to introducing special-ised performance-related interpersonal skills.

Nonetheless, you should be skilled in the fundamentals so obtain some basic information or training on the following personal and inter-personal skills—managing differences, questioning and listening, and bias and assumptions.

Managing differences

Each individual is different and the more you can manage each one for their unique qualities and character, the better they will perform. Differences that are worth managing include personal values, ethnic cultural values, work preferences and abilities, and psychological and behavioural preferences (commonly measured by the Myers-Briggs Type Indicator™ and the DiSC Behavioural Profile™ respectively).

Questioning and listening

Even before you begin to learn the specific skills of questioning and active listening, there is one fundamental rule you can take on board right now. Because of their position of authority and assumed wisdom, managers are far more likely to 'tell' than to ask or listen. This puts them at risk of poor communication and ineffective performance management. So, whatever specific skills you acquire, start now to practise the basic rule of 'ask and listen more, tell less'.

Bias and assumptions

Bias and assumptions will turn more performance interactions upside down than any other personal skills or attributes you may have. Your biases predetermine your reality of *how things or people are*, and your assumptions are the conclusions you draw about *how things happen or why people do things*. These human attributes are useful shortcuts to making sense of our world, particularly the cause–effect relationships between events, but when our biases and assumptions are wrong we can create a lot of strife for ourselves, our employees and our business.

Humans have a strong, almost uncontrollable tendency to see a cause–effect relationship between two events, even when they may be coincidental—this is our *assumption*. What we choose as the 'cause' component will be determined largely by our own *biases*. So, when a manager says to an employee who is late for work 'We need to talk about your attitude to work', the manager is *assuming* that arriving late means the employee has a bad attitude ('All employees have bad attitudes, don't they?'—the manager's *bias*).

You can't avoid having biases, but you can do some things to reduce their negative effects, and you can significantly reduce your misuse of assumptions.

- Know yourself—what are your biases and when and how often do you rely on your assumptions?
- Take care to gather factual information.
- Check that your *selection* of information has not been biased.
- Keep an open mind and take time to investigate or to hear the employee fully.
- Check your motivation before you act (including speaking) in critical situations.

Because there is an inbuilt tension in the nature of performance interactions, we need to be sure that we do not always assume employees are trying to defend themselves, and employees need to be certain they do not always assume that we are trying to downgrade their performance.

Strategy 3   Establish effective on-the-job performance management systems and processes

No matter how well you develop your own abilities, you will be hamstrung in your management unless you have effective business systems and processes for on-the-job management of performance. Such systems and processes might include planning, measurement, monitoring and performance data analysis. Throughout this book, systems and processes are presented hand in hand with management knowledge and skills. The main reason for systems and processes is to illustrate the use of the skills in practice; where you have no comparable systems and processes of your own, you may also wish to use or adapt these.

Business systems and processes support performance management in a number of ways, which we can conveniently group into management support, employee support and business support.

- *Management support* provides you with a basis for assigning work, setting targets or other performance parameters, monitoring performance and intervening appropriately to support individuals.
- *Employee support* gives your people a clear focus, an ability to discuss the pros and cons of the methods, a greater degree of control or influence over their own performance and the means to self-manage their work.
- *Business support* provides greater predictability and consistency of performance, a logical basis on which to plan and a framework for improved performance based on clear plans, good data and good analysis methods.

Strategy 4 Establish an effective approach to performance interactions

Each time you interact with an employee on a performance-related matter is a 'moment of truth' because every interaction has the potential to affect the employee's performance, for better or for worse. What you bring to such interactions is your abilities in business and performance management, your work content ability and your people-management ability. This strategy deals with people management.

Performance interactions will include formal meetings such as assigning new objectives for the year, but most will be informal on-the-job chats about work. Chapters 5 to 10 provide specific process and skill guidelines for particular interactions, but the overriding requirements that you should consider are:

- a facilitative approach;
- a discussion structure; and
- an agreement pathway.

A facilitative approach

Adopting a facilitative approach means that you take on the role of helping and guiding the process to a successful outcome, rather than issuing instructions, providing all the knowledge and making the decisions. Your aims in facilitating the process are to bring out the best in your employees and, progressively, to enable them to do more for themselves—that is, you enable their learning. Coaching, as described in later chapters, is a facilitative approach to performance.

For a facilitative approach to be effective, you need to exercise certain attributes and skills of your own.

Trustworthiness

Your employees won't be forthcoming with ideas and commitments if there is a lack of trust. Build trust by keeping to commitments about the conduct of the meeting—for example, don't switch into blame when you've said that this meeting is not about blame.

Supportiveness

Generally speaking, an employee in a state of discomfort will not contribute optimally to the interaction. You can avoid discomfort in your employees by reducing their perceptions of judgment, punishment or overly demanding tasks or objectives and replacing them with perceptions of support and understanding. In some cases you will need to maintain a controlled level of stress—for example, to enable an employee to address an issue more creatively, or for a difficult performer to participate.

Compassion and firmness

Sometimes a discussion is brought to a standstill because the situation becomes difficult for the employee. Difficulties may include tears, anger, self-pity and resistance to change. You should be compassionate while at the same time working firmly towards outcomes that meet the needs of both of you. Chapter 7 provides a process for this.

Questioning and listening

Two of the key skills in adopting a facilitative approach are questioning and listening. If you are going to help employees to solve their problems, you must be willing to step back from being the expert and to ask and listen in order to help them express and test their own ideas.

A discussion structure

One of the best things you can do to create more successful performance interactions is to have clear in your mind the *outcomes* you want to achieve and your *process* of getting there. Outcomes might include the performance objective, the problem to be solved or employees learning to help themselves more effectively in the future.

When it comes to planned process steps, the following approach brings successful results, even for informal performance interactions. The reasons for its value include:

- You stay on track, even if the meeting is disruptive.
- You will cover all you intended.
- You can focus on the person and the performance.
- You are more likely to reach agreement.
- Actions are more likely to be followed up.

These four steps provide a useful and proven discussion or meeting structure.

1. Beforehand
   - If your employee needs to prepare, give advance notice and be specific about the purpose and outcomes of the meeting.
2. Set-up
   - Confirm the purpose of the discussion.
   - Outline the outcomes and process or agenda.
   - Set time expectations.
3. Business of the meeting
   - Stay with the process or agenda. Avoid being drawn off into issues not relevant to the purpose or outcome.
   - Regularly check you are on track.
   - Anchor milestones reached by confirming each agreement along the way. This process creates a sense of mutual achievement and progressively improves the effectiveness of the interaction.

4. Completion of the meeting
   • Confirm outcomes that are reached and agreed, so that you have a shared understanding.
   • Agree follow-up actions. Be specific about who will do what and the time and other measurement dimensions.

Reaching agreement

You are far more likely to achieve sustained performance improvement in your people by reaching agreement with them than by imposing your will or by 'stick and carrot'. Employees who agree with the 'why', the 'what' and the 'how' will produce far greater results than those who disagree or don't even understand. During all stages of the performance cycle it is critical to reach agreement, although the content of the agreement may vary. For example, at Work Assignment, you both have to agree on the objectives, whereas in coaching you need to agree on changed behaviours or practices.

In discussing how to reach agreement we look first at potential barriers before exploring some of the steps and skills.

Barriers to reaching agreement

Potential barriers will vary according to the situation—for example, whether you are setting up a performance agreement or conducting a formal evaluation. What we can pull out of this is some generalised barriers.

Assuming it is automatic
Many managers assume that when they issue a performance requirement it is automatically accepted, but compliance does not necessarily mean agreement.

Employee resistance to the work
• The employee doesn't accept the value or rightness of the outcome and/or the method.
• The employee finds the work too challenging or uncomfortable.
• The employee fears failure, which might adversely affect reputation, remuneration or career.

Manager's ability

A manager's poor communication skills may result in an employee agreeing to the wrong things. For example, manager and employee may end up with different understandings of the goal, the method or accountability. Agreement may also be difficult to reach when managers can't act independently of their bias or prejudice.

Employee resistance to the result

A common barrier to agreement occurs when employees may agree that their performance is less than required but say that they were not responsible. The cause may be attributed to unplanned events, other people and you, all of which they regard as outside the requirement of the work. Another form of resistance may occur during formal evaluation where an employee agrees with the performance but not the attached evaluation.

Methods of reaching agreement

We can approach agreement along two pathways—a checklist or a model.

Checklist for reaching agreement

Here are some useful ideas suggested by other managers.

- Always check with the employee, don't assume.
- Use two-way communication, including questioning and listening.
- Fully understand the employee's perspective before attempting to change it.
- Be willing to put in the effort to reach agreement.
- Be willing to negotiate towards a 'win–win' outcome.
- Give the employee the 'why', the 'what' and the 'how'.

An agreement model

A model is a series of events that are connected to each other. Successful models of agreement, as used in negotiation, dispute resolution and selling, have in common a certain series of steps. The principle of the agreement model presented in Figure 2.2 is that final agreement on the chosen issue is far more likely if the process follows a sequence of five steps. The logic of the model is discussed in Chapter 7—here we present a simple example of the model in action.

Model	Model in action
Step 1 Agree to Participate	The employee agrees to discuss an additional task.
Step 2 Agree the Situation	Manager and employee discuss and agree that there has been a reduction in supervision of fare-paying compliance.
Step 3 Agree the Implication	They discuss and agree that fare evasion is likely to increase.
Step 4 Agree the Resolution	They discuss a range of ways to prevent fare evasion and agree what task the employee will undertake.
Step 5 Agree the Integration	They discuss and agree necessary changes to the employee's role and changes to the team to support the new task.

Figure 2.2 The agreement model in action

Strategy 5 Manage the 'unmanageable'

We noted in Chapter 1 the degree of tension between the old assumptions about work and the workforce and today's new reality, leading to a workplace that some have described as 'unmanageable'. The first step to regaining some management control is to understand the nature and degree of such tensions in your workplace. Only by knowing your own situation can you decide on the nature and extent of action required. Appendix 1 provides a useful diagnostic tool to help you do this.

Table 2.1 provides guidelines to the sort of changes to performance management that are needed to manage today's work and workforce. It is not an exhaustive list so, once you get the thrust of it, you should be able to come up with your own 'more of/less of' list.

To absorb these guidelines fully and understand how to adapt them to your own needs, imagine yourself in a situation that is more extreme than you currently envisage your own to be. Perhaps think of yourself suddenly put in charge of a business under serious threat, a situation that neither you nor the business has encountered before, where the dynamics seem to be continually changing. You can't rescue the business; only your people can, with your management and leadership. What would you do to manage the performance of this team?

Table 2.1 Guidelines for managing today's 'unmanageable' work and workforce

Manage with more . . .	Manage with less . . .
• Big picture direction	• Allocation of work without any explanation
• Clarity of what is expected	• Assumption that they should know
• Focus on outcome, not on activity alone	• Rigid activity requirements that are not linked to specific levels of outcome; rigid 12-month goals; reports that don't add value
• Integration across role and functional boundaries	• Sticking to their own job, 'silo' protection—competition with other functions
• Recognition of teamwork	• Competition between colleagues
• Discretion to act locally	• Reliance on you to make or approve key decisions, to be the source of all information and expertise
• Recognition for managed risk-taking, allowance for mistakes	• Advocating risk aversion, punishing mistakes, shooting the messanger
• Personal support—feedback, coaching; influence and leadership	• Supervisor/overseer role; command and control
• Physical support—information, systems, methods, tools, other resources	• Reliance on people to make up the slack
• Development to go beyond current needs and to enhance work fulfilment and career development	• Sufficient development to serve only the current need
• Management by values and principles	• Management by rules
• Recognise and manage differences	• 'One size fits all' style
• Trust	• Distrust
• Partnership between you and your people	• 'Them and us'

Strategy 6 Create a performance management culture

'Culture' in this context refers to the collective ideas we have about the right or best ways to go about managing the performance of people, ideas that lead to how we behave and the decisions we make. Such a culture usually arises by people learning 'what gets recognised and rewarded around here' and is expressed mostly as *values*—for example, 'Good work gets recognised'.

Why create a performance management culture? Because the prevailing culture determines behaviours and decisions and we have to be sure that it supports good performance management practices rather than runs counter to them. For example, in a supportive culture managers and work colleagues always give recognition to someone who does a good job, leading to the associated belief that 'Good work gets recognised'. In a non-supportive culture, no matter how good a job someone does, there is never any recognition of it (but it is mentioned when you do a bad job). Jokes are symbols of cultures and the relevant joke here is 'You know you're doing a good job if the boss hasn't said anything'.

Establishing a supportive culture

Working with culture change in a whole organisation can be a long and complex process, but you can create and sustain your own local performance culture by simply applying the method of 'what gets recognised and rewarded around here'. The method has three steps:

1. Define the sort of culture that will support performance in your work group or business unit.
2. Check on what the current culture is.
3. Form a plan to create or sustain your desired culture.

What does a supportive culture look like?
Start by thinking about what sort of beliefs and behaviours your people should demonstrate in order to fulfil your idea of a high-performing work group. You might ask yourself (and/or your team): 'If my team was performing at their best, (a) what would be their beliefs and (b) what would they be doing (their behaviours)?' Table 2.2, columns A and B, provide some examples. If your organisation has a published set of values or beliefs, start out by checking what sort of ideas already exist.

Table 2.2 Examples of the process of defining and establishing a performance culture

A Business or organisational need	B Your desired culture: what you want your people to believe	C What you do to create and sustain your desired culture
• Increased productivity and quality • People are self-motivated to do their very best work • People are more fulfilled by their work	'Good work gets recognised'	• You do good work • You openly recognise and reward good work by your employees • 'Employee of the month'
• Achieve more effective outcomes of decisions • Speed up customer service by devolving decision-making	'Make decisions, and learn'	• You lead by example • You train your people to make decisions • You support their decision-making and help them to learn from their successes and their mistakes

What is the current culture?

Before you launch into creating your desired culture, it would be good to look at the current culture in relation to the desired culture. If your desired culture already exists, your focus is on sustaining it. If, on the other hand, there is a counter-culture, you have the job of undoing the old one before, or in the process of, creating the new. Unless you have an entrenched counter-culture it is always more effective to build upon the culture that already exists.

There are two ways you can approach this step—you can either observe what your people actually do (their behaviours) and/or you can meet with your team and test the current culture. Here's a suggestion for testing with the team.

1. Taking one issue (belief/value/behaviour) at a time, do they believe that the idea is a 'right' one?
2. How well do they think the idea is currently put into practice—is it something that is generally recognised or rewarded, or does it draw negative sanctions?

Desired cultural idea
'Make decisions, and learn'

1. **Is it a good or 'right' idea?**
✓ *It will speed up customer service.*
✓ *It will give us greater pride in our work.*

2. **Is it aligned/not aligned with the actual culture?**
✗ *Mistakes are punished.*
✗ *We have risk-averse procedures.*

Figure 2.3 Testing the desired and current performance culture

In the example shown in Figure 2.3, the team supports the idea but experience the reality to be different. *You* may be the cause of the reality or it may be created at a higher level. When the corporate values, as practised, are not the values that are presented, front-line managers are often caught in the cross-fire.

Plan your desired culture

At this stage you either sustain the culture you have or create something new. Remember, words are not enough; you need to create or sustain your culture by actions—what you do, the processes and practices you create or support—as shown in column C in Table 2.2. Note also that your actions need to be consistent so your people can trust that a certain action will always gets a certain response, and sustained over time as they will look to see if you are for real.

If your cultural ideas are not supported by corporate cultural practices (although you are in line with their intent), come back to what you can *do locally* and what you can *influence corporately*.

Strategy 7 Manage the change to a high-performance workplace

As soon as you start to improve things you are embarking on a change process and for that you need to be guided by some basic rules on implementing change. The final chapter deals with the detail of change management—once you have absorbed the preceding chapters and decided what changes you want to make.

Part II

Managing on the Job— Business Performance

Parts II and III deal with managing on the job—managing *business* performance and managing *people* performance. The distinction is an artificial one because, in achieving results through people, both parts are intertwined—you can't manage one without the other. The areas are considered separately simply for *emphasis*.

On-the-job management of people and their performance is the real work of management and cannot be replaced by what are commonly known as 'performance appraisal systems'. The arrangement of the chapters in Parts II and III (see diagram) is based on a real system of managing work performance. In this system, individual work is derived from enterprise goals and the achievement of work objectives is evaluated against their contribution to the enterprise.

Chapter 3 covers the beginning of the performance cycle, Work Assignment and work planning, which are the foundations of effective employee performance. Chapter 4 takes the principles of Chapter 3 and applies them to the two specific areas of employee development and formal performance agreements.

Once the work is under way, you need to be able to understand and respond appropriately to performance data generated by your employees, and this is covered in Chapter 5.

Chapter 6 makes a case for understanding and managing work as an open system and provides practical guidelines for doing so. The open system model applies to both business and people management but it's included at the end of Part II for two reasons: (1) so that you already have the fundamentals under your belt and (2) to provide a realistic context in

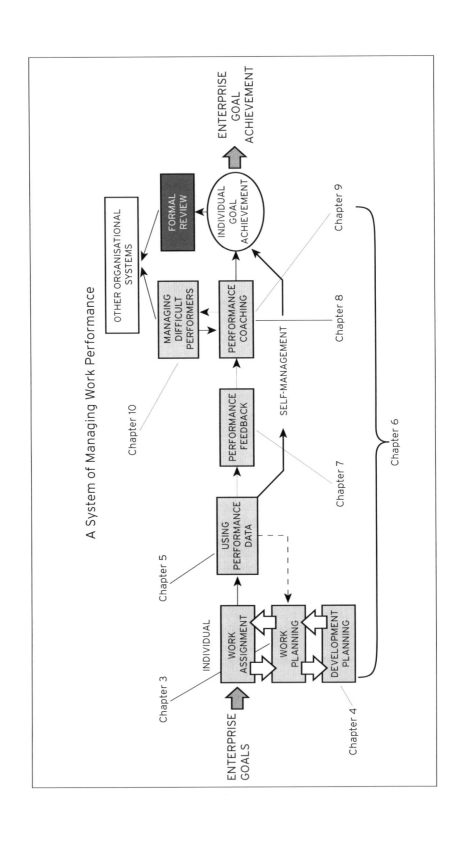

A System of Managing Work Performance

ENTERPRISE GOALS

Chapter 3

INDIVIDUAL

WORK ASSIGNMENT

WORK PLANNING

DEVELOPMENT PLANNING

Chapter 4

Chapter 5

USING PERFORMANCE DATA

PERFORMANCE FEEDBACK

SELF-MANAGEMENT

Chapter 7

Chapter 6

MANAGING DIFFICULT PERFORMERS

PERFORMANCE COACHING

Chapter 8

Chapter 9

Chapter 10

OTHER ORGANISATIONAL SYSTEMS

FORMAL REVIEW

INDIVIDUAL GOAL ACHIEVEMENT

ENTERPRISE GOAL ACHIEVEMENT

which to integrate the ideas about interacting with people in relation to their performance.

As each subsequent chapter is read, you will notice that we draw a number of lessons that refer back to earlier chapters. For example, when considering a good approach to feedback, you will find that a lot depends on the quality of Work Assignment in the first place. The consequence of this approach is that we attempt to provide basic information in each chapter and then build upon that information in subsequent chapters as the need for further refinement becomes apparent.

3 Off to a good start!— Work Assignment and Planning

You've probably heard the expression 'Garbage in—garbage out'. That expression could also apply to work performance because what your people achieve is only as good as how well you assign their work and facilitate their work planning in the first place. This principle is underscored by the large number of performance disputes that can be traced back to poor Work Assignment.

We assign work all the time and we take it mostly for granted, so that we may not always do it as well as required. This chapter discusses the importance of good assignment and details some processes for doing it effectively. We cover specifically *work assignment*, which deals with 'what' is to be done or achieved, and *work planning*, which looks at 'how' the results will be achieved. Two special types of assignment, employee development and performance agreements, are covered in Chapter 4.

The scope of Work Assignment

The term **Work Assignment** describes the process of delegating work responsibilities and accountabilities to your employees. It may range from simply confirming a role to assigning new tasks or goals and also includes any change to an employee's work. Common examples include:

- new appointee to an existing role;
- change in role requirements;
- new business planning cycle;

- new performance management cycle;
- targets are changed or a new task arises during the year; and
- new project.

Definitions of 'work'

To discuss Work Assignment we need a definition of 'work', which we can think of as something an employee has to *be*, *do* or *achieve*. Table 3.1 translates these three dimensions into the more common terms of *role*, *task* and *goal*. Each piece of work has elements of all three but the primary focus will be on one of them.

Most people have their work described by their *role*, which may be supplemented with objectives or standards. For some, work is a mix of

Table 3.1 Three dimensions of work

Primary focus of the work	Examples
What to *be* (role)	
• Description of work that is specific to a role, not an individual • Includes role/job/position descriptions and duty statements	• Sales order clerk • Journalist, Grade 3 • Customer Service Manager
What to *do* (task)	
• Specific task/s to be undertaken • A task refers to a piece of work that is finite in terms of time, resources and result	• Launch 'X' new product • Plan access to the new factory • *(for a manager)*: Complete staff development plan
What to *achieve* (goal)	
• Output or outcome of the work (usually referred to as 'goals' or 'objectives') • 'Output' is what is directly produced by an employee as a result of their work. The term 'outcome' is generally applied to a bigger result, a 'bottom line' result of the whole enterprise or one of its functional units. As distinct from an 'output', many people or functions directly impact upon the 'outcome'.	• *Output:* number of order entries processed per day, at 100% accuracy • contributing to a downstream *outcome:* all orders delivered on time • *Output (for a manager):* department achieves planned results

underlying role responsibility with occasional tasks to undertake as well—for example, a personal assistant who routinely administers her manager's work output but also has to arrange industry meetings and conferences. For other employees their work is mostly *task-based* or project-based—for example, an employee whose only current work is to determine the transport requirements for a new coal mine. Managers, particularly senior managers, represent many of those in the last group and have their work defined primarily by what they *achieve*. Others in this group include salespeople and piece workers.

Desired outcomes of Work Assignment

The overall reason for good Work Assignment is that your employees have the best potential to achieve the required performance. Specific benefits are that the employee

- has the understanding, ability and resources to do the work;
- is able to approach the assignment creatively and flexibly;
- is motivated, committed and has ownership of the work;
- is able to measure and adjust achievement towards the goal; and
- is challenged and thus able to grow in ability and confidence.

Quite clearly, your employee's success is your success but there are further benefits, specific to you.

- Your management improves through the use of a disciplined process of assignment.
- You should have fewer unpleasant performance surprises.
- You have a better base for coaching.
- You have a better foundation for monitoring performance.

The Work Assignment process

Most Work Assignment takes place as part of the annual planning cycle, with new or modified goals or tasks arising less frequently during the year. Whether it is a formal meeting or takes place informally on the job, the basic principles, processes and skills of good assignment will apply. They apply in the same way for assigning work to a team or an individual.

For Work Assignment to be effective there must be some form of two-way communication. Mostly this will be face to face but may include telephone or electronic means. The recommended process set out below is based on a face-to-face meeting but applies equally to other forms. The process is divided into pre-meeting and meeting segments.

Pre-meeting

These points are common sense to most managers and so are presented in point form, without discussion.

1 Advise your employee

Advance notice allows your employee to do some thinking before the meeting and thus make a better contribution. Advise:

- Purpose
- Required preparatory work
- Intended outcomes
- What to bring

2 Prepare

Your own preparation is to ensure that you know all the things you want your employee to know. The following checklist is a starter.

- How does the Work Assignment link to the business or operational plan?
- Are there any implications for the rest of the team or for other parts of the business or organisation—for example, will the employee need the cooperation of another work group? How will the output affect downstream processes?
- Are there any implications for the rest of this employee's work—for example, will it take time away from other work?
- What are the risks and consequences of non-achievement?

The meeting

The following six-step process may require some discipline until it becomes second nature. The effort, however, will be worthwhile as you are far more likely to get a favourable result using a structured approach such as this. The next section shows the process in action.

- Step 1 Establish purpose and relevance
- Step 2 Explore the current situation

- Step 3 Define the work
- Step 4 Specify authority and accountability
- Step 5 Ensure system and personal capability
- Step 6 Agree performance management of the work

A Work Assignment and Planning template is provided in Appendix 2.

Work Assignment in action

Because the descriptions are brief, you will benefit by selecting an actual Work-Assignment issue and testing each step against it as you read.

Step 1 Establish purpose and relevance

Your employee will make a better contribution to the assignment process and to the work if the 'Why?' question is answered. Therefore, discuss the context and relevance of the assignment—where it fits into the picture and why it's important. Discuss the business consequences of non-achievement.

Step 2 Explore the current situation

Before launching into a new Work Assignment it is wise to get feedback on the current situation. There may be some important things that you don't know—for example, this approach may have been tried before, the background situation is more/less favourable than you have assumed, the practice you have in mind is already in place. This is a time for patient questioning.

Step 3 Define the work

Define and agree the work being assigned, using three elements: description, dimensions and means.

- **Description.** Start with the basic, summary description of the role, goal or task—for example, 'I want you to increase the amount of on-the-job coaching that you give the field staff.'
- **Dimensions.** You achieve a better assignment if your description includes the dimensions of the work, usually according to Quantity,

Quality, Resources and Time (QQRT). Providing the dimensions, or scope, gives the employee more idea of the breadth, relative priorities and potential internal conflicts of the assignment. Whereas Step 6 ties down the details tightly, here we use measures to open out the thinking.

Sometimes you may assign priorities to goals or tasks, or designate one or more as 'critical' to indicate that these are to be achieved above all others.

- **Means.** Whenever the *method* of achieving the result is important, it should be specified—for example, 'I want you to report back to me before you implement the plan.'

Step 4 Specify authority and accountability

An essential part of the assignment, particularly in a dynamic environment, is how far the employee *can* go and how far the employee *must* go in order to ensure that the assignment is successful. This aspect is often overlooked.

- **Authority** will usually involve the discretionary use of resources, including people, or modifications to methods.
- **Accountability** will either specify what must be done (expectations) or will include everything 'except' (limitations). One critical expectation is to agree what employees are to do when they can no longer control achievement of the goal. This is usually a requirement to advise you, which enables you to bring alternative resources or strategies into play to ensure that the goal is achieved.

Step 5 Ensure system and personal capability

You would not want to discover, after the event, that either the employee or the work system lacked sufficient capability to deliver the work assigned. It's an obvious risk to assume that, as long as the employee understands the work and has the will, everything will work out fine. You need to discuss these issues as part of the Work Assignment so that, if there is a potential weak link, it can be taken up in the work planning.

- **System capability.** Investigate whether there are work or organisational factors that might hinder the work—for example, other functional areas may not provide support, IT system capability may be inadequate, quality of the product may not be up to the promise, critical legislation may not be passed.

- **Personal capability.** Provide a means for employees to evaluate their personal ability to fulfil the Work Assignment. You will have to consider some form of skills development if the employee is not capable. If it is clear that *personal development* is required, this may affect the time frame or rate at which the employee can fully deliver. If the employee is confident but you are not, check by asking focusing questions such as 'What could be the most difficult part?'

Step 6 Agree performance management of the work

Before leaving the assignment, you need to set up an agreement about how the performance of the work will be managed. This includes discussing and agreeing what performance *measures* will be used, what *level* of performance is required, and how and when the performance will be *monitored*.

- **Performance measures.** Measures describe what is being measured and may be outputs, outcomes or a mix, depending on the nature of the work or the level of authority. Performance measurement is covered in detail in Chapter 7.
- **Level of performance required.** The level is described as a goal, objective, target or standard. Each enterprise has its own meanings for the first three, while standards refer to a performance level that applies to a role or a process, affecting more than one person—for example, 'delivery within 24 hours'.

  Even if an employee is accountable only for an output, also specify (and monitor) those *outcomes* to which the employee's work contributes, to keep the purpose of the work in the picture.
- **Performance monitoring.** This deals with how, and how often, the data will be collected and reviewed. It should also include what employee *reporting* is required. Data needs to be frequent enough to anticipate results.

Check shared understanding and agreement

At the end of each step, ensure that you both have a shared understanding and an agreement to date. You can use probing questions to make sure that the employee is not simply nodding for the sake of it—for example, 'What will be the most challenging part?' 'Are you willing to stake your bonus on that objective?'

Giving it form—a statement of Work Assignment

Should Work Assignment be documented? Things such as the scope and importance of the work and the experience of the employee will usually determine the answer. Documentation is also a useful cross-check of understanding and commitment. Documentation for formal agreements is covered in Chapter 4.

Figure 3.1 presents two illustrations of a summary statement of Work Assignment. This format provides a link to planning as it can form the front end of either a work plan or a performance agreement. Column 1 is a statement of the higher-order goal to which this work contributes, providing relevance and alignment. In this example, the employee has two tasks (column 2), both contributing to the one goal. Relevant measures and targets (or objectives) are given in column 3. When an assignment has a priority order of goals or tasks, this should be noted in a separate column.

Assignment and the corporate planning cycle

Although you may need to assign work at any time, the most intense period is in association with the annual corporate planning cycle. Although not explicitly covered in this book, it is a prerequisite that you have an operational business plan or work plan for your own business unit, work group or team that has been cascaded down from the corporate plan. It is from this local plan that you will derive the work for your people. It is uncommon these days for any new cycle to start without some change in the group's plan—goals, methods, or both. For example, there may be an increase in targets, fewer resources/same targets, new products or a need to integrate new methods.

Business unit, work group or key process goals	Individual goals and/or tasks	Measures and targets or standards
Increase in-store promotional effectiveness— gross off-take and off-take per store	1. Increase coaching from current 1/2 day per month to 2 full days per month with each person, in order to obtain more and better deals, in absolute terms and in comparison with our competitors	• 2 full days per month per person • coaching is directed to improving sales staff's ability to negotiate better promotional deals in store • (weekly/monthly support meeting with sales manager)
	2. Working with a team of other supervisors, prepare a report on a means to obtain daily in-store promotional off-take, in order to respond more effectively to badly performing promotions	• includes review and recommendations • complete by (date) • travel and WP budget of $3500

Figure 3.1 A statement of Work Assignment

To assign the new business requirements you can allocate them to individuals yourself or you can use the preferable method of working with your team to translate work-unit goals into individual requirements. The second method gains you greater understanding and greater commitment from your people. There is one disadvantage, however, of using the team. A change in your business plan presents an opportunity to review and perhaps change for the better the way your work group does things (refer to the open system of work model in Chapter 6). This may mean that some people have to change their roles, a process that may be uncomfortable. It is difficult to get acceptance for such ideas in a meeting of the people affected. You can compromise by evolving alternatives by yourself and then putting them to the group for discussion and critical evaluation.

Employees who have routine and predictable jobs are often stuck where they are because of the nature of the role. Just because an employee has a permanent, routine job you shouldn't simply 'roll over' the work into the next period, but rather work towards both business and personal improvement, particularly if you operate in a fast changing or competitive environment.

Employee performance planning

While Work Assignment deals with *what* goal or task is required, planning deals with *how* it will be achieved. As a result, Work Assignment and Planning are integral partners. At the individual level, planning is not always required; when it is, the type and complexity will vary according to the need. Your role is to facilitate the performance planning of your employees.

Why plan?

Employee work planning is underutilised and the resultant cost to business in today's dynamic environment is high. Some very good reasons for employees to plan their work are:

1. Planning increases the probability and magnitude of success.
2. Planning often brings returns beyond the original assignment, such as cost reductions or improved service.
3. Planning develops business abilities, which drive performance in other areas.
4. Planning provides a sense of meaning and contribution.
5. Planning enables the premeditation that allows us to review and improve our business assumptions.

From a business perspective, there are two basic considerations to guide whether your employee needs to plan for a particular Work Assignment.

1. How critical is the assignment?
2. How much does planning increase the probability or magnitude of success (the 'pay-off')?

The logic is that (a) critical assignments have to be achieved, and (b) resources put into planning might yield better gains elsewhere. Thus, for an extremely critical issue, the use of planning resources might be good business even if the increased probability of success is small. The other side of this logic is that, even if planning would produce a 'high' to question 2 for a non-critical issue, you may not wish to expend valuable resources on planning when it may add only a slightly increased benefit. Figure 3.2 summarises the planning decisions.

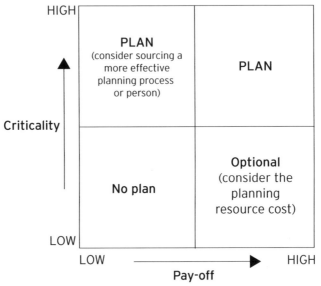

Figure 3.2 Planning choice matrix

In the notion that planning should increase the chances or magnitude of success is the implication that *thought*, *choices* and *decisions* must be involved. Many groups go through the motions of planning but all they are doing is filling out a mandated corporate form, with no thought as to how this planning process will help them to achieve a better result. They are producing a plan, but not actually planning! This is a waste of time and produces a complacent approach to achievement.

Planning situations—when to plan

The usual situations where employee planning should be considered are at Work Assignment, when objectives are not being met or when there are changes in the operating environment.

- *Work Assignment.* The most common reason your people will have for planning is Work Assignment, including not only the original assignment but also any change to the goal or task during the performance period.
- *Objectives are not being met.* When the employee is doing everything that was expected but the results are not there, you need to question your assumptions and this may require the exercise of planning.
- *Change in the operating environment.* Planning is often indicated in response to a change in the internal or external environment—for example, people, systems, methods, resources, products, markets, customers. An issue that is often missed by managers is a planned response to reduced numbers of people to do the work and/or increases in workload and/or competing priorities. Simply to carry on unchanged on the assumption that people will just work harder is a high-risk strategy.

Employee work plans

Some organisations have their own business planning format for employees. For managers whose organisations don't have a format, this section will provide you with a basic set of ideas to implement with your employees. For those in organisations that do provide a format, you may acquire some ideas that help you to use your own system better.

Business and performance planning is a large topic, even at the level of individual planning. The purpose in this book is to establish the importance of employee planning and to provide enough methodology to give managers and employees a start on the road to more and better work planning. We need to know how employee plans fit into the business planning framework, what basic types of employee plans are available and how to use the basic elements of these plans.

Employees' work plans derive from their work group's business plan, which in turn is cascaded from higher-level plans (Figure 3.3). An individual's work plan is analogous to that of a team. The following is a brief description of the plan for each group.

- *Work group plan.* For our purposes, this is the plan from which an individual's performance requirements are derived. It generally applies to a subdivision of a function—for example, the Cost

Accounting group in the Finance function—and is usually put together by the work group manager or supervisor.

- *Employee plan.* The employee plan relates to the work of an individual and includes work planning and personal development planning. A role plan is an individual plan that applies to a number of people filling exactly the same role, all with the same goals and tasks.
- *Team plan.* A team plan relates to a fully or semi-autonomous group, distinguished by *mutual accountability.* A team plan is treated much the same as an individual plan because each team member is accountable for the goals of the whole team.

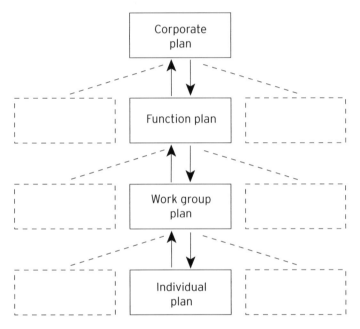

Figure 3.3 Cascade of the corporate plan through to the individual plan

Basic work plans

Employee work plans usually follow one of three basic planning models, which should suffice for most employee planning needs. Each type is defined by its relative focus on *objectives, strategy* and *activity* in the planning process.

Focus on objectives—statement of Work Assignment

The *statement of Work Assignment* (described earlier in this chapter) is a plan insofar as it provides clarity of requirement (purpose and goal or task), focus on where to expend effort (priorities and measures) and details of how much is required (targets or standards). In this way, it increases the probability of success.

Focus on activity—activity plan

An *activity plan* builds on the statement of Work Assignment, adding the key steps and timings, and possibly resources that are needed to achieve a particular task or goal. The activity plan assumes that the strategy for executing the goal or task is known and considered to be effective. The plan's primary purpose is to ensure that all key steps are listed in a logical order, with their completion dates. The activity plan makes the achievement of the goal or task more likely and enables better use of time and resources.

Focus on strategy—analysis-strategy-action plan (ASAP)

This planning process assumes that the best means of achieving the goal are not known and so part of the process is to analyse the situation, create and evaluate strategy options and, finally, to choose one. This form of planning ensures a greater probability of success in an unknown or uncertain situation.

We group these three types of plans under the heading of 'work plans' because they relate directly to the execution of an employee's day-to-day work. In addition to these three plans, there are three others that are relevant to individuals.

The *personal development plan* is covered in Chapter 4. Next, there is the *business plan*, a term generally applied to plans that include both a strategic and a financial case or argument. Within the context of performance management, business planning is likely to involve a task—for example, 'Prepare a recommendation on ways to obtain earlier reports from overseas agents.' Finally, project teams generally employ a dedicated *project planning* system, which is beyond the scope of this book.

Using work plans

The three types of planning models comprise a mix of four basic elements (Figure 3.2). One of these, statement of Work Assignment, has been discussed so this section takes you through the remaining three so that you can facilitate and coach your own people through the process.

Table 3.2 Elements of the three basic types of individual/team work plans

Elements of the plan	TYPE OF WORK PLAN		
	Statement of Work Assignment	Activity plan	Analysis-strategy-activity plan
1. Work assignment	▨	▨	▨
2. Activity steps		▨	▨
3. Critical issues analysis			▨
4. Strategy development			▨

Activity steps

The common elements of an activity plan, or schedule, are key action steps and targeted completion time. Additional elements are milestones, responsibilities, measures and results. Figure 3.4 is an illustration of an activity plan, demonstrating use of these elements.

Key action steps

Key activities, or action steps, are listed in order of due completion date. Employees are often unsure how far to break down a task into smaller tasks for listing. Generally, if a series of tasks naturally go together and are performed more or less without interruption, this is one key task. For example, all the components of 'Review current reporting' may not need to be listed.

Milestones

When a Work Assignment comprises a large number of key steps, the plan should highlight those points that represent the completion of a related set of steps. These points are appropriately called 'milestones' and provide a short-term focus in a long or complex task. Many people get caught up in whether it is best to start with the action steps or the milestones but the choice is an individual one, based on preference. Step-wise thinkers tend to start with the steps and then group them; big-picture thinkers tend to start with the milestones and then fill in the steps.

Timing

'Timing' lists the target completion date of each key activity. Sometimes, a second column is included for revised dates so that the original plan is

WORK ASSIGNMENT

Team task: *Prepare a report on a means of obtaining daily off-take data, in order to respond more effectively to badly performing promotions*

Measures and targets:
- Includes review and recommendations
- Written report
- Complete by 18/12
- Budget of $3500, incl. travel

1	2	3	4	5
KEY ACTION STEPS + MILESTONES	TIMING	RESPONSIBILITY*	MEASURES	RESULTS
Task assigned	10/10			
1. Review current reporting	17/10	Harry	on time	on time
2. Interview sample of sales staff	24/10	All	on time/4 staff	on time/3 staff
3. Draft analysis	27/10	Tricia	on time	3/11 (+ 7)
4. Finalise review	30/10	All	complete/on time	10/11 (+ 11)
REVIEW COMPLETE	30/10	(Tricia)		10/11 (+ 11)
5a. Investigate software options	14/11	Carmel	accurate, complete, on time	
5b. Investigate IT hardware	14/11	Tricia	ditto	
5c. Investigate other options	14/11	Harry	ditto	
6. Evaluate alternatives	21/11	Harry	accurate, on time	
ALTERNATIVES EVALUATED	21/11	(Carmel)		
7. Write draft report	30/11	Harry	complete, all time	
8. Write final report	14/12	All	on time	
9. Present report	18/12	Harry, Carmel	meets QQRT	
REPORT COMPLETED	18/12	(Harry)		

* Supervisor Sydney: Harry; Supervisor Melbourne: Carmel; State Manager Brisbane: Tricia

Figure 3.4 Example of an activity plan

not lost in the alterations. The traps for most employees are (a) over-estimating their capability, given their other commitments, and (b) not allowing for dependent activities or for scheduling, which may have them performing too many activities at the one time.

This overcommitment causes slippage which tends to increase as those managing subsequent steps have to reschedule and can't always maintain the original turnaround. Note below how in Column 5 a delay of seven days at step 3 has magnified into being 11 days late at the end of step 4.

Person/group responsible

When people other than the employee are involved in executing key steps, they should be included on the plan. This applies to team projects or where your employee is dependent upon others for completion of a work assignment. The inclusion of responsibilities highlights the steps where the work is passed from one person to another. These handovers are important to monitor and manage as they are potential fail spots.

Measures

Target completion times are usually the only measures but it is important to be aware, and to note, when other types of measures such as quality are also required.

Results

The activity plan should provide for recording of the actual results achieved against the assigned objectives, for the purpose of both management and evaluation.

Critical issues analysis

When an assigned goal or task requires some employee consideration of the 'how', it is important that the employee analyse the factors affecting achievement. *Critical issues analysis* is a discipline in its own right but, as a basic approach, the following method is simple and effective. The various tools associated with *quality improvement* are also an excellent source for this purpose.

It is useful to think of analysis and strategy as a pair. *Analysis* opens the issues out wide while *strategy* brings them back down to a sharply focused solution.

1. **Analyse the problem.** To solve the problem or achieve the goal effectively the employee must first become very clear about its full nature and extent. This means stating the problem or goal in specific rather than general terms. Refer to Figure 3.5.
2. **Identify possible influences.** Next, the employee should list all the possible contributors to the problem or goal/task outcome. (The open system of work model in Chapter 6 is very useful for this task.) Statements should be specific, not general—for example, not 'time lag' but 'usually 3–5 days before office is aware'.
3. **Sort the influences.** There are several approaches from this point but one of the more useful is for the employee to arrange the influences according to whether they have a positive or negative influence on the targeted outcome (see Figure 3.5). Once this is done, it is easier for the employee to begin devising strategies.

Analysis of the problem or goal
1. Estimated cost of problem is $1.3m, in lost sales and additional time spent in responding
2. Most poorly performing promotions are in larger, rather than medium, stores
3. Usually 3-5 days before office is aware
4. Usually only find out because of low or no reorder

Analysis of possible influences	
POSITIVE	**NEGATIVE**
• Field staff contact office within 1 hour of becoming aware	• Field staff workload does not allow time to call back on stores to check
	• When field staff contacts office, often engaged or messages not passed on to supervisor
	• Store managers fail to keep agreements

Figure 3.5 An example of critical issues analysis

Strategy development

Strategy development is based on the dual assumptions that (a) there is more than one path to an outcome and (b) the outcome of any chosen path is a matter of judgment, not certainty. This means that *alternative strategies* should be devised and evaluated and then the chosen strategies, together with the reasons for their selection, should be clearly articulated so as to allow discussion and reconsideration at any point of the work (see Figure 3.6).

For larger tasks, more than one strategy may be needed to reach the goal. These might be implemented side by side—strategy A alone produces an 80 per cent result but A plus B produces 100 per cent (Figure 3.6). At other times you may need to see the results of one strategy before you can begin the next; these are called *sequential* strategies.

Strategy development

Strategy alternatives

Strategy A   No change

Strategy B   Improve the existing telephone voice contact system, e.g. mobile telephones, office message machine

Strategy C   Provide field staff with laptop and modem

Strategy D   Redesign field staff schedules to allow a call back the following day

Multiple, side-by-side strategies

1. Replace current voice telephone reporting with laptop/modem/mobile system
   and
2. Redesign field staff schedules to allow a call-back the following day

---

Figure 3.6 Strategy development

Selecting the best strategy

Each strategy should be evaluated against a set of criteria that are relevant to the outcome. Some of these criteria will be 'costs' and some will be 'benefits'. Examples include speed of implementation, speed of results, reward, risks and probability of success. To help decision-making, each of the strategies can be rated on a scale against each of the criteria. Rating scales are either numeric—for example, 1 to 5—or descriptive—for example, High–Medium–Low.

We may regard some criteria as more important than others, in which case these select criteria can be 'weighted'. For example, if 'speed of implementation' is more important than other criteria, then strategies that favour speed stand out as the first choice.

Choosing the right plan

In the process of facilitating employee planning, you will advise your employees on the most appropriate type of plan. In its simplest form, the choice is based on whether the assignment's success depends most on *objectives* or *activity* or *analysis/strategy*. Table 3.3 provides summary guidelines.

Table 3.3 Guidelines for selecting a planning format for individual work performance

Environment of the assignment	Recommended focus
• There is high certainty of achievement • There is a prescribed method or the method is consistent with current methods and experience • There is no current or anticipated change to the operating environment • Nil, or few factors external to the employee are likely to influence achievement	Objectives
As above, plus when • There are multiple key action steps or stages • The work has a long cycle time • There is more than one person involved • One or more steps or stages are time critical • The employee has difficulty with time management	Activity
• Achievement is less than certain • Any number of factors external to the employee may influence achievement • Changes to the operating environment are anticipated • The existing situation needs to be more fully understood before planning responses • There may be more than one way of achieving the result and/or of dealing with the barriers	Analysis/strategy

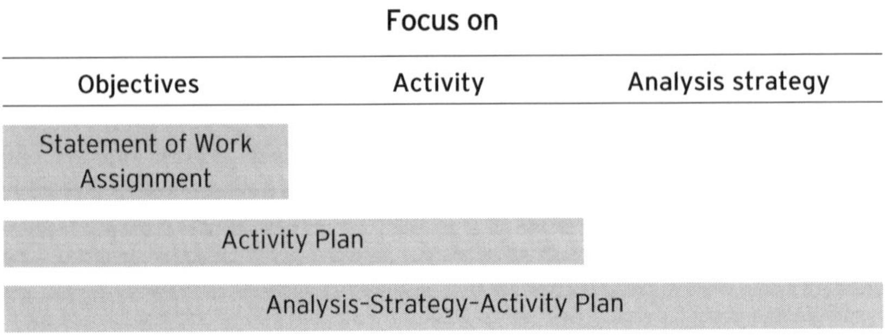

Focus on

Objectives	Activity	Analysis strategy

Statement of Work Assignment

Activity Plan

Analysis-Strategy-Activity Plan

Figure 3.7 Focus of the three basic employee plans

Once you are clear on the planning focus, the choice of plan is straightforward, as illustrated in Figure 3.7.

When the plan has been chosen, do a final reality check by returning to our original premise of planning—'What extent of planning is needed to improve the certainty or the magnitude of success?'

Facilitating the planning process

As in the case of Work Assignment, your role is more than advising your employees to 'go forth and plan'. You have to facilitate the process (a) to ensure that each employee's work planning is effective and (b) to help develop their planning ability. The following four–step process covers the essentials of facilitating an employee's planning to its best outcome. The process is included in the Work Assignment and Planning template in Appendix 3.

- Step 1 Review and confirm the Work Assignment
- Step 2 Specify what planning is required and provide methods and tools
- Step 3 Ensure employee's personal capability to plan
- Step 4 Review the plan

Step 1 Review and confirm the Work Assignment

Generally, assignment of the planning takes place at the time of Work Assignment, in which case this step is redundant. If the assignment of work planning takes place at a later meeting, review and confirm the

Work Assignment beforehand. Above all, don't get an employee to start work planning until you have properly assigned the work.

Step 2 Specify the planning required and provide method/tools

- Determine what type of plan is appropriate, as discussed earlier.
- Give your employee your reasons for (a) requiring planning in this case, and (b) choice of a particular type of plan.
- Provide the planning methods and tools, based on this chapter, or refer the employee to the organisation's methods.
- Set a date (or dates) for review of the plan.

Step 3 Ensure employee's personal capability to plan

The quality of the planning is only as good as the employee's ability to plan. Your role is to assess, educate and train, and to coach.

- **Assess.** Don't assume that employees are adequately skilled in the planning process, even though they may have used it before. (Sometimes a colleague has helped in the past, which is ideal, but may hide the true capability of the individual.) Use open questions to get employees talking about their ability.
- **Educate and train.** Provide education and training in the use of the planning methods. You may do this yourself or use someone else. If the latter, keep in touch with what the employee is learning because you will be coaching and reviewing the actual planning process and you and the employee need to be on the same wavelength.
- **Coach.** Your aim is to ensure (a) a plan that enhances performance and (b) ongoing development of the employee's planning ability. For either or both of these reasons, stay in touch with the planning process and support the employee, particularly with more complex plans. Once you have done the difficult task of assigning the work and the planning, it is easy for other work to distract you from the equally important follow-through.

When an employee is not very familiar with or capable at planning, other employees who have used the format can be asked to act as additional coaches.

Step 4 Review the plan

If you were assigned a task with implications of many millions of dollars for the organisation, your boss would definitely want to see your planning before you went ahead. The principle is the same at the local level. The risk and the benefit might be smaller but, multiplied across all employees, it is huge. The principle: if you ask your employees to plan, review the plan.

Two basic review approaches are valuable. First, you can go through the plan yourself; or you can use questions to get employees to talk about the plan, so that you can pick up the quality of their thinking, logic and thoroughness.

It's sometimes easy to overlook or take for granted the effort and skill an employee may put into planning. You are more likely to get the assignment off to a good start if you acknowledge the quality of the planning—it encourages effective planning in the future and sets up an expectation that a successfully executed assignment will be recognised.

People-management skills

Chapter 2 presented some core people-management skills, discussed in general performance terms. Work Assignment and Planning presents you with an actual task and it would be beneficial to review Chapter 2 in the light of that task. The following checklist is not a suggestion that you go through every item, but rather a prompt to where you might want to go.

For each of the people-management topics listed below, and in relation to Work Assignment and Planning, consider:

- Where might it be important to use this skill effectively?
- Your strengths?
- Your weaknesses?

1. **Managing differences**
   - personal values
   - handling information
   - making decisions
2. **Questioning and listening**
3. **Bias and assumptions**
4. **Facilitation**
   - Helping the discussion along
   - Reaching agreement

4 Employee development and formal performance agreements

In this chapter we cover two special cases of Work Assignment and Planning—employee development and formal performance agreements. Each of these situations will benefit from the use of the principles discussed in Chapter 3.

Employee development

Closely aligned with the notion of work and performance is the idea of *personal effectiveness*, which describes the contribution to performance made by the person as distinct from that made by the rest of the work system. It is one of the reasons why we observe different outputs between people in identical work situations.

Personal effectiveness comprises two basic elements—intention and ability. This chapter works with *ability* while intention is covered in Chapter 8.

Ability

We first look at the terms commonly used in connection with personal ability. The logic that gives each term its own meaning and relates them to work performance is displayed in Figure 4.1.

- **Ability**—describes what a person is able to *do*—for example, 'She's good at listening' or 'He knows the registration process'. It comprises task skills, knowledge and attributes.

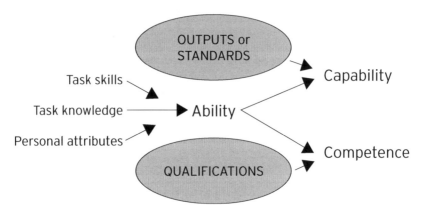

Figure 4.1 Dimensions of personal ability

- **Capability**—describes the *ability to achieve* targeted results or standards, with the focus on *relative* ability—for example, 'He always brings in a job on time'. This term is more work-focused because it refers to the achievement of objectives.
- **Competence**—means being able to meet *role-specific* standards or requirements and may be used to imply being qualified—for example, 'He's completed team skills accreditation' or 'She's fully trained in customer service'. The term 'competencies' is used to define a set of generic behaviours or attributes, associated with a particular type of role and believed to underpin effective performance, independently of the particular task focus. An example of a management competency might be: 'Leadership: able to conceptualise, identify cause and effect, apply logic and make decisions.'
- **Attributes**—refer to an employee's *intrinsic* ability to perform, whatever the work. They are personal characteristics and include beliefs and values, intellectual processes and behaviours—for example, integrity, lateral thinking, self-starter. Many organisations have defined sets of attributes that they require employees to have. In such cases, there is usually one set for all staff and an additional set for managers.

There are times when it is clear that an employee's personal effectiveness needs to be improved. When this involves a planned, structured process, it is generally referred to as 'employee development' and encompasses the common development methods of education, training, coaching and job rotation. In this way it differs from the manager spotting a problem on the job and helping the employee through it at the time. Because all employee development is a cost, it should be for a worthwhile purpose and should be effectively and efficiently carried out. To meet these requirements, employee development should be commenced with the same Work Assignment and Planning principles as are applied to the business side of work.

Development needs

The need for development is likely to arise during Work Assignment, work planning, on-the-job monitoring or formal periodic reviews. Indicators of the need will include the following.

1. In assigning or planning new work—role, goal or task—it is clear that the employee is currently not capable.
2. The employee is not meeting performance expectations and non-personal work factors have been eliminated.
3. There is an agreed process of ongoing improvement in personal effectiveness, linked to ongoing improvement in work performance. This occurs mostly in conjunction with a formal review process and/or the commencement of the annual planning cycle.

The inclusion of a personal development plan in an annual performance review requires comment. Although the plan provides a perspective of a whole year's work, development needs arise mostly *during* the period, not *after* it. Therefore, the most appropriate time to consider development is the point at which work is being assigned and planned or when performance is not meeting expectations.

Because this book is directed towards management of work, there are two types of employee development situations we don't cover. These are the acquisition of competency standards and career development.

Assignment and planning of employee development

The Work Assignment and Planning framework we use for employee development is illustrated in Figure 4.2 and discussed in the following sections. The process follows the principles of Work Assignment and Planning but is rearranged slightly to make more sense for employee development.

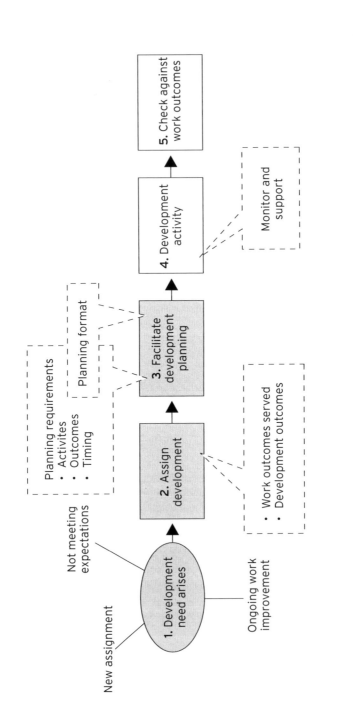

Figure 4.2 Assignment and planning of employee development

Step 1 Establish purpose and relevance of the intended development

When a development need arises at the time of Work Assignment, the purpose is automatically established—for example:

> 'The aim is to improve community uptake of our projects and we've agreed that an increase in your negotiation ability is key to achieving this.'

When an employee is failing to meet performance requirements, the purpose is similarly established:

> 'We've agreed that all other indicators are on track so we have to conclude that your negotiation effectiveness seems to be the issue. Let's discuss how to get this up to an effective level.'

Step 2 Explore the current situation

Before assuming that some form of development is needed, ask questions to get the employee's perspective. There may be reasons other than low skill that are the problem. Overriding factors may be personal problems, disagreement with the task or goal, or a cyclical slow spot.

Once you are sure that it is a skill factor, keep exploring to identify the actual ability that is the problem. In the example in Step 1 it may not be negotiation skills but rather interpersonal skills or a poor knowledge of community needs.

Step 3 Assign the development

We use a framework that is in common practice and provides a good business and development logic. For illustration we use a Personal Development Plan template (Figures 4.3a and 4.3b), which is shown in full in Appendix 2. The first two stages of the plan are applied as follows.

1. *Work outcome served* (Figure 4.3a). The reason for undertaking development is to improve work performance and so the development must relate to specific work goals or tasks—for example:

   > 'The aim is to improve community uptake of our projects from 10 to 20 per annum.'

Sometimes it may be relevant to note the *priority* of each work outcome. This helps if the employee's time or development resources need to be rationed.

2. *Development outcomes required* (Figure 4.3a). Express the development as outcomes, so that (a) they can be related to the work need and (b) the effectiveness of the development can be measured. For example, 'able to demonstrate improved negotiation skills' or 'able to demonstrate improved outcome of negotiations' or 'reach competency standards of the negotiation skills course'.

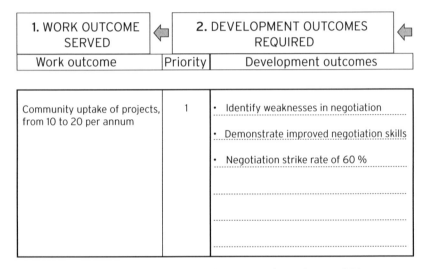

1. WORK OUTCOME SERVED		2. DEVELOPMENT OUTCOMES REQUIRED	
Work outcome	Priority	Development outcomes	
Community uptake of projects, from 10 to 20 per annum	1	• Identify weaknesses in negotiation • Demonstrate improved negotiation skills • Negotiation strike rate of 60 %	

Figure 4.3a The assignment portion of a Personal Development Plan

Step 4 Discuss performance management of the work

You have to manage this development assignment as you would any other work. First, you have justified the development on the basis that work outcomes depend on it and, second, the development is a cost, which must be well managed. The sorts of measures you might use include:

- development outcomes achieved—measured by observation on the job, course results, etc.
- completed on time; advises manager if any time slippage;
- resource utilisation (expenditure, employee time) is within plan.

Step 5 Specify planning requirements and
provide a planning process

Now that you have established the need and assigned the development, the next step is to consider the extent of planning required. Much assigned employee development never happens because it was not planned for. The implications are underperformance and employee cynicism.

As with other work, the means may be simple or complex and thus determine the extent of planning. At the simple end, the manager may decide to supervise the employee on the job and provide some coaching. This is something to be done in the normal practice of work, which will consume no extra resources and therefore does not require any more planning than agreeing how, where and when. At the other end of the scale, an employee in a remote location needs to acquire database skills. This clearly has both logistical and resource implications, and so is likely to fall into a hole if not well planned.

A common and effective planning process is shown in Figure 4.3b, which is a continuation of the 'assignment' portion shown above. This is stage 3, *Development activity*. Always consider alternatives: how many ways can you think of to get the same development outcomes? Then choose the one that is most certain, most cost-effective and meets your time availability. The following three components describe the development activity.

- *Activities*. Describe what will be done to undertake the development—for example, attend a course, observe a colleague, self-study, get a mentor. If the employee has to make inquiries, include this as a part of the plan—for example, 'get dates and costs of public courses in our area'. It is often failure of these predevelopment activities that bring the good intentions to a halt.
- *Resources*. Attending a course is not the only or necessarily the best way to undertake development. A full list of suitable resources includes:
  - self-study materials (books, videos, CD ROMs);
  - professional magazines or journals;
  - libraries;
  - in-house training courses;
  - external training courses;
  - time spent working with others;
  - assignment to a special project;

- other people in the organisation—to observe, coach, mentor or train the employee; and
- other organisations.
- *By when.* Realistic dates are an essential start to ensuring that the development takes place within a time that allows it to have an effect on performance. Be aware that, if the employee needs to acquire the ability to deliver 100 per cent on the target performance, the 100 per cent target should not kick in until the planned time that the ability is developed. This will mean starting targets at a lower level and increasing them in line with planned development.

3. DEVELOPMENT ACTIVITY		
Activity	Resources	By when
• Source external courses	Training Dept	1 July
• Attend a course	To be located	1 August
• Source self-study material	College library	1 July
• Complete self-study	Self	1 September
• Source role model/coach	To be located	1 August

Figure 4.3b The planning portion of a Personal Development Plan

Bringing the plan to fruition

As noted before, many development plans die. The message for you as a manager is (1) don't encourage an employee to embark on a development process unless both of you are willing to put in the work to see it through, and (2) monitor any development agreements you make with your employee. You are more likely to ensure that the agreement happens if, as part of the assignment, you make it the employee's responsibility to report to you on progress, either regularly or by exception, and certainly at completion. When the development is complete you need to check that the planned abilities have been achieved and that they are having the intended impact on performance.

Some common killers of development are listed below. If you are aware of these, you should be able to manage them more effectively.

- Undertakings that are not feasible given resources and work pressures;
- Development plans that are 'nice to have', not 'must have';
- Employees who are not willing to take shared responsibility for the plan eventuating;
- Managers who don't follow up on the plan but leave it totally to the individual; and
- Managers who go through the motions because it is a performance system requirement.

Formal performance agreements

Most performance systems have a formal objective-setting component for individuals which, when agreed between employee and manager, is often termed a performance 'agreement' or 'plan'. This objective-setting process has two aims—business and system—and, unless approached thoughtfully, one or the other aim may be compromised.

When goals are set primarily as part of the system they are often treated as an administrative task, with the primary focus on a favourable review rather than an optimal business outcome. As a consequence, their impact on the actual work and business is frequently compromised. Therefore, it is best that you approach Work Assignment and Planning from a business perspective in the first instance and then, when that is complete, translate relevant content into the performance agreement.

From the system perspective, the implications of formally assessing the work extend beyond meeting business results to the employee's reputation, remuneration and career. Therefore, you have to undertake the Work Assignment to meet the requirements of both sets of per-spectives. As we dealt with assigning work to achieve business results in Chapter 3, we now concentrate on translating this into meeting the needs of a performance agreement.

Requirements for a good performance agreement

If Work Assignment and Planning has been carried out as described earlier, they will represent 80–90 per cent of the requirements of a good performance agreement. Some special considerations include the following five essentials.

1. A good performance agreement reflects the business needs.
2. It is achievable.
3. Authority and accountability are specified.
4. It can be evaluated.
5. It is fair and equitable.

It reflects the business needs

Although good Work Assignment and Planning will reflect the business needs at the time, annual formal agreements tend to be inflexible. This means that you must build enough flexibility into the process so that the employee can adapt to ongoing changes in business needs, the assignment or priorities, without being constrained by the formal agreement.

Where *priorities* apply to the business needs, transfer them to the performance agreement. Priorities are sometimes reflected in weightings—for example, the achievement of a goal with a weighting of '2' carries twice as much value as one with a weighting of '1'. As a final check, ask yourself: 'Does the rating and reward structure of this agreement focus the employee on achieving highly in areas that are priorities for the business?'

It is achievable

Set up your employees to be able to achieve their goals. Unachievable goals risk a loss to the business and a loss of employee trust in the system. This is not saying that you shouldn't set 'stretch' goals, but that such goals should be accompanied by the *means* of achievement.

When setting measures, employees should be accountable only for those over which they have some reasonable degree of control. For example, say the intended outcome of a project is to change community opinion. The manager has the skill, the authority and the resources to have significant influence over the outcome, whereas an employee's influence is limited to the production and placement of PR activity. Therefore, the manager's agreement would include outcome measures while that of the employee would include PR output measures.

A further aspect of achievability is that it has a *manageable number of goals or tasks*. Some people seem to have so many things to do that they end up with an overwhelming, unfocused 'shopping list'. For the sake of a performance agreement, four or five goals or tasks are about as much as can be managed for evaluation purposes. If the number is greater than this, see how well they can be grouped. You will find that most people in this situation end up with two or three major goals or tasks and then a number of smaller ones. Figure 4.4 gives an example of the Work Assignment of a scientist who has many research projects to manage and complete within the performance cycle, where all of them have been rolled up into the first two goals.

Authority and accountability are specified

One of the major causes of disruption in the formal review process is the employee's claim: 'I didn't achieve the objective, but it was outside my control.' This is a short-term gain for the employee (who is adhering to

Goals: Business unit, work group or key process	Individual goals and/or tasks	Measures and targets or standards
Contribute to the Institute's Biochemical Research Program	Manage staff in execution of assigned research projects	• Completion, on time • Professional standards, met • Interim and final reports, complete and on time
	Complete own assigned projects and present reports	• Completion, on time • Professional standards, met • Interim and final reports, complete and on time
Achieve effective and efficient technical effectiveness	Contribute to the project team on laboratory systems improvement (mutual accountability)	• Meeting attendance, all • Contribution, full • Team report, complete and on time
Operational effectiveness	Carry out administrative roles and tasks	• Timeliness, accuracy and service, meet agreed standards

Figure 4.4 The Work Assignment section of a performance agreement

the system) but a loss for the business and a loss for the relationship. It underlines the importance of specifying the expected use of authority and discretion and accountability for managing goals at risk, as described on page 33. The dual principles here are that the goal will be met and the employee's performance will be evaluated fairly.

It can be evaluated

Whatever goals are agreed must be capable of evaluation within your own review system. This means that you must think ahead, look at each goal and measure, and come to an agreement with your employee; for example: 'In 12 months' time, how will we know if this goal has been met/exceeded/rates a 3?' If you aren't in agreement at the time of the agreement, it will be even more difficult when it comes to the evaluation.

It is fair and equitable

Three contributors to this requirement have already been discussed: a flexible plan to allow for ongoing changes in the work, achievable goals and evaluation criteria agreed up front. Other issues in relation to fairness and equity include all employees being given equal *opportunity* to achieve and all employees being *evaluated* under the same terms. Both of these are established during the performance agreement phase.

Attributes

In addition to goals and tasks, many performance review systems include targeted *attributes*—that is, things that people have to *be*, such as resourceful, cooperative/team player, self-starter, good leader, etc. Most organisations that have specified attributes also have a predetermined method of accounting for the attributes in their performance management system, so we do not deal with them in this chapter.

Compliance with organisational values should not be included in performance agreements as this turns them from group-owned principles into hierarchically enforced rules and, thus, the antithesis of cultural values.

Performance agreements for managers

While following the same principles as those applying to non-management staff, there are some distinguishing aspects of developing a performance agreement with managerial or supervisory staff. The aspects that distinguish managers in relation to performance management are listed in Table 4.1, together with an indication of how you translate them into a performance agreement. The inclusion of items does not mean that they should all be included in a manager's performance agreement, they are there to provide some guidance if they apply to your situation.

Table 4.1 Distinguishing aspects of managerial performance agreements

Distinguishing aspect	Illustration of individual goals, tasks or measures
A) Managers are accountable for the results of their own people. The major component of the agreement should reflect the above.	**A Goal:** 'Achievement of planned objectives by management of (unit/department).' **Measures:** Measures and targets should reflect what is in the work unit plan and could be re-expressed here but preferably referred to; e.g. 'Measures and targets, as per (unit/department) plan', so that the agreement doesn't require modification with every change in the work unit plan.
B) In addition to (A), managers may have special goals or tasks for which they alone are accountable.	**A Goal:** 'Achieve a stronger alignment of departmental staff to the company's core values.' **A Task:** 'Review the order fulfilment process and recommend efficiency improvements.'
C) Managers are accountable for business health—processes, systems, resources, products and services.	**A Goal:** 'Maintain (or develop) operating efficiency of (unit/department).' **Measures:** 'Measures and targets, as per (unit/department) plan.'
D) Managers are accountable for organisational health—people, organisational culture, communication, morale, structure.	**A Goal:** 'Maintain (or develop) the organisational health of (unit/department).' **Measures:** 'Measures and targets, as per (unit/department) plan.'
E) Managers may be required to possess and practise certain management and leadership attributes, e.g. decision-making, planning, providing direction.	These are usually expressed as a framework of competencies or behaviours, to which the performance agreement refers. **A Goal:** 'Demonstrate the *Business and Leadership Standards*.'

5 Performance data—what you don't know could hurt you

> There is a story about an Air Force instructor who would upbraid his trainees whenever they performed badly. A senior officer challenged him to compliment the trainees whenever they performed well rather than punish them when they performed badly. The instructor was able to produce statistics to prove that (a) punishment worked because on the next flight they always performed better and that (b) acknowledgment didn't work because every time he tried complimenting them for a good performance they would turn right around and produce a bad flight next time.

This apocryphal story is one of overreaction to random data and underlines the fact that much management time is wasted and many poor decisions are made because of poor understanding of performance data. As managers, we need a sound understanding of measurement to be able to manage the performance of others.

During the assignment of work to an employee you will have set up performance measures and the means and frequency of monitoring. This chapter is about how you and your employee can make the best use of the data you generate and begins with the management implications of different types of data. It continues with a model process for interpreting and responding to data, through knowing the right measures and having the right data and the right understanding. This chapter will also add to your ability to set up good measures during Work Assignment and Planning.

While our focus is on managing performance data as a day-to-day means of improving work performance, the principles extend to two other areas—to formal review and evaluation and to the management of business performance data.

Most of the explanatory examples use data-rich situations to make the point easier to understand. While it is simpler to work with data-rich situations the principles apply equally to all situations; it is the *application* of the principles that is sometimes easier, sometimes more difficult. The benefits apply equally.

Performance data and their management implications

> *To know what you are measuring has everything to do with how you manage it.*

Distinguishing between different types of performance data has implications for (a) selection of the best measures during Work Assignment, (b) setting performance targets during work planning and (c) interpreting and responding to the data generated. Our first look at performance data is from five overlapping perspectives:

1. the end and the means: Outcomes–Outputs–Drivers;
2. three types of outputs: Activity, Effectiveness, Efficiency;
3. personal effectiveness and work performance;
4. team measures; and
5. objectivity, quantity, cycle time.

The end and the means: Outcomes–Outputs–Drivers

Employee work generates outputs that are part of a chain of value adding from the start of the process right through to the bottom line. We can distinguish three basic types of data along this process or value chain— outcomes, outputs and drivers—each of which requires its own form of management (Figure 5.1).

Outcomes
Outcomes refer to those 'bottom-line' performance measures that are specified in corporate or business unit plans—for example, revenue, costs,

profit, market share, customer satisfaction, staff satisfaction, programs delivered, tonnes shipped.

Outputs

Outputs are what people and processes produce as a direct result of their inputs and efforts. They are not bottom-line results in themselves but are precursors to such results: for example, business plan completed, right people recruited, sales appointments made, service level agreement completed.

Drivers

All outputs should drive results but we reserve the term **key performance drivers (KPDs)** for those outputs that are the most critical or have the highest leverage in producing the final result. Performance drivers are often usefully referred to as 'lead indicators' and outcomes as 'lag indicators'.

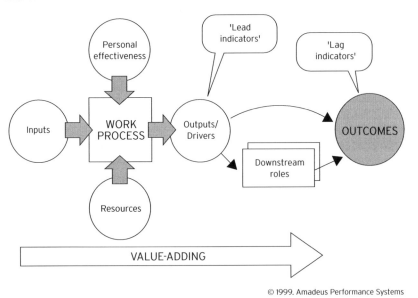

© 1999. Amadeus Performance Systems

Figure 5.1 The performance data mix—outputs, drivers and outcomes, viewed from a work process perspective

Implications for management

There is a wise management axiom, *Monitor the outcomes, manage the outputs*, which is our guideline here. The principal performance objective of the enterprise is to achieve planned results and so you must monitor results, or outcomes. However, you cannot *manage* results, you can only manage outputs, and so your performance management focus should be on those outputs that you identify as the key drivers of downstream results. This focus is needed when you plan, when you review and respond to performance and when you review your planning assumptions.

Three types of outputs: Activity, Effectiveness, Efficiency

When you review the work output, you are dealing with two types of data—activity data and/or achievement data. Understanding the difference has implications for objective-setting, planning and the management of performance, including distinguishing between work performance and personal effectiveness.

Activity

Activity is something you *do*, your workload, and is a measure of the number of items or tasks completed. It is characterised by a measure which includes 'the number of . . .'—for example, number of applications processed/customer inquiries handled/press releases issued.

Achievement

Achievement refers to something you *produce* as a result of your work. Achievement is a concept and is employed mostly in terms of its components—*effectiveness* and *efficiency*.

Effectiveness is the result achieved, or the extent to which it is achieved, particularly in relation to a target, such as customer satisfaction, tonnes mined or percentage achievement against budget.

Efficiency refers to productivity and it measures how well inputs are converted into outputs—for example, sales to cost ratio, units produced per hour, cost per unit produced.

Activity and achievement are demonstrated in the following two examples and can be put into the work context very simply by using the work process model (Figure 5.2).

Examples of activity and achievement

Activity:	Made 50 telephone calls to seek sales appointments
Effectiveness:	Achieved 30 sales appointments as a result of telephone calls
Efficiency:	Achieved a strike rate of 60 per cent (50 telephone calls yielded 30 appointments)
Activity:	Completed annual plan
Effectiveness:	Plan complete in detail and on time; approved by the Executive
Efficiency:	Consumed 55 hours to complete; incurred direct costs of $1500; no lost time on other work

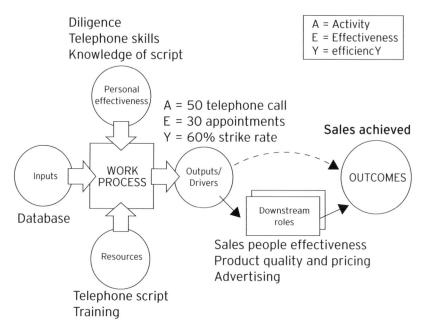

© 1999. Amadeus Performance Systems

Figure 5.2 An example of activity and achievement in the work process

Implications for management

The differentiation of activity data and achievement data affects the management of work performance, as well as objective-setting and work planning. In the telephone example, 'effectiveness' is the driver of downstream outcomes and is therefore a component of planning, but activity and efficiency are the measures that are managed on a day-to-day basis.

Personal effectiveness and work performance

We concluded in Chapter 3 that the person is only one part of a larger performance system—in some circumstances the greater part, in some the lesser part. This means that there will be times when you will want to separate personal effectiveness measures from whole-of-system performance—for example, for work planning, to test your planning assumptions, for employee development, or for on-the-job management of performance.

Measures of personal effectiveness are those over which the employee has some degree of control, giving us a spectrum, ranging from higher control (personal attributes) to lower control (bottom-line outcomes), as shown in Figure 5.3. Preceding or underpinning each of these measures, but not shown on the chart, is the employee's intention, or 'will', to do the work.

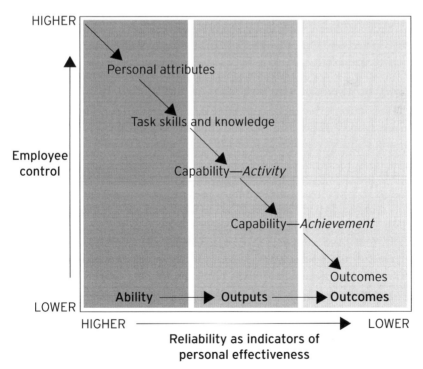

Figure 5.3 Spectrum of personal effectiveness measures

Implications for management

The two major areas of implication are how personal effectiveness influences performance, and how it can be measured.

In its *link to performance*, the management implications of personal effectiveness apply to both your employee and to you. The basic principle is (a) to manage employees for what they can influence and (b) manage other parts of the work system where the employee has no/low influence. Returning to the telephone example, you manage the *employee* for diligence, skills and knowledge and you manage the *system* for an accurate and timely database and effective telephone scripts. Finally, be selective with these personal effectiveness measures, using only those that you identify as key performance drivers.

Some cognitive and behavioural attributes and skills tend to be overlooked because they are not particularly visible. However, the evolution of business (see Chapter 3) indicates that these skills are becoming increasingly important in all workplaces.

The *measurement* of personal effectiveness may appear to be difficult but there is usually a way—for example, reflective discussions with the employee, observation, interviews with customers. Your own organisational or human resources specialists should be able to advise you.

Team measures

As before, when using the term 'team' we are referring to an autonomous or semi-autonomous group with shared goals and identity and mutual accountability; it does not include the typical work group reporting to a supervisor or manager. *Measures of team performance* are governed by the same principles and include the same sorts of measures as those outlined for individuals. In addition, you will need measures that are specific to the team environment, spanning *outputs*, *task ability* and *personal attributes*.

- *Outputs*. Among the KPDs should be drivers that describe the successful functioning of the team. For example, a measure on team or subgroup meetings occurring *on time* and with *full attendance* might be critical to maintaining *time schedules* and to ensuring necessary *communication* between parties involved.
- *Task ability*. Project management skills are the most obvious item here but you should also consider such things as cross-functional technical knowledge, meeting processes and report writing.

- *Personal attributes.* Interpersonal behaviours, such as communication and collaboration, are the ones that stand out as being important inclusions in team measures.

Implications for management

Despite all the rhetoric about teams, very few managers actually manage true teams, according to our definition. Those who do are most likely to be overseeing project teams. A lot has been written about managing teams but, in relation to measures, you should differentiate those measures of *mutual accountability*, such as work outputs, and those that apply to *specific individuals*, such as communication.

Objectivity, quantity, cycle time

Objectivity, quantity and cycle time are three more perspectives on measurement, overlaying those we have already covered. The topic is presented in two columns so that you can immediately relate the type of measure to the implications for its management.

Objective or subjective

Description	*Implications for management*
Objective data is 'hard' data, measured impartially and objectively, e.g. diameter of items produced, number of customers who express satisfaction, work produced on time.	*Generally considered to be more reliable than subjective data but may lead to a false sense of 'rightness', even when it is measuring the wrong things or is poorly understood.*
Subjective data is a matter of opinion, which may vary from one person to another, e.g. 'a good report', 'effective policy'. Personal attributes data falls into this category, e.g. 'innovative', 'self-starter'.	*Generally held that this form of data is unreliable and less valid than objective data. However, its value is great if it is well set up in the first place, i.e. ask the right questions, and you know how to use it. It is underused but is becoming more important in line with the changing nature of work.*

A lot or a little

Description	Implications for management
Work that is 'data-rich' is generally easier to manage. The richness of data is a function of the repetitiveness of the work, length of the work cycle, and the number of people performing the same work.	*The amount of data, its frequency and its comparability determine the nature of your management.*
	When you are producing good quality frequent data you can:
Examples of data-rich situations include telephone call centres and supermarket checkouts; examples of data-poor situations include corporate planning and policy analysis.	• *test cause–effect relationships;* • *evaluate responses to changes in process or strategy; and* • *identify differences between and within people.*
	Learn how to become fluent at managing data-rich situations (borrow someone else's data, if necessary) and then apply the principles to any data-poor situations that you have.

Work cycle: long or short

Description	Implications for management
Cycle time refers to the length of time a piece of work takes. Generally, longer cycle times are associated with higher levels in the organisation and therefore with the impact and importance of the work. A production worker may have a cycle equal to the length of one shift, a CEO a cycle of 3–5 years.	*A long cycle time usually means that you have to look for some intermediate output drivers to measure and monitor.*
	You should also be aware that circumstances may change during the life of a long piece of work; as a result, the work should be reviewed and also the choice of measures.
Cycle time relates to the frequency of data and so the paradox is that many of the more critical pieces of work are the hardest to measure, being less data-rich.	

A model process for understanding and responding to data

Because misinterpretation and misattribution of data are so common, it is helpful to have a good knowledge of performance data as well as a structured approach to managing it. The following process represents a logic flow that makes it easier for you and your people to make sense of performance data. As an on-the-job guide, a work template, the Performance Data Model, is provided in Appendix 2.

When you want to understand and respond to some performance data, you need to address three critical questions.

1.   What are the right measures?
2.   What is the right data?
3.   What is the right understanding?

These three questions are addressed using a series of eight steps through which you cycle twice, once for *outcomes* and once for *drivers*.

The right measures
Step 1 Start with *outcomes*
Step 2 Confirm the agreed measures

The right data
Step 3 Data supports the agreed measures (valid)
Step 4 Comparable—'apples with apples'
Step 5 Reliable

The right understanding
Step 6 Cause and effect
Step 7 Variation
Step 8 Capability

Then, repeat from Step 2 and analyse the *drivers*.

Through a combination of human nature and the pressures of work, we frequently make decisions based on the wrong measures. The two steps of question 1 help us to get off on the right foot. Even when we know what measures we should be looking at, we all too easily select the wrong data to support these measures—mostly because our desire to create meaning overwhelms our discretion. Steps 3 to 5 help us to address question 2, 'The right data'. Lastly, we need to know what sense to make of this data and how we should act upon it. Steps 6 to 8 deal with cause and effect logic and extend our knowledge into multidimensional measurement in 'Variation' and 'Capability'.

The right measures

Even before you start thinking about how good your data is, you have to confirm that the data you are looking at represents the right measures in the first place. There are two steps in dealing with this question: the first is to start with the outcomes (not the outputs) and the second is for you and your employee to agree that these are the right measures.

The *right measures* is dealt with by the first two steps:

Step 1 Start with *outcomes*.
Step 2 Confirm the agreed measures.

Step 1 Start with the outcomes . . . then the drivers

Earlier in the chapter we presented the axiom '*Monitor the outcomes, manage the outputs*'; this suggests that you first look at the bottom-line results and then at the outputs that drive those bottom-line results. There are three business reasons for first looking at the outcomes:

1. Outcomes are the reason for individual work.
2. Individual outputs only make sense when related to the outcomes.
3. We are forced to consider the wider 'work system' or the 'performance mix'.

There is one further reason for linking individual outputs to outcomes—employee empowerment. The first empowering thing about the idea is that it demonstrates to individuals that what they are doing or producing in their daily work has a larger meaning. The second benefit is that it provides individuals with a broader focus for improvements in performance or the work system; it moves their horizons from 'doing things better' to 'doing better things'.

Step 2 Confirm the agreed measures

Imagine the outcome of reviewing the performance of a piece of work where you are placing emphasis on one set of measures and your employee places emphasis on another. Before you start looking at the data, you must both be clear exactly what measures are being used—they should be those measures that were agreed at the time of assigning or reassigning the work. Agreement on the measures means a greater likelihood of agreement on the data and, ultimately, on actions arising from the data. Furthermore, to introduce new measures or comparisons at random sends confusing messages to your employee as to where to focus attention.

This sounds logical enough, so why should there be a problem? One common problem is that the measures are not clearly agreed at assignment: they are either glossed over by the manager or the whole thing is not thought about deeply enough by either party. It is also quite common for a manager to react to *any* performance data that is seen to reflect on an individual, and to use that data to draw conclusions.

Note: The following topics, dealing with 'The right data' and 'The right understanding', apply equally to *outcomes* and to *drivers*, although mostly outcomes are featured in the examples. A wide range of examples is used to demonstrate the relevance of the principles across a spectrum of workplace situations.

The right data

Unintentional misuse of performance data is common; therefore you need to ensure that the data you are using is right for the purpose. This applies equally to outcomes, personal effectiveness drivers and other drivers within the performance mix. Your first response is likely to be that you would know if you were using the wrong data but the truth is that, in cases of good and bad performance, it is very easy to fall innocently into the trap of attributing data to the wrong causes.

Checking that you have the *right data* incorporates the next three of the seven steps:

Step 3 Data supports the agreed measures (validity)
Step 4 Comparability—'apples with apples'
Step 5 Reliability

Step 3 Data supports the agreed measures (validity)

The term 'paradigm' was first coined to describe the phenomenon where two scientists could take a piece of hard, objective data and each reach a totally different conclusion. The reason given was that they each had their own mindset and so they, quite honestly, saw the data in different ways. This 'paradigm' effect shows up in two principal ways when we select data—misattribution and bias.

Misattribution is easy

Be sure that you are measuring and monitoring what it is that you tasked your employee to achieve. It is very easy to grasp at related data and attribute it to the efforts of your employee. For example, your employee's task is to undertake computer training in spreadsheets, but later you draw upon data that relates to achievement of budgets to infer how well, or not, the task was executed. What happened?

In your own mind, when assigning this task, your logic probably went something like: '*He will achieve budget more consistently if his budget-ary planning improves, and a course in spreadsheets should fix that.*' Your business model looked like this:

So when you came across data on budget achievement, you readily attributed it to the measures of how well your employee performed on the assigned development task.

The bias trap

Misattribution of data is a particular trap when you have a bias, positive or negative, about an employee. Bias makes you even more susceptible to seeing the 'logic' in the data you have chosen. In the above example, if you had a favourable bias towards the employee, when it came to the end-of-year review, you might say: 'Well, you didn't actually complete the spreadsheet course as you were tasked to do, but you are achieving budgets far more consistently, so we'll give you a 9 out of 10 for that development task.' The negative bias impact on this type of interaction is a common cause of disputes—'Well, you did complete the spreadsheet course as you were tasked to do, but your budget achievement each month is still all over the place, so the best I can give you is a 5 out of 10' (for that development task).

Step 4 Comparability—'apples with apples'

Another common trap is to compare unlike data ('apples and oranges'). Once again, we seek data that supports our preconceptions or helps us reach a meaningful conclusion quickly (but not necessarily accurately). Three common ways of comparing apples with oranges are illustrated in these examples:

- *Comparisons between people.* 'Sue, Roger manages to process twelve applications per day but you manage only nine.' In this case, Roger processes proportionately more *personal* applications, Sue more *commercial* applications, which take longer.
- *Behaviour/attributes within the same person.* 'Last month I asked you to improve interactions with your colleagues, particularly to be more courteous and less abrupt. You obviously haven't made much of an effort because I now hear that you are not willing to help out when others are short-handed.' The events and behaviours may be related but the observations of unwillingness to help doesn't necessarily reflect lack of compliance with the original task.
- *Periodic comparisons* make comparisons of one period with another, such as this year against last year or this June against last June. For example: 'Your goal was to improve your time per customer call. Your weekly average last year was 72 seconds per customer, but over the first month of this year it is 81 seconds.' The problem here is that the supervisor is comparing a 12-month period with a one-month period. It is possible that (a) there is a natural cycle where more difficult calls come in at the beginning of year, or (b) there was an abnormal event that caused a lot of difficult calls to come at this time.

Step 5 Reliable data

The third dimension of having the right data is less to do with selection and more to do with *quality*, which we approach from two perspectives:

(1) how representative the data is and (2) the degree and influence of underlying bias.

Representative data

There should be sufficient data for you to reach valid conclusions and the data should represent what you are intending to measure. How much data you need depends on such things as the number of transactions/events, cycle time of the work, the stability of results and the impact of each event.

- *Number of transactions or events*. Remember the saying 'One swallow doesn't make a summer'? The same applies to data. You must have sufficient data to give a true representation of the work performance. For example, if an employee produces 300 machine parts per day you would not usually judge on the basis of one part but, if the employee produces one machine part per day, one defective part would be representative and therefore important. The same principles extend to *behavioural* measures and data—for example, one observation of an employee behaving in an authoritative way with their own team does not necessarily indicate a poor leadership style.
- *Cycle time of the work*. Ensure that the data reflects a complete cycle of the work, or a stage of the work. For example, a bank would not rely on measurement of a loan customer's total satisfaction before the loan approval process was complete. If, however, the bank wanted to measure an individual employee's contribution it could measure satisfaction against those stages over which the employee had influence.
- *Stability/instability of results normally expected*. Some performance is subject to influences that cause data to exhibit wide swings between highs and lows, or produce unpredictable spikes. This behaviour makes it difficult to act on any single measurement event; what you need in this case is to know the *pattern* of the data and to see how your piece of data fits. (Variation is covered in more detail in Step 7.) For example, the time spent on information requests varies greatly according to their complexity and sources of data. Therefore, the manager could not normally regard any single event as being intrinsically 'good' or 'bad'.
- *Impact or importance of each event or associated decisions*. The more important the decisions you have to make on the data, the more you

would want to know that the data is representative. For example, you detect a few recent cases where a competitor has offered its property management services at a lower than normal management fee. Because it is a big decision to decide to go into a price war, you would want to find out whether these are isolated incidents before taking action.

Underlying bias

Frequently, you and your employees will rely on feedback from others to determine the level of performance. Feedback is commonly sought from external and internal customers, colleagues, others who receive work from the employee (downstream in the process) and the person's own employees. This form of data is at risk of intentional or unintentional bias and so you need to apply some basic tests for bias.

- Formally solicited, structured feedback, such as that obtained by surveys, is mostly less susceptible to bias than impromptu or un-solicited feedback.
- Look for consistency between respondents if feedback comes from several people, such as customers.
- Look for consistency with other related measures of performance.
- Look for circumstances that might engender bias—positive or negative.
- Look for bias in your own questions as you seek the feedback.
- If employee behaviour is being examined, look also at the circum-stances of the situation.

The right understanding

Having established that you are working with the right measures and the right data, the next principle is 'right understanding'. *Right understanding* deals with how you make sense of your employee's performance data in a way that enables an appropriate and effective response. The first part of this chapter identified *individual* types of measures and considered the management implications of the data generated by each. This topic considers performance data within a work *system*.

The major components of understanding are dealt with in these three steps:

- Step 6 Cause and effect
- Step 7 Variation
- Step 8 Capability

Step 6 Cause and effect

Your work planning will have been based on the assumption that the achievement of certain drivers would produce certain outcomes—the cause–effect relationship. From the performance data that is generated, you now need to be able to:

- know whether you are on track;
- improve performance, if not on track; and
- test the validity of your planning assumptions.

Cause and effect is a big issue and is the framework upon which the other components of understanding are built. We work with two ideas—the outcome–driver decision tree and the mix of work performance drivers.

The outcome–driver decision tree

Having talked about the need to make decisions based on the driver–outcome relationship, we clearly need a framework for doing this. The decision tree in Figure 5.4 illustrates the interplay between monitoring and managing outcomes and those outputs that are drivers of performance (KPDs), indicating what to look for and what decisions or actions are required. This decision model is based on Step 1 in 'The right measures'—*Start with the outcomes, then the drivers*. In illustrating the use of the decision tree, the examples deal only with the *employee* outputs although, as we have already learned, drivers should include *all* key performance drivers in the work system.

The next section uses the logic of the decision tree and guides you through decisions and actions, depending on one of two scenarios—outcomes are on track or outcomes are not on track.

Outcomes on track

The overwhelming response to the outcome objectives being met is to forget about the 'how'. 'Who cares how we did it? It's the final result that counts.' But is it? If this was a one-off event, never to be repeated in kind, and if you weren't responsible for the performance of an employee, then

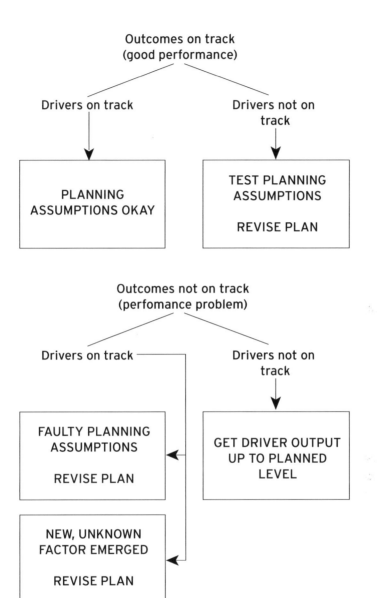

Figure 5.4 The outcome–driver decision tree

you might get away with it. However, you need to be able to repeat this success and the enterprise only survives by learning and adapting, so you do have to revisit the 'how'.

If the results for outcomes are on track, then the employee's primary purpose is being fulfilled. This leaves you with two worthwhile questions—how well is the employee performing against *output* objectives (an employee performance question), and how well do your planning assumptions still hold (a business, or work performance, question)? To answer these questions you now have to determine whether the key performance drivers are on track—that is, do they meet their objectives?

- *Key performance drivers are on track*. If the drivers are on track, the employee is performing to expectations and your original planning assumptions (about cause and effect) hold (Figure 5.4). Your decisions will now involve such things as whether to continue unchanged, or to look for ways to improve effectiveness or efficiency and/or to anticipate possible changes in the operating environment.
- *Key performance drivers are not on track*. If outcome objectives are achieved but your planned output objectives are not, then your planning assumptions do not hold and you have to review and revise them (Figure 5.4). If the employee's performance is below plan, respond either by downgrading the requirement in the light of a revised plan or by improving performance.

Outcomes not on track

Unlike the previous situation, if the outcomes are not achieved it is more natural to look for the causes. What we have to beware of is the common tendency to assume that the problem is personal effectiveness or, if that is clearly not the case, to blame the most obvious thing that looks wrong—our meaning-seeking at work again.

If the results for outcomes are not on track, then the employee's primary purpose is not being fulfilled. As before, this leads you to the key performance drivers to determine how well the employee is performing against *output* objectives, and how well your planning assumptions still hold.

- *Key performance drivers are not on track*. If the output drivers are below planned levels, the first response would be to get them performing and then review the effect on the outcome objectives (Figure 5.4). For example, our outcome target of x loan approvals per week might have been planned on the basis of a processing time of y. If we are not achieving x and we are not achieving y, it's likely that our planning assumptions are still okay—we just need to get the processing time back on track.

- *Key performance drivers are on track.* If the output drivers are being achieved, but not the outcomes, then the planning assumptions were wrong in the first place or there is another force operating, not known or not existing at the time—for example, a software problem is holding up the printing of the final loan approvals (Figure 5.4).

The mix of work performance drivers

In Chapter 6 we introduce an 'open system of work' model, which establishes that there are more drivers delivering an outcome than personal effectiveness alone. In continuing with our right understanding of performance data, we can use the open system of work model to add depth to the decision tree model by better management of the mix of personal and non-personal drivers.

The first lesson to be learned is not to jump mindlessly to the soft option of seeing work performance as a 'people' issue, but to be aware of *all* critical dependencies. The former approach ignores the possibility of other critical influences and may result in unjust or overgenerous treatment of the employee, a missed opportunity to exploit favourable influences or failure to correct a non-personal problem.

The task implicit in this recommended approach is complex—there are many moving parts and many levers to push and pull. However, economics and competitiveness have created an agenda of complexity in all work, and managers and their people have to rise to the challenge of managing it.

Step 7 Variation

Managers work mostly with performance data as a single number—representing an absolute value ('sales for last year jumped to $30 million'), or a relationship to a target ('last month's production was 12 per cent ahead of budget'), or performance requiring a response ('customer satisfaction dropped 0.7 per cent last month—we have to act quickly to stop the decline'). There is nothing implicitly wrong in these representations but they are a one-dimensional view of the data and they don't provide enough information for us to address such important questions as:

- Does this figure tell us everything that we should know?
- Can we predict future performance on the basis of this data?
- Should we act on this data? If so, how?

What these performance figures lack is a reference to *variation* or an associated concept, *capability*. Both topics are already the subject of many books in their own right and the scope of this book does not allow us a detailed discussion. But we can gain an understanding of what they mean and how, in general terms, we can use them to improve our management of performance.

What is variation?

When we make a series of measurements of a work activity, we find that the values are not all the same but move up and down in a mostly random fashion. For example, the turnaround times (hours) for a series of 20 in-house press releases are shown in Figure 5.5. 'Variation' describes this pattern of scattered data where the variation may be in time periods, people, machines, batches, samples, or a combination of any of these. Various ways to express variation in work performance include:

*   the *range* from highest to lowest value (16 to 2 hours);
*   the *mean*, together with the variation above and below (9.0 hours ± 7.0 hours); and
*   the *distribution* (75 per cent of the values are between 8 and 10 hours).

Press release turnaround times (hrs):
9, 7, 10, 9, 12, 10, 9, 7, 5, 2, 10, 12, 7, 9, 14, 6, 9, 8, 16, 9

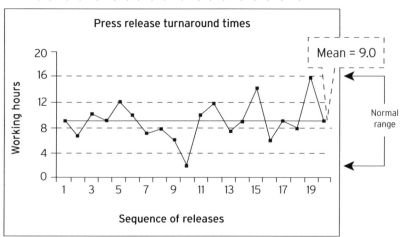

Figure 5.5 A graphic representation of performance variation

What we need to know about variation

Understanding the nature of variation, and how to respond to it, should increase significantly the ability of you and your people to manage work and personal performance. There are three things you should know.

- *Variation is normal* and does not imply a special problem in your work processes or your people. Variation occurs from one sample to the next, from one time to the next, from one person to the next and, for the same person, from period to period. The more influences acting upon a piece of work, the more it will be subject to variation. The vast majority of variation in any process is due to the random effects of a large number of influences—people, machines, technology, materials.
- *Variation is a cost to the enterprise.* Variation in performance is a cost to the organisation because the organisation is structured and resourced in order to cope with the range of performance. The larger the variation, the higher the cost.
- *The mismanagement cost.* Poor understanding of variation results in overreaction and underreaction to data, leading in turn to avoidable adverse consequences on the one hand, or wasted resources and constant 'tinkering' on the other. Common results of misunderstanding include:
    - management time wasted by seeking to explain away random variation in data;
    - shuffling of performance results, so as not to achieve less than or too much more than the target;
    - sacrificing one aspect of the business to ensure good results in another; and
    - endless excuses by individuals to ensure that they are not held personally responsible for shortfalls they did not create.

Responding to performance variation

Most responses look at improving the mean value or cumulative value. There are, however, further gains to be made in improving variation. The approach is to reduce variation overall and to case-manage performance that falls outside your 'normal range'.

Understand your business

In the same way that we analysed press release performance, above, you can look at the various aspects of your business. You are working towards obtaining a picture of what your business looks like when it is operating under normal conditions. In the case of the press releases, we could say (on the basis of the available data) that any value that falls between 4 and 6 hours represents 'normal business'. There are complex statistical processes for calculating 'control limits' but we can estimate them simply by looking at our data. We also refer to them as the 'normal range' (Figure 5.5). Dr Paul Walsh of Sydney University has coined the most apt phrase—'a business as usual' range. The normal range will shift in line with trend and cyclical effects.

Variation is most apparent when there are frequent data points to evaluate, but a great deal of work doesn't appear to generate much data, or very frequent data. However, although some jobs might seem, at first glance, to be immune from the traps of misunderstanding variation, many are subject to such risks and are not well managed, at a cost to both the business and the employee. Space doesn't allow us to discuss examples but it is recommended that you make an effort to understand all the important parts of your business, using the principles described.

Reduce variation

Independently of the day-to-day performance of your employees, you can continually look for ways to reduce the scale of variation in your business unit, in order to meet customer needs and reduce costs more effectively. For example, a shift in a response time from 59 ± 11 minutes to 51 ± 4 minutes indicates far greater effectiveness and efficiency than a change in the mean time alone.

Respond appropriately

The two costs are underreaction and overreaction. Underreaction means that problems go unresolved and overreaction means that the 'tinkering' consumes resources and often depresses the performance it is trying to correct. Appropriate management means (1) understanding the normal range of your business, (2) not interfering with normal business variation, and (3) case-managing data that falls outside your normal range limits.

Figure 5.6 illustrates a new version of the press release example data. There are two data points where a manager might be lured into an overreaction trap. In the case of a 16-hour turnaround, we might have had a 'serious talk' with the employee or changed the process, all for nothing because the result is within our normal range of performance.

On the other hand, we are likely to give the team lots of praise for a 2-hour turnaround, only to have them repay us by becoming progressively worse.

The 20-hour result is a different situation because it is outside our normal range. This means that a special event has occurred that is not part of our normal business environment. Our response to such results is to case-manage them by seeking the causes and either eliminating them or accepting them as a rare and unpredictable event.

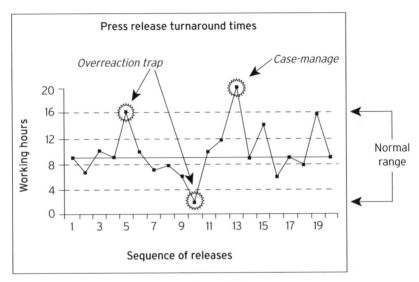

Figure 5.6 Management responses to variation

Variation in people-based measurements

Have you heard about the manager who said to his team: 'Some of you are average, some perform above the average and some of you below. By this time next week I want everybody above the average'? Unfortunately for this manager, variation within a work group is inevitable; within the natural range of performance outputs, some individuals will regularly perform towards the upper end, some towards the lower end and some around the middle. This normal range is the result of inbuilt variables such as work input, number of interdependent relationships, resources and customers as well as intrinsic personal effectiveness. We manage two types of people-based variation:

- variation *between* individuals across the group; and
- variation *within* each individual.

Variation between individuals. Knowing where each member of your work group fits into the spectrum allows you to take an individual approach to management of your people's performance. It means that you can first work on improving each one against their current performance, not against the top person in the team.

Figure 5.7 is a diagram of the variation between individuals in a work team. It shows two histogram curves, plotting the level of performance, on a scale of 1 to 10, against the number of team members who achieve at each level. Histogram A shows the team before improvement, with a mean performance of 5.5 and performance ranging from 1 to 8, a range of 7. Most employees achieve a performance of between 4 and 7, with fewer employees above and below this level.

In setting out to improve performance, the first step is to reduce variation across the team. In this example we would work on the lower performers to lift them up a notch or two. Our second step would be to shift the curve to the right—that is, to improve everyone's performance (histogram B). This step requires us to look at *non-personal* performance drivers because these affect all employees in the group. The outcome of both of these initiatives is that the mean performance has increased from 5.5 to 6.5 and the range has reduced to from 7 to 5—a good result.

Variation within individuals. Just as the whole team shows a range of performance, so too does each individual. Good understanding of this phenomenon means, first, that you won't be drawn into overreacting or underreacting to performance data. Second, you will undertake improvement in two stages:

1. Control and progressively reduce variation in individual performance; and
2. Progressively move the graph to the high-performance side.

This understanding also helps us to answer the question that perplexes many managers: 'Why does one of my poorer performers sometimes beat one of my top performers?' We may say it's just luck or 'a fluke', or we may take it seriously, express disappointment that our hero has fallen and create a new hero in the person who came from behind. The situation occurs when your top performer is performing at the lower end of his performance histogram while the lesser employee is at his top end and the curves overlap.

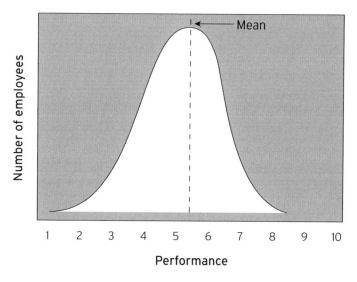

Histogram A. Team before improvement

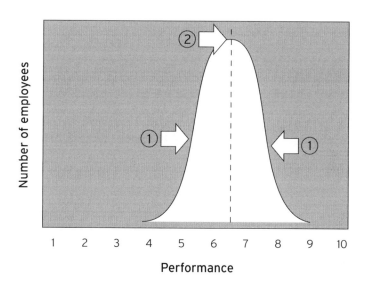

Histogram B. Team after improvement

Figure 5.7 Histograms of team performance

Step 8 Capability

We noted earlier that 'capability' is the level of achievement against performance objectives. We now want to expand our traditional thinking from just one-dimensional measures of capability to three-dimensional measures, which include both *range* and *limits*.

An example of a one-dimensional measure might be: 'average training course rating of 90 per cent'. The overall intention of this measure and target is no doubt to ensure that all clients are happy with the training courses, and the belief is that an average rating of 90 per cent should reflect that. However, this is not necessarily so, as shown in the report in Figure 5.8 where we can see that, while the trainer achieved the target average of 90 per cent, two participants, presumably unhappy, rated the course at 70 per cent and 60 per cent respectively.

This leads us to the notion that capability in this case is more than just an absolute value and must include a lower limit—that is, how far off

Training Satisfaction Scores

Data, 10 courses

Score	No. of participants
100%	30
90%	40
80%	28
70%	1
60%	1

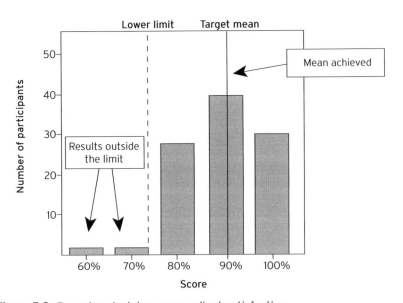

Figure 5.8 Report on training course client satisfaction

track can you afford to go without unacceptable consequences. Thus, the measure should have been something like:

Achieve an average course rating of 90 per cent, with no more than 10 per cent of ratings falling below 85 per cent and none falling below 75 per cent.

On the basis of this new measure, the trainer has not met the requirement (see Figure 5.8).

In this example we use mean values as the core measure. In the case of results that *accumulate*, such as transactions, customer contacts, production or sales, a lower limit may be placed on each of the measurement *periods*, so that the employee can't reach a point where recovery of the cumulative target is no longer possible.

6 Managing work as an open system

It used to be that many people were buried deep inside the organisation and produced their work in a very predictable environment. As long as they looked after their part, and others looked after theirs in the same way, the results would be okay. They operated within a relatively closed work system where the only major portals to other environments were the work inputs they received and the work outputs they produced.

At the other extreme were people who lived daily with a work system that was influenced by a bigger 'system'. For example, field salespeople could not get by with just knowing their sales territory, their product and their pricing. They had to contend with such unpredictable influences as product availability, competitors, their customers, the economy, the weather and the traffic in order to perform successfully.

The former operate in a relatively closed system of work where they have few interdependencies, while the latter are in a relatively *open system* of work where they have many interdependencies.

In Chapter 1 we considered social and business evolution within organisations, the challenges for managers and some guidelines for managing the 'unmanageable' workplace. One of the reasons for 'unmanageability' is that more and more people now operate within an open system. As a consequence they, and you, need to be able to *understand and manage work as an open system*.

An open systems perspective

What defines an open or closed work system? The one aspect that stands out is *interdependency*—that is, the degree to which work is dependent on outside factors and, conversely, the degree to which outside factors are dependent on the work. To illustrate the nature of interdependency, Table 6.1 presents some examples; they should also help you to identify interdependencies within your own work or business unit.

Table 6.1 Examples of work according to degree of interdependency

Less interdependent work system	
Work	**Systemic interdependencies**
TASK 'File of these invoices in alphabetical order of company name; where any are unclear, refer them to me.' **ROLE** 'Match invoices against purchase orders, tick when correct, refer to supervisor when not.'	There is limited outside interference with performance. Factors that might affect performance include: • competing priorities (manager controls) • inaccurate invoices or purchase orders (but a response pathway has been built into the assignment)

More interdependent work system	
Work	**Systemic interdependencies**
TASK (Customer Service Consultant) 'Ask each inquiring customer what make, model and year of car they drive. Report at the end of the week.'	Personal factors affecting performance: • degree of training or instruction for the specific task
	Non-personal factors affecting performance: • priorities—the exercise may slow the queue and customers become angry, leave the queue, won't answer the research questions, etc. • media is carrying stories that your company is about to enter the car insurance market by acquiring smaller lower premium firms and thus pushing up premiums in the market

From these simple examples it is also clear that the degree of inter-dependency tends to correlate with work *complexity*.

Although interdependency is the dominant characteristic of open systems, it also determines secondary characteristics that differentiate them from closed systems. These secondary characteristics are the ones we recognise more readily and the ones that provide some insight into the differing performance management requirements. Table 6.2 provides a basic comparison of closed and open work systems.

Two particular management implications of open systems should be apparent from Table 6.2, affecting you and your employees. From the

Table 6.2 A comparison of closed and open work systems

	Closed system	Open system
WORK		
Interdependency– where the major influences on output lie	within the work and the workplace	within the work, the organisation, customers and suppliers, competitors, the economy, etc.
Degree of worker direct influence over the output	higher	lower
Predictability of operating environment	more predictable	less predictable
Level of risk	lower	higher
Performance monitoring	less frequent: task focus	more frequent; outcome focus
Typical planning horizon	operational: annual strategic: 3–5 years	operational: shorter than annual strategic: 1–3 years
WORKERS		
Level of work, business and relational skill required	lower	higher
Employee development focus	skill in managing immediate and stable environment more efficiently	skill in managing environments that are multiple, dynamic and uncontrollable

	Closed system	Open system
MANAGEMENT		
Management of the work	work mostly rolled over—minimum new assignment; little or no planning; activity-based monitoring; scheduled performance review	more detailed and interactive assignment of work; greater level, more dynamic planning; emphasis on outcome-based monitoring and management; performance reviewed on an ongoing basis
Management of the employee	limited employee discretion; implicitly accepts responsibility for all outside of the employee's immediate work environment; limited personal feedback	wider, clearly stated employee discretion and contingent accountability; ongoing personal feedback

managerial perspective, you are required to take an active interest outside your own 'patch', meaning that you manage inputs, you manage external influences upon your outputs and you manage how your outputs are further transformed.

In relation to your people, given the changing nature of work, there is clearly an increasing need for more and more employees to exhibit the attributes normally associated with senior managers or entrepreneurs. For example, in an open work system the employee must deal with uncertainty, manage risk, deal with several dynamic environments simultaneously, make more decisions, exercise greater discretion and accept greater accountability, all behaviours that are not generally currently associated with the front line.

An open system work model

We'll build our open system work model from two components. First, we'll take a process view to see *how work generates value*, and then we'll superimpose the work's *global environment* to create a model of an open system of work.

How work generates value—a process view

In Chapter 5 we introduced a 'process' view to understand different types of measurement. We now use this same process perspective as a starting point for understanding your work within a larger system. Your work will invariably consist of several processes and some or many of these processes will be one part of a larger process (Figure 6.1). To illustrate the process view we consider just one process you might do—let's say it involves *the preparation of a monthly management report that goes to your manager.*

Your **process** is that you take data from the market, from some other functions in your organisation and from your own business unit, and then you analyse the data and write a report. In executing this process, you take **inputs** (the raw data from your suppliers—internal and external) which you process (analysis and writing a report) and produce an **output** (your report). Your report goes to your manager who completes a **downstream** step of this process by adding an overview and distributing it to other function heads in your organisation.

Beyond this process, but in the same value chain, the report provides **input to other roles** (valuable decision-making information) so that they

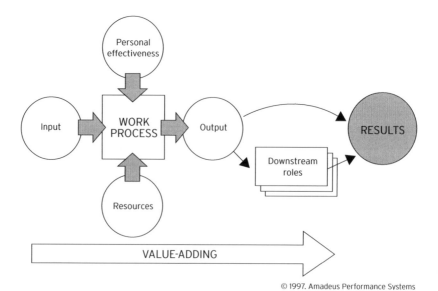

© 1997. Amadeus Performance Systems

Figure 6.1 A simple process view of work

can add value in their turn, ultimately creating an enterprise **result** (for customers, shareholders, staff, etc.).

In addition to this activity flow, you use **resources** (your people to collect the data and your computer to do the work) to enable your process, and your **personal effectiveness** (ability to acquire good data, to supervise your own people, to provide good analysis and write good reports) influences the quality of your work. All along this chain of work, from the input, through the intermediate processes and outputs to the final enterprise results, **value** is being **added**.

Some people look at a process view of work and say, 'That makes sense. I knew all that but never really put it all together.' The significance of the process view is that it is a start to knowing what needs to be measured and managed in order to ensure that results are achieved.

The work environment—a global view

The process view is largely linear—that is, we start at the left side of the page and move in a line across to the right-hand side. We need to stretch the view again to take into account the operating *environment* of the work. To do this, let's use as an example the Earth and its atmosphere. As humans we go about our living on the surface of the planet—the equivalent of our immediate work environment. Heavier gases are closer to the Earth and the lighter ones are at the outer edge of our atmosphere. For day-to-day living we need oxygen for breathing and this is readily available at sea level. At the outer edge of the atmosphere are lighter gases, one of which is ozone. Although we don't think about it every minute, ozone is critical to our ultimate survival because it reduces the lethal levels of ultra-violet radiation that would otherwise reach the Earth's surface. So what we have here is distant ozone, which may not change your life today, but is critical to achievement of your longer-term goals.

Similarly, your work and that of your people operates in a global 'atmosphere'. For example, going back to the 'analysis and report' process, **management support** enhances your work when your own manager provides clear Work Assignment, feedback and coaching. You depend upon **enterprise ideologies and infrastructure** (culture, policy, strategies, IT and communication systems) and the **external environment**, in the form of the market, competitors, community, governments and the economy, also influences your work. More detailed examples of the work environment are given in Appendix 1.

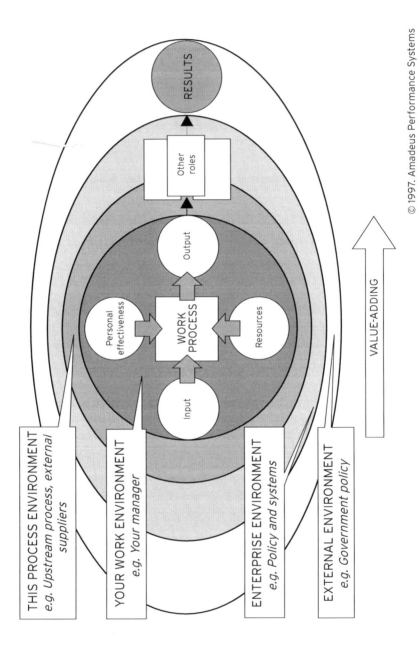

RESULTS

Other roles

Output

Personal effectiveness

WORK PROCESS

Resources

Input

THIS PROCESS ENVIRONMENT
e.g. Upstream process, external suppliers

YOUR WORK ENVIRONMENT
e.g. Your manager

ENTERPRISE ENVIRONMENT
e.g. Policy and systems

EXTERNAL ENVIRONMENT
e.g. Government policy

VALUE-ADDING

© 1997. Amadeus Performance Systems

Figure 6.2 A global view of work

If we overlay the *process* view with the *global* view, we have the basis of a model for effectively understanding the performance of any piece of work buried within the enterprise (Figure 6.2).

Figure 6.2 shows graphically that an individual's immediate work environment is continuous with, or interdependent with, other environments, both internal and external to the enterprise. It displays some of these interdependent environments, more or less arranged in relation to the degree of environmental proximity or control available to the individual. The distinctions between environments are arbitrary but they are a useful way of understanding how to influence work results and plan work more effectively.

To turn these ideas into practice, we now look at managing an open system of work and introduce a performance management tool, the *work system model*.

Managing an open system of work

Having proposed an open system approach as a good thing, the next step is to turn it into management practice. First, we need to know the specific performance situations where this approach adds value. Next, we need a suitable model to use as a practical management tool and, finally, we need to consider the people-management implications of an open system approach.

Where do you apply an open system approach?

The use of an open system approach makes even more sense when you look at its impact on the common performance management tasks: Work Assignment and Planning, measurement and monitoring, feedback and coaching, and the formal performance review.

Work Assignment and Planning

When you assign to an employee a role, task or goal, it should include an agreement about what degree of discretion the employee is expected to exercise over what degree of the work system. The full extent of accountability is then taken into account when planning the work.

Measurement and monitoring

Taking a view of the whole system helps to make clear the critical factors that need to be managed, and therefore what is to be measured and monitored. These decisions will also affect planning and the interpretation of the performance data.

Feedback and coaching

Feedback and coaching both work with personal effectiveness. An open system view helps you and your employee to differentiate between personal effectiveness and non-personal performance drivers.

Formal performance review

As with feedback, you are able to distinguish between personal effectiveness and non-personal performance drivers when it comes to formally reviewing your employees. You are also clear in advance of the scope of accountability for achievement, including what alternative actions were to be taken to address goals at risk. All this leads to a more straightforward resolution of reviews and a more just outcome.

Applying an open system of work model

The model illustrated in Figure 6.3 should look familiar because it pulls together the process view of work and the global view of work into a form that makes it easy to use as a tool in managing performance. The model is a gross simplification of the complexity of modern work but it illustrates the management concept and provides the basis for a checklist that you can use.

In the open system view each element in the model has a relationship with every other element. If we were to illustrate this with double headed arrows the model would be unreadable, therefore, what the model shows is arrows tracking the underlying process pathway. To make use of the model we ask ourselves what influence each element has upon the other, determine the significance of any influence and then, any management action that is required. In order to illustrate the model in action, we will apply the check list approach to our earlier process example, the *preparation of a monthly management report*. Because of the interrelationships of the elements there is no 'right' place to start. In the absence of a known area of risk, I tend to start with the bottom line objective, which is to use a planning logic, and which is the way we will go with this example.

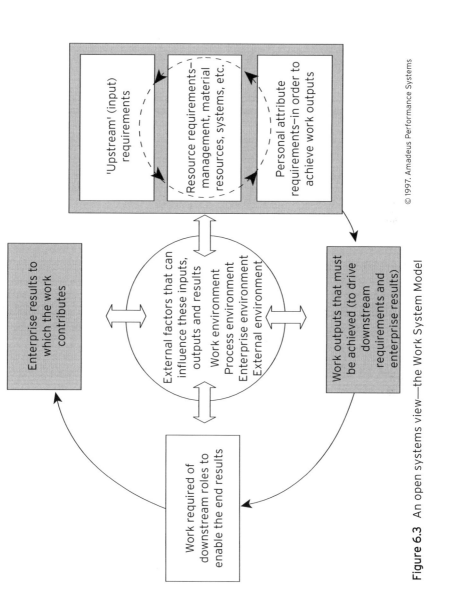

Figure 6.3 An open systems view—the Work System Model

'Upstream' (input) requirements

Resource requirements—management, material resources, systems, etc.

Personal attribute requirements—in order to achieve work outputs

External factors that can influence these inputs, outputs and results
Work environment
Process environment
Enterprise environment
External environment

Enterprise results to which the work contributes

Work outputs that must be achieved (to drive downstream requirements and enterprise results)

Work required of downstream roles to enable the end results

Enterprise results to which the work contributes

One result to which your report contributes may be, for example, a measure of 'customer satisfaction'. With this in mind you have a focus for managing the output of your task and the way in which your output is subsequently used—'How well does this output address issues of customer satisfaction?' This examination could lead you to fine-tune your output, to influence what others do with your output or even to question the task itself.

Your requirements of downstream roles

You could produce a report that meets the expectations of your manager or some other downstream user and then say that you've done your job. But what if your manager is late in distributing your report or one of the users applies your report incorrectly—is that no longer 'your business'? In the interests of the enterprise, and in keeping with open system management, you would monitor and manage these downstream steps, preferably proactively rather than reactively.

Outputs required by downstream roles

You must balance your view of the enterprise purpose of your report with a good understanding of the needs of those who actually use it. Determining these needs will often involve you in negotiating expectations with your downstream users or 'customers', extending you beyond your simple task process.

Upstream requirements

You depend on the quality and timeliness of the data you use to write your report and therefore you have to manage upstream. You have to be specific about your requirements, set standards, put monitoring or checks in place and establish responses for when the report is put at risk because of input shortcomings.

Resource requirements and personal attribute requirements

Although resources and personal attributes might seem to be stable requirements, they are *interdependent* with each other and other components of the system. For example, if input quantity falls, you may use greater resources to pick up the slack, or if input quality falls you may require greater personal skills to correct it.

External factors that can influence inputs, outputs and results

In your **work environment** you have to manage your staff to meet the work requirement. In the **process environment** you have other functions providing input data so you have to ensure that their input is not compromised by lack of time, other priorities or faulty computer systems.

In order for your reports to influence enterprise results, you depend on other people in the **enterprise environment** to use them and understand them and, therefore, you have an interest in company policy with respect to their required use and in the skills of users.

In the **external environment**, if the needs of the company's clients change, the conclusions in your report may become irrelevant or misleading.

Already you begin to see how complex and overwhelming is the number of influences on your work and that of your employees. You don't have to manage all these influences but you *do* have to manage those that are *critical* or *at risk*. This means that, first, you have to be aware of all the influences so that you can identify the critical ones.

Activity 6.1

Work system model

Using the open system of work model, take one important aspect of your own role, a task or a goal, and analyse it from an open system perspective. Think about the range of influences on your chosen work focus and on the downstream results you expect from this particular piece of work.

1. What are these situations and how are they evolving?
2. Identify those influences that have the most impact on your ability to achieve your results.
3. Which of these are the most difficult to predict or control?
4. How many of these do you currently monitor?

Implications for people management

Adopting an open system approach affects not only your management of work performance but also your management of your people's performance. The implications can be thought of as being of three types—skills, systems, and differentiating between the two.

Skills

These were referred to early in the chapter and include such skills as managing multiple, dynamic and fast-moving environments, influencing others, managing uncertainty and risk, exercising greater discretion, making more decisions faster and accepting greater accountability.

Systems

The above description of requisite skills is already an indicator of the sort of systems and information that are necessary to support such personal effectiveness on the part of employees.

Improve the system, not just the people

What the open system view shows us very clearly is that people are just one part of the system necessary for achieving work performance, yet we tend to focus on getting better results from our people at the expense of improving the rest of the system. It is a paradox that, although many managers say that managing people can be difficult, they also avoid managing the work system.

The following memorable statement from author Peter Scholtes underscores the implications of failing to manage work as an open system. This view is also supported by the quality management axiom which states that 85 per cent of performance problems are in the process (system) and only 15 per cent are people problems.

> *Develop outstanding systems which excel with the efforts of ordinary people. Stop believing that you must have outstanding people whose heroic efforts will compensate for the inadequacies of your dysfunctional systems.*
> (Scholtes 1995)

When there is an unrealistic expectation on people to perform under closed system management, the following problems arise.

- Business performance becomes less responsive to personal effort and people appear to be less responsive to incentives (positive and negative).
- The individual loses the 'touch' of being a significant influence on the work. Motivation inevitably declines and the employee is likely to go elsewhere to get both self-fulfilment and market-relevant skills.

- The organisation invests in developing the 'old' skills to a greater level—doing the wrong things better!
- At performance reviews it becomes harder to be sure what we are rewarding.

So, if you manage work as an open system and distinguish between personal effectiveness and system effectiveness, your people and you can manage their personal effectiveness more skilfully. The following are some of the benefits.

- You can address personal performance more precisely and effectively; you can focus on defining where people best add value as distinct from where the system best adds value.
- You make allowances less frequently because something was beyond the employee's control.
- Your people are better able to make sense of the complexity and unpredictability that they observe influencing their daily work.
- You make sure that, if a particular employee is not managing to exert a significant influence on the results, then someone else is.
- Your people are more in control of their output and results and more positively motivated.
- Your people are willing to be more accountable.
- Formal performance review takes place on a more sound and agreeable basis.

Making the transition to an open systems approach

If you have gained an understanding of work as an open system, and if you can see what it will add to the performance of your work unit, then you have made a good start. In this section we touch briefly on some of the considerations in making the transition.

- *Work design.* It is possible that the design of work in your work unit is based on an older, more stable, more independent environment and that you will need to redesign to suit the new operating environment.
- *Challenges for you.* To manage people effectively in an open system of work may require that you are willing to change. You should identify

and work with such personal challenges. You might also identify your strengths in this regard.

- *Encourage your staff.* Some staff will readily adopt the new way; others will need encouragement. You will need to answer the question *Why would we want to change?* as well as dealing with reasons why they *wouldn't* want to change.

Part III

Managing on the Job—
People Performance

Chapters 7 to 10 deal with what many managers regard as the most difficult part of performance management—feedback, coaching and managing difficult performers. Part III is a continuation of the system of managing work performance that was described in Part II, and covers the part of performance management that is focused more on the interpersonal components of the performance interaction.

Between them, Parts II and III (Chapters 3 to 10) cover all the practical requirements for you to manage the performance of your people on a day-to-day basis.

In a similar vein to Part II, you will notice that we draw a number of lessons that refer back to earlier chapters. For example, when considering a good approach to feedback, you will find that a lot depends on the quality of Work Assignment in the first place.

7 'I wish I hadn't said that!' Performance feedback

I had a problem with a young graduate whom I'd appointed to a project team working on a strategic review. In reviewing report drafts, I noted that his section mostly didn't follow our format and that some of it was quite radical. I reached the conclusion that he was bored with the project, more interested in expressing his own ideas, and was probably looking for a better job. In the end I called him in and let him have it—about the immorality of sponging off the company while looking for another job, how it let down the team and how he'd better not ask for a reference. I was embarrassed and shocked when he told me (1) that he was very happy here because he was learning so much from the principal specialist who (2) had been coaching him in the radical approach the specialist considered necessary for this important section of the report.

This classic was courageously shared in a management workshop and is typical of the 'I wish I hadn't said that!' war stories of feedback that nearly every manager could tell. In this chapter we provide guidelines and processes that will make feedback easier and more productive for both you and your people. We start by looking at the place of feedback in the work environment and then consider the key elements of good feedback, bringing them together in a feedback model. We conclude with an approach to managing difficult feedback situations.

Feedback at work

Performance feedback is a management task that is both critical and complex. It is critical because, like performance data, it provides your people with information to evaluate and modify their performance. It is complex because, on the one hand, you have to be a task expert and manage the data and business aspects, while on the other you have to execute skilfully what is, for most managers, a difficult person-to-person interaction. Performance feedback is also an opportunity gained, or lost, for building trust and respect between you and your people.

What is performance feedback?

We can start by defining 'feedback', using the classic analogy of the thermostat in a room heater. The thermostat is set to a certain desired temperature (*performance target*) and, while the room temperature is below that level (*actual performance*), the thermostat registers the deficiency (*measures the performance*) and keeps the heater on (*responds*). As soon as the set temperature is reached, the thermostat switches off the current and the heater stops. When the room temperature falls, the thermostat once again switches on the current and the cycle repeats.

The essential elements therefore are a performance target, actual performance, measurement of performance and an action response. In applying the notion of feedback to people at work, we make two additions. First, we consider the delivery and receptor method, which is human, imperfect and sensitive. Second, we include the open system of work model, which allows us to question the *underlying variables* that not only determine performance but also test the rightness of the objective and strategies (Figure 7.1).

This process of not only keeping on track but being on the right track has been called 'double-loop learning'.

Feedback is personal

Because of the hierarchical relationship, any reference that you make to your employee's work is implied feedback about their personal effectiveness. For example—'How's it going?' 'When do you think you'll have finished section 3?' 'I notice that (competitor) has switched from TV advertising to radio.' 'Sales are slow, are you still happy with your

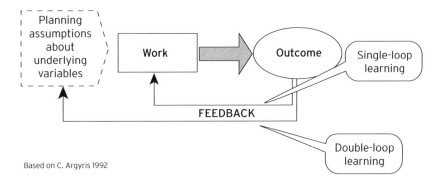

Figure 7.1 Using feedback to test planning assumptions

strategy?'—all have an implication about how well the employee is performing. Any dialogue about the work involves explicit or implicit feedback and so the principles learned in this chapter apply to much more than formalised feedback or review interactions.

Giving feedback is also a moment of truth for you because you get to find out about the quality of your own assignment of work and the quality of your management and coaching support. Use it as an opportunity by facilitating two-way communication during performance feedback, which will allow you to correct and fine-tune your own management abilities.

Although this chapter focuses on *you* as a source of feedback, it is feedback directly *from the work itself* that should mostly guide your employees on a daily basis. Develop employees' ability to self-manage, with your role being to focus on the finer points of their performance, those small things that can make a very big difference.

Why give feedback?

If you played blind man's bluff as a child, or with your own children, you will know how it is made easier when people are calling 'you're getting colder, you're getting hotter'. Most tasks don't move in a perfectly straight line towards their goal but are more a case of act, measure, check against target, correct, act, etc. It is sometimes said that the first rocket sent to the moon was on course less than 5 per cent of the time; the rest of the time it was correcting its course in response to feedback on its trajectory.

The same situation applies at work, where the main reason for giving feedback is to let your people know *how* they are performing so that they can correct, or affirm, their actions in an *informed* manner.

The reasons for giving performance feedback can be presented as seven specific benefits.

1 **Correction and consolidation.** The most basic benefit of performance feedback is either (a) to ensure that what your people are doing or achieving is on track to reach their objectives, or (b) to reinforce or improve effective performance.

2 **System development.** The outcomes of feedback should extend beyond the employee to the whole of the work system. By using the open system of work model you can test the underlying variables on which you planned your objectives, as well as how effectively those variables were implemented.

3 **Coaching.** Before you can coach, you need to have identified and agreed on the subject at issue and this can only be done by an effective feedback discussion on current performance.

4 **Learning and development.** All personal development depends on *learning*, which in turn involves having an experience, observing the consequences of our actions and then reflecting on cause and effect. Feedback is critical to being able to observe the *consequences* of our actions.

5 **Recognition and reward.** To give convincing recognition to an employee for good performance you have to give good-quality feedback. This requires more than a 'Good job' comment in passing. For example, 'Good job on the report, Kathy' is not as powerful as 'Kathy, the analysis of section 3 is very thorough and opens up more opportunities than we'd thought of'. Praise given without knowing or communicating exactly what it was that the employee did to achieve a good result can be used occasionally, but used too much your people will start to believe that you do it only to make them and/or yourself feel good.

6 **Discipline.** Discipline procedures in relation to poor performance are dictated mostly by company policies. However, whatever procedures you have in place, if performance-related discipline is based on a series of well conducted feedback meetings with the employee, you are more likely to get a performance-effective and industrially acceptable outcome.

7   **Evaluation**. Most formal reviews or 'appraisals' include a form of evaluation where each employee's performance over a period is reduced to a single measure that allows all types of employees to be compared with each other. An effective process of ongoing feedback is essential to an accurate and fair evaluation.

Elements of effective feedback

Whenever a group of managers discuss feedback, the list of what makes good feedback is pretty well universal. Our first approach to feedback is to explore that list. Some of these points are discussed again later, in the context of a feedback *model*.

Act with respect
Giving feedback is an opportunity not only to improve the outcomes of the work but also to build your employee's self-respect and dignity, whether as a result of good work done or of their confidence in being able to improve their work performance.

Manage your motivation and mood
Each time you approach a feedback situation, check your *motivation*. If you try to give feedback with a 'hidden agenda', such as demonstrating your authority or 'getting even', nobody wins.

   If you are aware of *mood* issues before you start, you can make allowance for them rather than letting them run the meeting. If your underlying emotions include being angry or upset in relation to your employee's work, you can express these, but do it within the feedback framework. If you are feeling out of control or fearful—you might be under pressure in your own job or troubled by a personal issue—you can either postpone the feedback to another time or, if you can't do that, continue to be aware of the possible influence of your feelings.

Be honest
Your employees can deal with the truth but not with half-truths or hidden truths. Sometimes managers attempt to spare an employee's feelings or avoid a confrontation by 'pussyfooting' around an issue, which means less chance of a resolution. In a more worrying situation, a manager withholds comment on adverse performance until a later time,

sometimes to make a point, at which time employees feel their manager has been 'living a lie' and this undermines trust.

Separate the problem from the person

By this statement managers mean don't make it personal—that is, don't attack the person, attack the problem. Employees generally regard any feedback on adverse work performance as a judgment of them personally.

Direct, not indirect

Sometimes managers will give feedback indirectly by making a snide comment, whingeing about an employee's performance or withholding favours. Sometimes an employee receives unfavourable feedback via the grapevine. Indirect feedback is counter-productive because the employee is not clear what the problem is and so can't do anything about it.

Give *and* receive

Once you set up a culture of good, direct feedback, be prepared to get direct feedback *from* your employees. Employee feedback is an opportunity to develop your own management, if you can move yourself beyond seeing it as a criticism.

Avoid 'a great job, but . . .'

Managers often try to soften bad news by giving good news first, but employees say that this doesn't work. When you have to give both positive and negative feedback there are ways to avoid the problems.

- Deal with positive and negative on different occasions.
- Tell your employee that you have both good and bad news. This way you can both put full effort into the positives without at the same time preparing yourself for the negatives. (I don't believe that 'good' first or 'bad' first is anything more than a personal preference.)

Keep it manageable

Avoid giving feedback—good or bad—on too many issues at one time, or too frequently. The receiver becomes overloaded and desensitised, with results that include:

- disbelief (positive feedback);
- information overload;
- giving up on self (*Am I really _that_ bad?*); and
- giving up on you (*_Nothing_ will please him.*).

'Just the facts, ma'am'

If you focus on *objective* facts, such as actual behaviour, outputs or outcomes, you are less likely to lead with your *assumptions* (Chapter 2) about why your employee might have done something. Leading with assumptions is the *worst* move that can be made and unfortunately it happens right up front, sabotaging some interactions completely. 'You arrived at 9.30 this morning (and your starting time is 8 am)' is a statement of fact that will definitely be more productive than 'We need to talk about your attitude to work'.

Be specific

Don't generalise by using 'always' or 'never' as this paints your employee into a corner. Better to approach multiple underperformances with a statement like 'I've noticed that each of your last four weekly reports has been two days late'.

Keep to recent events

There are two good reasons not to postpone your feedback. First, when there is an unresolved problem you need to intervene quickly to protect enterprise performance. Second, you need to provide feedback close in time to the event so that your employee and you can recall enough detail to analyse the problem.

Involve the employee

The more the employee is involved in exploring both the situation and the resolution, the better the quality of the actions arising and the employee's commitment to them.

A model process of performance feedback

Feedback is one of the more challenging parts of your management role and one that has significant implications for performance and for mutual trust and respect. This means that you can't afford a 'hit and miss' approach—you need some form of structured approach or process to give you the security of the *form* while you focus on the *content* and the other *person*. If you observe, you will find that managers who are 'naturally' successful at feedback will be using some form of structured process (although they may not be aware of it). Some managers who get on well with people often seem to achieve a relaxed interaction but don't necessarily get the results they intend because they lack the focus and structure to turn the good relationship into a work outcome.

The Agreement Model of Feedback

A model for reaching agreement on performance issues was introduced in Chapter 2. It is the ideal platform for performance feedback because it is logical, ensures clarity of understanding and creates a non-threatening atmosphere that encourages employee commitment to the process and outcomes.

Figure 7.2 shows the agreement model, configured for use when giving performance feedback. The five process steps begin with a mutual agreement to participate, progress through reaching agreement successively on the Situation, the Implications and the Resolution and end with a mutual agreement to integrate—p S I R i. The following are two simple examples of the feedback model, using the core S-I-R steps.

1. An example of feedback about a need for **correction**:

    Situation   *John, the monthly sales result is below budget.*

    Implication   *If we don't correct any problem and pick up the deficit, we won't be able to meet our annual target.*

    Resolution   *I'd like to discuss how we might solve the problem.*

This example is presented as a monologue but feedback needs to be a *dialogue*, a conversation between you and your employee, reaching *agreement* on each step before moving on to the next. The next example is a simple illustration.

2. An example of feedback to give **recognition**:

    Situation   *Kathy, the analysis of this chapter uncovers more issues and opens up more possibilities than we had previously thought of.*

    (Dialogue and agreement follow)

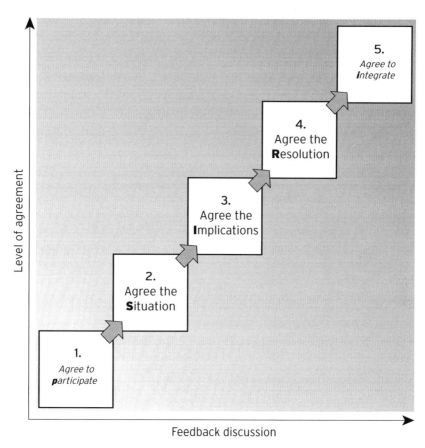

Feedback discussion

© 1997–2002 Amadeus Performance Systems

Figure 7.2 The Agreement Model of Feedback—p S I R i

Implication   *This will mean a much better community impact and recognition for our work.*
(Dialogue and agreement follow)
Resolution   *I wonder if you are now ready to tackle some of the more difficult analyses?*
(Dialogue and agreement follow)

When giving positive feedback, the **R**esolution step does not always need to include some development or future work activity. It may simply involve some form of acknowledgment or recognition, such as saying 'Thank you'.

Although the three core steps of *Situation–Implication–Resolution* are where most of the discussion time will be spent, remember that all five steps are essential for a successful result. For example, it happens often enough that an employee does not want to engage in a feedback discussion and, unless you gain agreement to *participate*, then nothing beyond that point will work out. Similarly, unless both parties discuss and agree the *integration* of the resolution into the workplace, even the best solutions risk falling over.

Logic of the feedback model

In Chapter 2 the logic was that you couldn't move on to the next level of discussion without having reached agreement on the previous level. This means that if you encounter either open or hidden disagreement at a point, and proceed without resolving it, you are effectively seeking participation in solving a problem and commitment to actions that you alone have determined. In these circumstances you have less chance of a sustained improvement in performance or, indeed, any improvement at all.

The logic is based both on the way we think and the way we feel. We are more able to deal with a need for correction when we understand and agree the reasons; therefore we start at the point of most likely agreement and move towards the point of least likely agreement. We are also more able to deal with feedback when we feel justly treated; the model allows us to form a trusting relationship on the more objective items before moving to the more personal.

We start by agreeing the Situation, because:

- this is the area where we are most likely to be dealing with objective and verifiable data and therefore able to reach agreement;
- being an objective topic, we are less likely to harm the relationship with our employee;
- without agreement on the 'facts', we are not in a strong position to move forward to correction or consolidation.

Next we need to agree on the Implications, because:

- the actual performance is only relevant to the employee if the consequences are also relevant; this takes care of the potential 'so what?!' response;

- before we can move on to actions arising from the Situation, we need to know what it is we want to change and, generally, the primary focus is the Implications of the performance, not the performance itself; and
- before we can move on to Resolution of the issue, the employee will need to agree with the implications, otherwise there is limited reason or motivation to take any action.

Finally, we are able to agree on a Resolution, because:

- now we have agreement that there is a need or an opportunity for action, we have agreed what Implication we want to change, and there is a clear and committed focus on the Resolution.

The following example illustrates these points in action.

Manager: *Robert, your monthly reports are due in the first week of the month and for the last three months they have arrived in the second week.*
(Dialogue and agreement. Robert may also offer reasons for the delays.)

This is an objective statement. The manager may be right or may be wrong but the facts are verifiable and seeking agreement on the Situation will not damage his relationship with his employee.

Manager: *The problem is that, when your reports are late, we are late getting consolidated data to Production, which means their schedules are delayed, causing low stocks in the warehouse and some retailers actually being out of stock.*
(Dialogue and agreement)

Robert's late reports are not the real issue here, even though they irritate the manager. The real issue is the impact on stock levels and, ultimately, sales. By seeking agreement on the Implications, the manager has provided a valid reason for Robert to want to address the problem, and a more worthwhile motive than simply keeping the manager happy by getting his reports in on time. In addition, even if the manager's logic on the Implications is wrong, it is discussable and they have still maintained a good relationship.

Employee: *Well, if that's the problem, and given that it's difficult for me to meet the deadline over the next six months, how would it work if I were to email my figures directly to Production, without waiting for the other information I need for my report?*
(Dialogue and agreement)

What we have now is a focus on Resolution to address the *real* problem, which in turn creates the potential for better, more innovative solutions, maybe not just to this problem but to improve the current system.

Receiving feedback

Performance feedback is about both giving and receiving. The Agreement Model of Feedback is for use whether you are the giver or the receiver.

In a feedback situation, the receiver can ensure that the process is being followed. When the manager initiates the process, it may sometimes require that the employee bring the process back on track. Here are two examples of the receiver applying the Agreement Model of Feedback.

Feedback dialogue	Receiver applying the agreement model
Example 1	
Manager: *You're getting a bit careless about your reports.*	Manager's feedback is indirect, non-specific, and makes an assumption ('careless')
Employee: *I'm not sure what you're referring to. Can you be specific?*	Employee doesn't become engaged in defending the 'careless' assumption but probes for the Situation
Manager: *Your monthly reports are due in the first week of the month and for the last three months they have arrived in the second week.*	Situation is expressed; now they can get started
Etc.	

Feedback dialogue	Receiver applying the agreement model
Example 2	
Manager: *Your monthly reports are due in the first week of the month and for the last three months they have arrived in the second week.*	Good Situation statement
Employee: *I'm sorry about that. My involvement on the project team means I'm unable to do the report in the normal time frame.*	Employee confirms agreement on the Situation
Manager: *Well, you'd better sort out a way to fix it. Maybe you should reconsider being on that project team.*	Manager leaps straight into attempted Resolution
Employee: *My understanding is that the aims of the project are more important than my reports being on time. What's the actual problem or implications with their being late?*	Employee seeks to establish what the Implication is, so that they can balance the competing requirements
Etc.	

Applying effective practices to the feedback model

Earlier in the chapter we explored the key elements of effective feedback. We now consider how to integrate them with the agreement model, making the model more effective and more a reflection of real-life interaction. A work template for conducting a performance feedback meeting is provided in Appendix 3. The template incorporates material from this chapter, as well as from other chapters.

1 Agree to participate

An unwilling employee is not a partner in the feedback process but either a rebel or a victim, meaning that any agreements and commitments to action will be only token. Another value of this step is that it serves as an introduction and gives your employee a moment or two to get in sync with you. When attempting to provide feedback to your own manager, gaining participation can be difficult if they are not receptive.

In gaining your employee's participation there are four issues to take care of: timing, place, intention and language.

Timing
Schedule the meeting, and any prior advice, for when the employee will be most receptive; for example:

- when they have the time—at the end of the day or a shift is not so good;
- when they are feeling okay about their work—it's not a good time when they are upset or angry; or
- when it's close in time to the actual work event so that recollection is fresh.

In situations that require your *urgent intervention* your actions to correct the problem will also implicitly give feedback to your employee. Two points to keep in mind are:

1. Even on the fly, stay with the principles—better, 'Something doesn't look right; can we have a word?' than 'What the hell is this?!'
2. After an urgent issue has been resolved it is important to have an immediate feedback session.

Place
It sometimes works well to give *positive* feedback in public, but at other times the receiver is embarrassed by public acknowledgment. Use your knowledge of individuals and of your own work culture to tell you what is appropriate. Invariably, *negative* feedback to one person is best given in private.

Intention
Be clear about what you want to get out of this feedback interaction—a clear and well-founded intention at the start will help to engage the employee. If you have a personal agenda—for example, to put this

employee 'in his place'—this intention will be evident and will create an unwilling participant.

Language

Participation can be expected when it comes to feedback on good performance but resistance starts to build early when 'bad news' is anticipated. In such cases, use neutral but relevant language: for example, 'John, can we have a talk about last month's sales result?' If necessary to allay anxiety, add reassuring phrases or words such as 'work together to fix it . . .' or 'see if I can help you . . .'. Body language is also important so use reassuring behaviour and posture and particularly avoid intimidating gestures.

2 Agree the Situation

Your desired outcome here is to ensure that all the facts are on the table and that you both have shared understanding and agreement. Four of the 'key elements' are important here: deal with the facts, be specific, keep to recent events and be honest.

To make this step work well:

- Deal with facts, not assumptions.
- Think of yourself as an explorer and be hungry for information; ask lots of questions.
- Leave aside all conclusions and judgments.
- Don't leap prematurely into Implications or Resolution.
- If dealing with underperformance, avoid 'rescuing' the employee by 'pussyfooting' around the truth or softening each issue with mention of some good performance.
- Confirm agreement before moving to the Implications step

3 Agree the Implications

Agreeing the Implications means taking the employee's performance (the Situation) and relating it to its *consequences*. This step provides the motive to change, the context for change, and the separation of the person from the problem. Three of the 'key elements' are important here: deal with the facts, be specific, and separate the problem and the person.

To make this step work well:

- Keep it non- (employee) personal—better to think and say, 'Your reports are late, which affects production planning' than 'Your reports are late, therefore you are a bad worker'.
- Don't confuse Implication with Resolution; a common trap is 'Your reports are late and (the implication is) you need to start preparation earlier'.
- Your employee must see the implication in terms of its enterprise consequences and to be more than just keeping the boss happy or 'off my case'.
- Ensure that the consequences are directly related to the performance.
- Keep any judgmental thoughts or comments on the employee out of the discussion—for example, 'Because of you . . .'.
- Provide a context for change by exploring the whole picture. For example, if you tell your accounts clerk that her processing backlog is affecting payments to suppliers, she may see several ways of resolving the problem.

One consequence that may be uncomfortable for you to discuss is any impact on *you*. From time to time your employee's performance may embarrass, frustrate or anger you, or make you happy. Your employee needs to know about these consequences, for all the reasons above, and so it is both okay and important for you to disclose them. Keep to how *you* have been affected, and *don't assume* your employee's motives. Using an earlier example, here's how to handle a positive impact on you.

Situation	*Kathy, the analysis of this chapter uncovers more issues and opens up more possibilities than we had previously thought of.*
Implication	*This will mean a much better community impact and recognition for our work It will also reflect well on my project management when I take this to the Committee.*

4 Agree the Resolution

By this point you've both agreed what happened (Situation) and what the consequences (Implication) are and you now need to agree a *Resolution*, which means bringing the issue to completion. This could be in the form of a verbal conclusion, an immediate action or a decision on a subsequent action.

As managers, it is very easy to respond without actually resolving anything, which usually means that we are avoiding an interpersonal or intellectual challenge. To help to make this step work well, Table 7.1 illustrates some types of responses that occur and the differences between responses that lead to resolution and those that don't. The examples will help you to review your own tendency to respond ineffectually or to resolve performance issues.

Table 7.1 Responding and resolving

Examples of responses	Degree of resolution achieved
Verbal conclusion	
Manager response to incorrect data: *Obviously the figures are not what they seemed and so we can say that you are still on track.*	*Resolved* by agreeing no problem in the first place.
Manager response to good performance: *I want you to know that you've done a fine job and that this reinforces my confidence in you.*	*Resolved* by way of recognition.
Manager sanctioning poor performance: *Well I don't agree with how you handled it and I'm certainly not happy with the result.*	No agreement on how to either recover the result or to avoid in future. *Unresolved*
Immediate action response	
Manager responding to good performance: *As a result, I'm recommending you for a salary increase.*	Assuming the employee agrees, the situation is *resolved*.
Manager sanctioning poor performance: *I've decided to keep you on this job a little longer, rather than promoting you now.*	Not agreed what it is the employee needs to do to learn better ways. *Unresolved*
Decision on a subsequent action response	
Manager responding to good performance: *I'd like to meet with you tomorrow to talk about some ways we could make use of this particular strength of yours.*	Leading towards *resolution*.
Manager responding to poor performance: *Well, we'll just have to sort it out sometime.*	*Unresolved*

In seeking Resolution, it is particularly important to balance directing and discussing. Some of your employees will need no encouragement to participate in problem-solving, while for others you will need to facilitate their process. Depending on the situation, you might leave all options open: for example, 'What do you think you can do in future?' Or you might lead with one idea, as a thought jogger, and then open it out: for example, 'A laptop computer might be a possible solution but I'm really more interested in your thoughts and ideas.' You are likely to get a much better result from these two types of approach than with a purely directive one such as: 'I think that laptop computers are the solution so how about you trial one and we'll see if that fixes your problem?' Avoid the extreme of *underreaction*, which occurs when you believe that simply highlighting the problem is enough to motivate and educate your employee on what to do in future.

Although joint solutions are generally preferable, there are times when the balance will shift more towards the 'direct' side of the scale, such as when your employee does not have the required level of ability to deal with the situation. In such cases, *explain* your reasons for there being no discussion so that your employee doesn't feel undervalued and thus becomes uncommitted to your decision.

5 Agree to integrate

It is disturbingly common for parties to reach an agreement on actions without considering how these actions will be sustained back on the job. A common example is to agree to employee training when neither the time nor training resources are available.

To make this step work well:

*   Agree on what was agreed. In simple cases there is likely to be a shared understanding of agreed actions, but in more complex feedback situations, as you cover each new issue, the previous agreements may become distorted or simply forgotten. You should also confirm that the agreements on Situation and Implication are shared. If an employee leaves the meeting having forgotten the performance gap and the consequences, the agreed action becomes a little isolated and unattached to anything except that it's something that 'has to be done'; it then easily slips onto the back burner.

- Determine what system resources are needed to be able to meet all the commitments made in the feedback session and whether the resources are available. Particularly, don't be too cavalier about how your employees will be able to 'squeeze' such and such new commitment into their daily work, at least without some help in setting priorities.
- Reaffirm any conditions that must be met to enable your employees to complete their part of the deal—for example, you will be available each Friday to discuss progress with them, or you will ensure specialist assistance from another department. Unfortunately, as readily as managers assume that their employees can fit in 'one more task', they also take on more assistance than they can easily deliver. You need to be sure that you can keep your side of the bargain.

Managing difficult responses

When you set out on a feedback session, what you hope for is a nice, easy straight-line path from beginning to end. The reality is often quite different and you find yourself following more of a winding, up and down path, at times not sure where you're going—rather like a theme park ride: 'Feedback, the Adventure'. Common situations that make performance feedback something of an adventure are shown in Table 7.2.

Basic principles of responding

The sample responses in Table 7.2 have much in common with being lost while driving in the country. When you know you are in trouble, you acknowledge that you are lost and then you stop, so that you don't become further lost. Next you take a deep breath (don't panic!) and try to remember the last place where you were sure of your position. Lastly, you don't blame the map. This analogy provides an overriding philosophy for managing difficult responses, a task that calls upon the full range of task- and people-management tools and skills.

Figure 7.3 is an overview of the basic approach to take with difficult responses, and discussion follows, together with examples.

1. As with getting lost, first acknowledge that you're in trouble, stop and don't panic. Then regroup.

Table 7.2 'Feedback, the Adventure', and some sample responses

The Adventure	Sample responses
'Red herrings' You are led off on a tangent, either intentionally or unintentionally, by your employee; you find yourself involved and arguing irrelevant issues that have nothing to do with where you want to go.	Immediately re-establish focus, without alienating your employee. As soon as you are aware, stop, acknowledge the importance of the topic to the employee, but not relevant to this discussion. Note it down for future discussion if necessary. Return to the feedback where you left off.
Roadblock You have struck unresolvable disagreement or passive resistance and you can't seem to go anywhere.	Take both of you back to what you both agree and then work forward again, maybe along a different path. If there is passive resistance, go back to working on *Agreement to participate*.
Confusion You are thrown off balance, you've lost the thread. You're not sure what you've agreed or what you've covered; this usually happens after pursuing a 'red herring'.	Stop, go back to a point where you were clear, then, with your employee, go forward, retracing your forward steps.
Swamp You become bogged down and either thrash about or sink in: (a) too much data; or (b) your employee's concerns or emotional responses (anger, blame, self-blame, hopelessness, etc.)	(a) Data—acknowledge that you are swamped with data and reach agreement that you will both work towards isolating a smaller selection. (b) Emotion—first acknowledge the emotions, and then direct the employee back to the issues at hand.
New information Your employee introduces new information and you haven't had time to comprehend it.	First, determine whether it is relevant; if you're unsure, ask your employee to justify it. If it seems to be relevant but you can't grasp it on the spot, reconvene when you have.

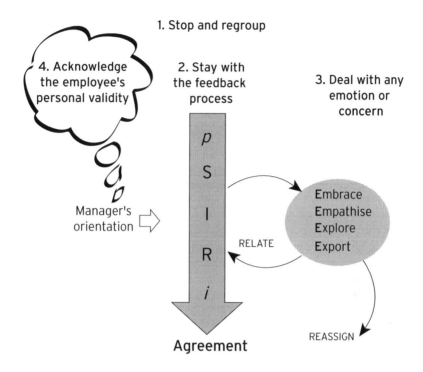

© 1997–2002. Amadeus Performance Systems

Figure 7.3 Recovery model for managing difficult responses to feedback

2. Stay with the process that holds the feedback together, the Agreement Model of Feedback (S-I-R). Once you have regrouped, *handle the issue within the S-I-R framework*. When confronted by a red herring or roadblock, clarify the employee's issue and then *come back to the central topic of the feedback*. Sometimes you will feel that you sound like a broken record—'I understand about the . . ., but coming back to the teamwork problem . . .'.

3. Sometimes, the issue causing the employee's neglect of performance will be something of *real concern* to the employee and may be accompanied by strong emotion. The micro process for handling this, giving the best outcome for both, is as follows.

   • **Embrace** the problem. Many managers are uncomfortable or impatient when confronted with these 'distractions' and attempt to deal with them by avoidance (change the subject or drop the issue), denial (carry on regardless) or suppression (accuse the employee of making excuses). Quite clearly, this is not effective in resolving the feedback issue. It is far better to get used to the fact that the game has changed and to enter the fray whole-heartedly and skilfully.

- **Empathise** with the employee's concerns or emotion.
- **Explore** the detail so that you understand fully (don't assume).
- **Export** the issue in one of two ways. Either:
  —RELATE it back to the feedback process if the issue is relevant;
  or
  —REASSIGN it to another time if the issue is real but unrelated to the feedback topic.

4. Overall, keep in mind that most difficult employees are driven by valid views from their perspective so, unless you have contrary evidence, that's what you should assume.

We have covered a complex management task in a very short time, so here are two examples that may help.

Example 1

Employee: *You're picking on me because I'm the only one here who's not a graduate.* (**Red herring or swamp**)

Manager: *I acknowledge it would be bad to feel picked on. What makes you think that I would do that?* (**Embrace, Empathise, Explore**)

Employee: *(Response)*

Manager: *Going back to the miscalculations that we agreed were occurring, are they related to your not being a graduate?* (**Export—Relate to S-I-R**)

Employee: *No, but . . .* (**Red herring or swamp**)

Manager: *What I'd like to do is firstly to agree to meet with you separately to deal properly with your concerns about being picked on.* (**Export—Reassign**). *For now, I want to continue discussing the miscalculations and the problem they're causing our forecast-ing.* (**Export—Relate to S-I-R**).

Example 2

Manager: *Your last three weekly reports have been late.* (**Situation**)

Employee: *This new project doesn't allow time for anything else because they've got the specification totally wrong.* (**Red herring**)

Manager: *Are you aware that the regional report has to wait for your report and this in turn delays the production forecast?* (**Implication—stay with S-I-R**)

Employee: *Well, the problem belongs to Head Office because they didn't consult with us in the first place about how this project should work.* (**Red herring**)

Manager: *I'd like to stay with the issue of your reports. Do you acknowledge the importance of not delaying production forecasts?* (**Stay with S-I-R**)

Employee: *Yes, but . . .* (**Red herring**)

Manager: *We can talk about the project and Head Office later. About the production forecasts . . .* (**Stay with S-I-R**)

Employee: *But it's not right, they think they can get us to drop what we're doing because of their whim. How would they like it done to them?* (**Emotion, personal values to the surface**)

(Once it is clear that there is a major concern or a strong emotional component, it is time to change tack and **Embrace** the concern or emotion.)

Manager: *You seem to believe that they're taking advantage of us?* (**Empathise**)

Employee: *(Response)*

Manager: *What's your major concern if they are taking us for granted?* (**Explore**)

Employee: *(Response)*

Manager: *In view of your concerns, this is something I'm happy to talk over with you, and I suggest that we fix a separate time for this.* (**Export—Reassign**) *Right now I need to know that you are aware of the importance of the production forecasts.* (**Export—Relate to S-I-R**)

Etc.

8 Manager as coach

So far, we have looked at ways to assign and plan work, to develop our people, to understand performance data and to give feedback. Our experience is that many managers are not confident about the next step—that is, how you personally can influence the performance of your people. When managers give feedback about performance that needs to be improved, common remedial approaches are:

1. Tell them what they are doing wrong and let them fix their performance in their own way.
2. Tell them what 'they need to do'.
3. Send them on a training course.
4. Get them to 'try harder', either by 'motivating' them (meaning to inspire them), by offering them an incentive, or by threatening or denigrating them.

With the exception of threat and denigration, all these approaches have a place but each one is an incomplete solution. For example, they are all characterised by a lack of involvement or engagement with the employee, either by undermanaging ('a training course') or by overmanaging ('tell them what to do'). What is missing is the role of the manager as a *coach*, where managers become involved with their employees to develop the employees' capability to meet the requirements of the work.

In this chapter we look at your role as a coach, at the sort of situations where coaching is appropriate and at the principles and processes that will make you effective as a performance coach. In the chapters that follow we apply the principles to a range of on-the-job situations.

Manage *and* coach

When the subject of coaching is raised, one of the most common questions is, 'Am I supposed to be a coach or a manager?' The answer is that you should be both—coaching is a particular way of managing by focusing on the *performance development* of your people. We begin to become a coach by understanding what performance coaching is, why it is a worthwhile means of developing employee performance and when it should be used.

What is coaching?

Coaching is a *relationship* between you and your employee, with defined *roles and responsibilities* and a defined *purpose* that relates to the employee's performance development. We now examine three ideas from this definition—relationship, roles and responsibilities, and purpose, with the final two ideas being covered in further detail later, within a coaching model.

Relationship
The coaching relationship is a formal one, differing from your regular manager relationship with an employee. It needs to be deliberately commenced and finished by both parties, because of the special expectations of both parties within the coaching relationship.

Roles and responsibilities
The coaching relationship is based on mutual agreement about the coach's role authority and the employee's role as learner. Coaching authority has nothing to do with management authority because it applies equally to anyone who is being a coach, and you can't force an employee to 'be coached'. As a coach, your responsibility is to bring out the best in the employees, while your employees' responsibility is to be willing to give of their best.

Purpose
The purpose of coaching, irrespective of the problem, is that the coach will guide the employee towards solving their own performance problem, in order to help the employee learn from the coaching experience how to solve future problems.

There is often confusion about the difference between a coach and a mentor and the following saying sums it up very well: 'A mentor is someone who gives us the best of themselves; a coach is someone who gives us the best of ourselves.'

Why coaching?

At the start of this chapter we propose that coaching should be a preferred response to performance improvement. This section describes some of the more important benefits that you will gain by being an effective coach. They encompass both immediate and long-term benefits for the business and for your employees.

Effectiveness

When employees are able to solve their own problems (the purpose of coaching), more problems are solved, better solutions are produced, problems are solved more immediately and performance is more consistent.

Return on resources

The aims of managing your work unit performance are to ensure that enterprise goals are met and also to achieve the greatest return on resources, including those represented by you and your people. If we consider management spanning a continuum ranging from 'coaching' at one extreme to 'control' at the other, Figure 8.1 shows the resource implications of each extreme.

We can see from Figure 8.1 that a coaching style of management is ultimately easier for you and, without any doubt, produces superior business and professional development results.

Better work understanding

Through your coaching, you and your employees become more aware of which drivers, personal and non-personal, are the most critical to work performance, an awareness that greatly enhances work understanding and planning. Awareness extends to a greater identification of the small things that make a large difference (the 80/20 rule), further enhancing understanding and performance.

Managed interdependence

In Chapter 2 we touch on ways to manage the new world of work, a world characterised by a workforce and a business environment that are less manageable according to traditional management methods. In such a world, a more interdependent workforce is essential to being able to deliver best value at lowest cost, and this is where coaching is valuable. Coaching enables you to move your employees away *from* either total dependence (they can't do anything without you) or independence (they

INPUT

Management input required

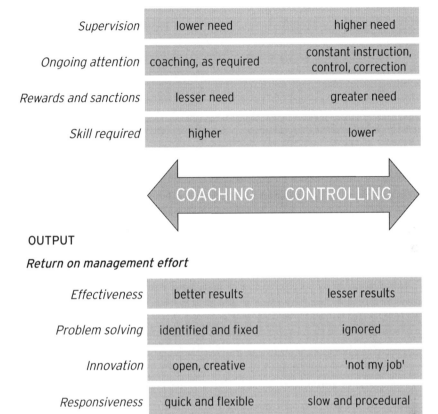

Supervision	lower need	higher need
Ongoing attention	coaching, as required	constant instruction, control, correction
Rewards and sanctions	lesser need	greater need
Skill required	higher	lower

COACHING   CONTROLLING

OUTPUT

Return on management effort

Effectiveness	better results	lesser results
Problem solving	identified and fixed	ignored
Innovation	open, creative	'not my job'
Responsiveness	quick and flexible	slow and procedural
Employee dependence	lower	higher

Figure 8.1 Business returns along the coaching–controlling continuum

don't need you at all) to interdependence (you both need each other but you also support each other).

Management development

When we move into management there is always the risk that we will lose touch with the business. This is why the CEO will walk the factory floor, visit customers and go out into the field with staff. Very few coaches would say that they are not continuously developing their own skill and judgment through the process of coaching others.

Relationships

When you develop an effective coaching relationship with your people you will also strengthen your overall relationship, including improved communication, greater trust and a greater alignment on business thinking. Such improvements in the relationship will result in better decisions, greater cooperation and greater employee willingness to take risks and expend discretionary physical and mental energy.

When to coach

Now that we have established that coaching is a most effective way for you to directly influence your people's performance, the question is 'when?' In response, one trigger is according to the *need* and another is according to the point in the *work performance cycle*. These triggers overlap.

The need

It's useful to think of three basic indications for coaching—addressing underperformance, an employee's intention for self-improvement and ensuring performance.

- *Addressing underperformance* is the most common trigger that managers recognise and it arises when performance is not meeting planned or agreed targets. The personal effectiveness component will become apparent through the process of feedback.
- *Employee self-improvement.* There are times when employees wish to achieve their 'personal best' independently of whatever performance target is set. This is commendable but be cautious that this effort is not at the expense of achieveing other targets.
- *Ensuring performance.* Coaching is also indicated when you want to make sure upfront that employees will achieve their targets, rather than waiting until they fail. This includes ensuring sound planning and skills development.

The performance cycle

The need for coaching may also be indicated according to a point in the performance cycle. Following is a brief description of the place of coaching at some points of the cycle (except for on-the-job review, which is covered in Chapter 9).

- *Assigning work and work planning.* At this point in the cycle you want to ensure good performance in the first place. If an employee seems not to be totally on top of what is required or how to go about it, this is a perfect opportunity to do less 'telling' and to coach them to *learn to solve their own problems.*
- *Employee professional/skill development.* Once the means of development has been identified and the process planned, you can actively support the development process by being a coach, in the content and/or by aiding your employee's *learning process.*
- *Formal review.* The often-perceived judgmental or adversarial nature of formal reviews tends to work against an aligned approach to the issues being discussed. However, there is an equally important role for coaching here—not so much about work performance, because that should have been handled on the job, but more to do with helping your people to become more skilled at the formal review process itself.

A model of coaching

There are probably as many ideas on the 'what' and 'how' of coaching as there are coaches. With this in mind, we have pulled together a coaching model, based on sound coaching theories and on observation of the on-the-job methods and styles of effective managers.

Coaching advice often focuses on the *process* of doing what a coach should do. Our coaching model is not only based on a process but also includes the *intrinsic abilities* of both the coach and the employee being coached, providing a rounded, or complete, approach. As you would hope, many of the principles, skills and processes used in the model have already been covered in earlier chapters. Together with some new ones, they are now rearranged to present a performance coaching model (Figure 8.2).

In the *performance coaching model*, coaching is driven by the interaction of three principal dynamics: the manager's coaching capability, the employee's capability and the coaching process. This chapter describes the model and how to use it, in general terms. Chapters 9 and 10 present examples of the model applied to a range of on-the-job coaching situations. A work template of the performance coaching model is provided in Appendix 3.

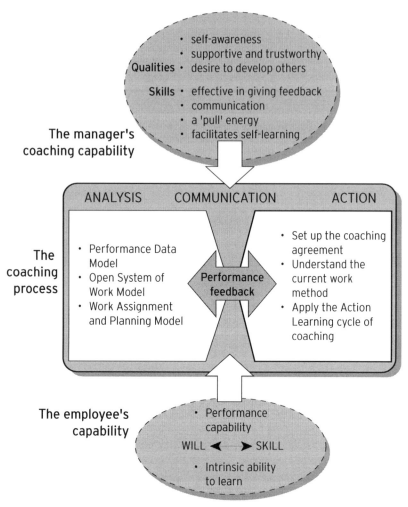

Figure 8.2 The performance coaching model

The manager's coaching capability

How capable you are at coaching depends on how well your coaching qualities and your coaching skills meet the need of the occasion.

Coaching qualities

The qualities of an effective coach include personal *self-awareness*, *trust-worthiness* and a desire to develop your employees, including their development of *increasing levels of self-management*.

- *Self-awareness.* To enable the special relationship that exists between coach and coachee, you need to know yourself well. You need to be aware of your preferred way of dealing with information and decisions, your personal values, and your biases and assumptions. For example, if your preferred information style is big picture over detail you may have a strength in encouraging exploration of options, but you may have difficulty when it comes to asking the employee to focus on one thing to develop.
- *Trustworthiness.* The employees make a commitment to the self-learning process, which means a willingness to push themselves, to take risks and make mistakes. If your employees don't trust you to respond supportively to their efforts and go the distance, they will pull out of the commitment.
- *Desire to develop others.* Good coaches are motivated by the development of their pupils and the increasing *interdependence* in the relationship. This is also a cause of fear among some managers because they see their importance diminishing. To be effective, you must be willing to let go of the 'controller/expert' role and assume the manager–coach role.

Coaching skills

Of all of the skills that a coach should possess, the following four are regarded as the most significant. The first two have been discussed already.

- Effective in giving feedback;
- Communication;
- A 'pull' energy; and
- Ability to create a learning culture.

- *Effective in giving feedback.* Feedback is the critical coaching link between work and the employee's development. It's no good having all the other coaching qualities and skills if you can't effectively communicate performance to your people.
- *Communication.* Apart from feedback, important communication includes giving instructions, questioning (open questions) and listening. Instructions should be clearly given and explained so that they are executed correctly and the effectiveness of the task can be evaluated and thus provide learning. Questions are particularly important in assisting employees to recall the specifics of what they did and what happened as a consequence. This also means that you need to listen actively.

- *A 'pull' energy*. We've talked a lot about facilitating your people's ability to *find their own solutions*. Some time ago I heard a colleague refer to this as a 'pull' rather than 'push' energy. This means, for example, that if someone is watching you coaching an employee, they will get a distinct impression that you are focused on guiding the employee to explore, to test alternatives, to stretch himself to find a solution. What the observer would *see* is the employee solving his own problem but what they would *sense* is that you are the creator.
- *Ability to create a learning culture*. If you are a good coach your employees will value and be practised at *learning from experience*. To achieve this you will make it safe for them to take risks and you will always have them reflect on what was learned before trying the new approach.

Activity 8.1

How ready are you?
Before launching into the *process* of coaching, it would be worth creating a snapshot of your coaching capability.

For each of the seven qualities and skills we've covered above, think about and identify the following.

1. **Your greatest strength and how it will enhance your coaching ability.**
2. **The first thing that you should work on to improve your coaching ability.**

The employee's capability

Once you have addressed your own capability to coach, you need to consider your employee's capability to be coached. We can look at this capability under two headings—*performance capability* and *learning capability*.

Employee's performance capability

Having determined that the employee's personal effectiveness does not meet the agreed level, the two fundamental issues that influence coaching decisions are the employee's 'will' and 'skill'. We are already familiar with skill, but an employee's 'will' is different and refers to the commitment they feel and display towards work, or a particular piece of work. In the case of coaching, 'will' also describes the commitment employees have towards addressing underperformance.

The will–skill dynamic

The interaction between level of *skill* and level of *will* determines what type of coaching approach you will take (Figure 8.3) and leads us to three basic types of coaching decisions. Are we faced with a need for:

1. coaching an underperformer, one *who has the will, but not the skill*;
2. coaching and managing a *good performer*, one who is meeting or exceeding expectations; or
3. managing a difficult performer—one who is not meeting agreed performance and who *hasn't the will* (whether or not they have the skill)?

Alternative 1 is the most common situation—you or your employee have underestimated the skill needed, or overestimated the level of skill available, and coaching is geared towards addressing the skill gap. Alternative 2 is a tricky one for many managers—what do you do with a 'star' employee? This employee is certainly not short on skill but will frequently want to achieve more, so you need to have special ways of coaching them. Alternative 3 is the one that most managers dread— an employee who does not want to perform. This situation requires a combination of both management and coaching.

As there are different approaches for each of the three scenarios, we need to be able to distinguish the employee's level of will and skill.

Assessing skill

Assessing the level of skill is easier than it is for will. The Work Assignment and Planning process is designed to reveal actual skill requirements and current skill level and/or plans to acquire the requisite skill. Indicators of skills capability include:

* demonstrated skill in the past, in the same situation;
* has been trained in this skill; or
* has achieved competency level for this task.

On the job, or when reviewing the work in process, you will have opportunity to gauge the employee's level of skill by such means as direct

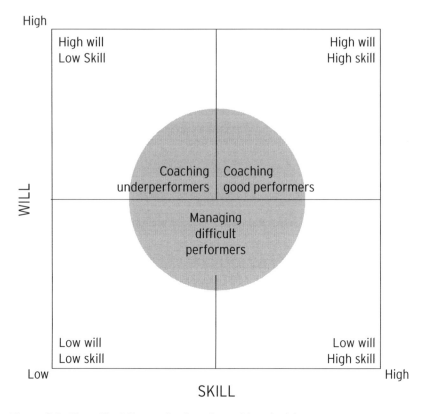

High

High will
Low Skill

High will
High skill

WILL

Coaching
underperformers

Coaching
good performers

Managing
difficult
performers

Low will
Low skill

Low will
High skill

Low

High

SKILL

Figure 8.3 The will–skill coordinates of coaching decisions

observation, feedback from peers or customers or conversation with the employee. Be aware that you can't evaluate personal skill from work performance alone—you will need to evaluate other contributors to the system, such as resources and inputs.

Assessing will

It is usually more difficult to determine whether employees are unwilling to perform at their best, either because they are good at hiding it or because the background circumstances are complex. Indicators of low will include:

- personal effectiveness has dropped suddenly;
- unwillingness to explore the issue;

- defensive or aggressive; blames others, the product, the systems, etc.;
- invokes privacy;
- appears upset over a performance issue;
- known personal problems outside work; and
- indicators of being a misfit in the organisation, technically, ideologically or socially.

A word of caution here. There are managers who actually create some of the 'low will' responses listed above, simply by their manner in dealing with work performance issues. Therefore, remember to apply the relevant principles covered in earlier chapters, such as:

- don't *assume* it's low will;
- use open questions;
- listen; and
- apply the performance feedback model.

Employee's intrinsic ability to learn

Earlier we said that the object of coaching includes enabling your employee to learn to improve, as distinct from being told what to do. Some of the intrinsic attributes that will enable an employee's learning, and which you must create and support, include:

- a will to improve, as described above;
- previous good learning experiences; confidence;
- knowing themselves well—professionally and personally;
- trust in their manager—manager's coaching ability, willingness to accept mistakes, etc.;
- ability to be aware of what they are doing, so that they can critically observe and reflect on their current practices and new practices;
- ability to follow an agreed plan or process;
- perseverance and diligence—willing to stick at it; and
- willingness to risk, to make mistakes.

As part of setting up the coaching agreement (see below), you should explore each of the above attributes, discuss them and include them in the process of the coaching agreement.

The coaching process

The process describes what you do over the period of the coaching inter-action, whether it lasts five minutes or five months. Figure 8.2 shows the process as three linked components—Analysis, Communication and Action. Analysis ensures that you have an understanding of current performance, at the beginning and in response to changes implemented as part of the coaching; this stage uses the work tools we have already covered. Communication involves performance feedback as the bridge between problem and solution, and Action deals with the procedure involved in the actual coaching. At this stage it worth noting, if you haven't already, how performance management is linked together as a system. We are now discussing coaching and find that it depends on all the other management roles in the work performance system.

Analysis and communication

Because performance analysis is a two-way process we can't separate it from communication and so the two are dealt with together. The need for coaching begins to emerge as you and your employee agree that (1) performance is lower than agreed, (2) the employee cannot self-correct and (3) the shortfall is one of personal effectiveness. The first process step is performance analysis, using an integration of the work models that you have already covered. In particular, the performance data model (Chapter 5) provides you with the *right understanding* by dis-tinguishing between performance outcomes and performance drivers, and the open system of work model (Chapter 6) by distinguishing between personal and non-personal drivers. The Work Assignment and Planning model (Chapter 3) is a check that the issue isn't poor Work Assignment or flawed planning assumptions.

Actions

So far we've covered a lot of familiar ground, reassembling some of the already learned skills and processes into a coaching environment in order to be sure that we are prepared, that we know our employee's capability and that we know what performance data we wish to feed back. This is a long build-up to the actual 'helping' activity but it is all an essential part of being an effective coach. There are three elements in the Action stage—set up the coaching agreement, understand the current work and apply the Action Learning cycle of coaching.

Set up the coaching agreement

We have described coaching as a relationship with agreed roles and responsibilities, and this requires some form of coaching agreement to be created. For ongoing sessions, the 'agreement' step will be a check of how the original agreement and method is working, leading to a confirmation or a discussion of any change needed.

Three steps are suggested for setting up an agreement.

1. *Confirm the overall aim, or purpose.* Given that you have completed a process of performance feedback, the personal effectiveness issue will be already on the table but it is worth restating it within the coaching context: for example, 'We are going to develop your production scheduling ability in order to reduce the current stock problems . . .'.
2. *Commit to the process.* The coaching agreement also includes discussing and agreeing the commitments. Your commitments will generally be those described earlier in 'coaching capabilities'. You will then need to describe what is needed from the employee—a commitment to enter into a coaching relationship, which means a willingness to learn, to push themselves, to risk and to make mistakes, and to trust you to respond supportively to their efforts and to go the distance.
3. *Discuss and agree the coaching method.* This step involves discussing and agreeing the mechanics, such as when it will happen, the steps, how often and the other people involved.

Understand the current work

You can't improve what you don't understand so don't begin to explore solutions until you know exactly what the problem is. (Remember the performance feedback model—no Resolution until you are agreed on Situation and the Implication.) The method for understanding the current work is to use the five steps of the Action Learning model (described below), which would be applied as follows.

In Step 1 the employee you are coaching explains what she currently does in the work being improved. Get her to talk through the specifics; for example, 'When you say you use the spreadsheet to estimate demand, what do you do exactly?' Following this, she performs this part of her work (Step 2), either observing herself or being observed by you (Step 3), then continues on through the Action Learning cycle, as described below

(Steps 4 and 5). When you *observe*, ask lots of questions, and don't openly challenge any of the current method at this stage—your objective is to understand.

The Action Learning cycle of coaching

The action model we use for developing employees is derived from a method called *Action Learning* because, in Action Learning, as in performance learning:

- the participants are dealing with new problems and unknown solutions;
- it involves doing;
- it involves some personal (and business) risk; and
- it has to depend upon the existing knowledge and experience of the employee and the manager.

You might wonder about the 'new problems and unknown solutions', believing that your experience ensures enough certainty to be able to suggest and guide your employees along the right track each time. Your experience and guidance are important but, for each different person, and for you with that particular person, it is a new and individual journey. This means that it will always involve newness, uncertainty and risk, all components in which Action Learning has proved to be very successful. Turning from the learning perspective to the coaching perspective, *your role* is to educate the coachee in the use of the Action Learning process and to actively support them through it. Therefore, it makes sense that the action steps for your coaching are based on the learning steps that will be undertaken by the coachee.

For the purpose of performance development we have found it useful to show the Action Learning process as a cycle of five steps (Figure 8.4) and, like many such improvement processes, it is a continuous cycle. Below is a brief learner's perspective of the five steps; in the following section the five Action Learning steps are expanded to include specific coaching considerations.

1. In order to learn you must start with a clear *intention* of what is going to be done, and for what result.

2. Without known solutions, you first have to *act*, to do something from which to learn.

3. *Observing* is the judgment-free process of noticing the 'what', rather than the 'why' or 'what if'.

4. Now that you have factual data, this is the time to *reflect* on analysis and conclusions.

5. On the basis of your accumulated knowledge you can now ask 'what if?' questions—that is, *hypothesise* possible solutions.

At the end of Step 5 you have planned actions and targeted results, which lead you back to Step 1.

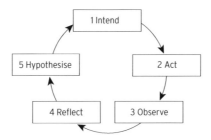

Figure 8.4 An Action Learning cycle of coaching

Applying Action Learning to coaching

Action Learning is applied to a wide range of situations and so it is worthwhile for us to consider some of the specifics that apply when we use it as a performance coaching framework.

As this is a process of learning, you must both start with a clear intention of what the employee will do and what outcomes will be created. Be specific, otherwise it will be difficult to be sure later whether the intention was actually carried out, which makes it difficult to judge cause and effect.

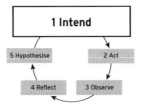

Work on/change one thing at a time

In the process of exploring solutions you will probably come up with more than one thing that needs to be done—for example, '. . . double check input stock data, improve system skills, improve analysis skills, etc.' For the coaching to be fully effective you both need to work on one thing at a time. The employee will improve faster and you will be a better observer if you limit your focus.

Being a performance issue, you will naturally want to get your employee up to speed as soon as possible but, remember, coaching is about bringing out the best in the person, not just solving the problem.

Talk through the new behaviours/practices

At this point employees should be very clear about what they are going to do. Getting a positive performance result without being clear about what caused it is no basis for learning. If the new method is an idea from your employee, you should clarify. If you are instructing, the requirements are as outlined earlier, under 'Communication'.

Demonstrate

Quite often what is spoken about is different from what the person meant. If you are giving instruction, demonstrate what you mean. Similarly, if the employee has the idea, ask them to demonstrate the idea in practice. You don't have to be the expert that the employee is, you can still demonstrate the method. Many managers are held back by fear of looking foolish at this point. This is a misunderstanding of the coaching role and poor role modelling of the risk we are asking our coachee to take.

The employee carries out the actions as agreed, with the focus on doing what was intended. Even if the employee has a 'better' idea part way through, neither of you can judge effectiveness unless the agreed actions are enacted first.

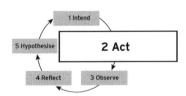

Monitor

Don't set up the process and then fail to keep your commitment, as this will undermine not only this exercise but your whole coaching role. Even if the performance result is a success, you still have the agreed purpose of developing the employee's learning ability. Busy managers who don't have time for coaching shouldn't dress up other forms of intervention as 'coaching', just because it is expected.

Keep focus

While you are observing, or while the employee is debriefing what has been happening with the new method or behaviours, there is an over-whelming tendency to comment on every aspect that might need improving. Remember to keep your focus on the one change that was agreed (other changes can come later).

There's a story that makes the point in a very visual way. Australian swimmer Shane Gould is walking alongside the pool, following a pupil in the water. Shane is making small, alternate up and down movements with her hands. She is communicating: 'Your feet, concentrate on your feet.'

When the action is complete, you agree on two things—what the employee *did* and what the *results* of the action were, including how others responded.

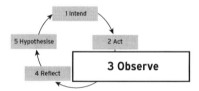

When to observe

When observation takes place is determined by the type of work and whether the manager is observing or the employee is self-observing. For example, if you are a manager coaching a customer service officer, you and she might observe the intended new behaviours in a role rehearsal, then the employee might self-observe after each customer interaction, or during breaks, then report back to you after several days. This example illustrates the wide range of options.

Intention does not automatically eventuate

Often the employee's actions will not be as you intended. Don't assume that what was intended to happen was what finally happened. Ask questions.

Suspend judgment

This step must be free of judgment, blame, new ideas or conclusions—
just plain old boring 'what' happened, not 'why'.

This is the time for analysis and conclusions, now that you have
factual data with which to work. You are both looking at possible
cause–effect relationships between actions and results. Results in this
case also include the way that other people responded to the employee.

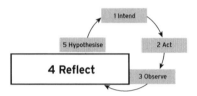

When intention is not enacted

If the employee's actions were different from what was intended, find
out why—it may be significant. For example, the employee may have
intended to telephone the upset customer, but wrote a letter instead. Is
there a problem with personal contact?

Plan or execution?

Look particularly at whether results were caused by the plan or the
execution.

Confirm success and learning

Once you have completed the coaching process, confirm what it was
that worked. This is reinforcement for the employee's efforts and has
implications for work practices.

Also investigate and acknowledge what the employee has learned,
beyond simply finding a way to solve this problem.

Assuming that the problem is still not fully solved, this is 'what if'
time. What do your own experience and the recent learning of the
employee tell you about possible new ways to approach this?

At the end of this step, you should have planned actions and results
that you firm up back in Step 1, 'Intend'.

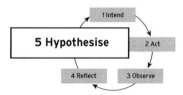

What if we change the objective?

Before looking at the method, it is always worth challenging whether you have the best objective; for example, 'What if analysis skills are not the key. What if it's interpersonal relations with the production staff?'

What if we change the plan?

Reflection leads you to analyse whether there were limits to the plan and/or the execution. If it is the plan, a good place to start is your assumptions; for example, 'What if we're wrong about Production's needs?'

What if we change the execution?

What you are looking for here is better ways to translate the plan into action on the job; for example, 'What if I have a prompt on my screen?'

Making the transition to employee self-management

> There is a saying that the mark of a great leader is when the followers celebrate a success and say 'We did it'.

Earlier in this chapter we explored the benefits of employee 'managed interdependence'. The transition, however, from a more controlled and dependent workforce takes more than a management decision. The overriding requirement is that you are an effective coach, but there are also four potential barriers that you must manage.

1. *You* must be willing to let go.
2. *Your people* must be willing to self-manage.
3. *You* must have the means to manage interdependent employees.
4. *Your people* must have, or acquire, the requisite skills to self-manage.

You are willing to let go

Letting go means that you trust your people (a) not to abuse the situation and (b) to possess the knowledge and skills. Letting go also means that you need to 'empower' them, an idea that has two strands to it. You structurally empower them by giving them more management responsibility, but you also encourage their own personal empowerment.

In the work context, the idea of personal empowerment, or self-determination, embodies employees' belief that they have control over their own performance and achievements, which develops their sense of personal responsibility. An extension of empowerment is the idea of 'self-efficacy'—the employees' belief that they can perform, which you will develop as a result of effective coaching.

Your people are willing

Some of your people will jump at the chance of self-management; for others, it is a responsibility they don't want. In order to reassure the less sure and reinforce the leaders, you will need to provide a promise of benefits to them, demonstrate that they can trust you not to punish them if it doesn't work at first and give them confidence in their ability to do it. When things are under way, you must recognise and reward good self-management as well as results.

You have the means to manage interdependent employees

All the processes and skills described in this book equip you to be able to manage this task. For example, good Work Assignment and Planning gives you the confidence that your employees know what and how and also provides you with the reference points to monitor. Similarly, your coaching process and skills enable you to be engaged in employees' work process, without controlling them.

Your people have the requisite skills

If your people achieve some level of mastery of the processes in Work Assignment and Planning, and the performance data model, and are skilled in receiving feedback and being coached, they will be well equipped. In addition, they should develop a level of decision-making and problem-solving ability commensurate with the work, as well as skills in negotiating with peers, suppliers and customers (internal and external).

9 Coaching on the job

This chapter is all about taking the principles and tools from Chapter 8 and applying them to day-to-day performance situations. The three basic on-the-job coaching situations described in Chapter 8 were:

1. Coaching an underperformer, one *who has the will, but not the skill*;
2. Coaching and managing a *good performer*, one who is meeting or exceeding expectations; and
3. Managing a difficult performer—one who is not meeting agreed performance and who *hasn't the will* (whether or not they have the skill).

Although the coaching environment differs in these three situations, the performance coaching model applies throughout, adapted to different content in each case. In the case of high performers ('overachievers') and difficult performers, coaching is one of a number of performance management responses that we discuss.

As an introduction to this chapter, Figure 9.1 is a decision tree that summarises how to determine which type of coaching situation is facing you. It is a visual summary of Chapter 8, incorporating what you have already learned about managing performance from earlier chapters.

Coaching underperformers

We have been using the term 'underperformer' to describe an employee who is not meeting planned levels of personal effectiveness and where,

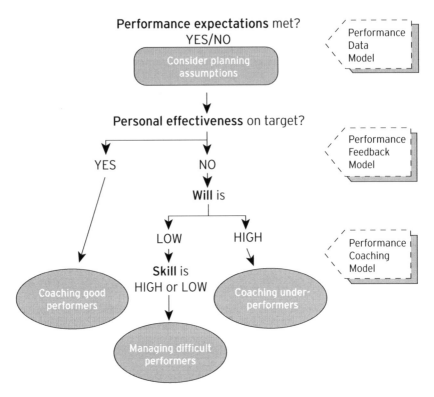

Figure 9.1 Performance coaching decision tree

through the process of feedback, we have concluded that the cause is 'low skill'. This is a case for the most straightforward of the three coaching situations and the method to follow is that described for the performance coaching model process in Chapter 8.

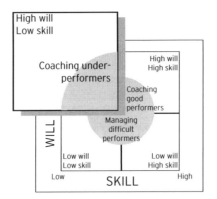

The performance coaching model in action

Leading up to the first coaching session, managers should review and ensure their own coaching *qualities* and *skills* and review the performance data and outcomes of the feedback session. Because there is nothing more to add to our knowledge of the coaching model, the best way to understand its use in the case of an underperformer is to look at an example. Following the example is a list of the key learning points that arise from it.

Example 9.1 Coaching an underperformer—the performance coaching process in action

Situation

The *employee* is a customer service consultant who deals directly with customers over the counter and whose performance is lower than agreed. The *coach* is the Customer Service Supervisor.

The measure of performance: The agreed maximum error rate of transaction discrepancies is 1.2 per full-time day, averaged over one month, with no more than three on any one day.

Performance: Over the last month, the consultant has averaged 1.8 errors, with two days reaching three errors and, on one day, reaching five.

The model	The execution
Set up the coaching agreement	
	The manager sets up the *coaching agreement*, as described in Chapter 8. Both parties confirm that the purpose of the coaching is to enable the employee to perform within the error target.
Begin with the current work method	
Apply the five Action Learning steps to the work	Beginning at Step 1 they establish that the employee knows the correct procedure and agree that the supervisor will observe the employee on-the-job. At the de-brief—**'Observing'** (Step 3)—they note the following *specifics*:

- keying in hurriedly
- mis-keying and re-entering
- frequently looking at customer instead of looking at the keyboard
- not looking at the screen to check

- the employee's customers often become agitated
- employee appearing to be stressed
- employee feeling stressed

Example 9.1 (continued)

In **'Reflecting'** upon what was happening (Step 4) they conclude that the employee is feeling stressed by increased queue lengths causing the change in behaviour in keying in and in handling customers.

Once they believe that they have a good understanding of what is currently happening, the supervisor says that they are ready to proceed to improvement. They then undertake Step 5, **'Hypothesising'**, or 'what if?' They come up with a number of ideas for reducing the errors, both changes to the method and some means to remind the employee of the changed behaviours when they are immersed in the job.

Having now better understood the current work method, the manager and employee apply the Action Learning cycle of coaching to the new methods and behaviours.

The Action Learning cycle of coaching

1. Intend

Work on or change one thing at a time	After discussing a range of changed practices, they agree that the one thing to work on is *uninterrupted focus on keying in transactions*, particularly if the customer seems agitated about the wait.
Talk through the new behaviours or practices	They discuss precisely what the employee will do in order to maintain focus. They begin to talk about the employee also practising appearing relaxed, not anxious, but the supervisor recalls the 'one thing at a time' principle and they agree to leave this until later.
Demonstrate	During a slow period, the employee demonstrates the idea in practice, with the supervisor role-playing the customer. They discuss and modify, as necessary. The supervisor demonstrates a couple of alternatives for consideration.

2. Act

Monitor	As agreed, the employee monitors and records his behaviour. Although they plan to meet at the end of the two days, the supervisor has also kept in touch on an informal basis.
Keep focus!	At a lunch break, the employee reports back that there is a problem with customers rushing their instructions because they are anxious about the time. The supervisor acknowledges the comment for future action and *brings attention back* to the agreed new behaviours.

Example 9.1 (continued)

3. Observe	
What happened– *(what was done* *and what was the* *result?)*	When they reconvene the supervisor first asks the employee to talk about what he *did*—in relation to the new task.
	Assuming that the employee followed the intention, the supervisor then asks what happened as a *result* of the behaviours—accuracy, customer behaviours, cycle time, how the employee felt.
Intention does not *automatically* *mean action!*	If the employee replied '*I did what we agreed*', the supervisor would ask the employee to *describe*, *step-by-step*, what he did, to check that intention and action matched.
Suspend judgment!	The supervisor knows that this step must be objective, so when the employee begins to talk about queue lengths, and the supervisor wants to know *now* why the employee didn't follow the intention, they put these questions aside until both have a clear view of the 'what'.
4. Reflect	
Cause and effect	They look first at the employee's *personal effectiveness.*
	• Was the employee able to key in transactions with uninterrupted focus? What *caused* it to be possible? • Was the employee successful in some circumstances but not in others, e.g. a customer asks him to hurry? What *caused* the difference?
	Next they look at the *results* of the actions.
	• Error rates are down—was this *caused* by the employee's new actions or were there any other reasons? • There were no adverse customer reacations—what *caused* this?
When intention is *not enacted*	If the employee did not stick with the intended actions, what was the *cause* of the employee doing something different?
Confirm success *and learning*	(When the new behaviour/skill is finally mastered and the performance is back within targeted range, they review the process and confirm that the coaching aims have been met.)
5. Hypothesise	
What if we change *the objective?*	They ask whether the original objective of coping with time pressures is still valid, and conclude on the basis of

Example 9.1 (continued)

	what has happened so far that it is. They know it is not an accuracy problem because the employee is accurate during less stressful periods.
What if we change the plan?	The plan was to maintain uninterrupted focus and this has worked most of the time. For customers who show that they are in a hurry, they ask 'what if we . . .?'
What if we change the execution?	If they decide that the plan is valid, even for rushed customers, they want to know how the employee can make it work with these customers, so they ask 'what if we . . .?'

What we learn from Example 9.1

As well as illustrating the application of the performance coaching model in a high will/low skill performance situation, this example demonstrates the importance of certain coaching behaviours and capabilities. This list is a short reminder.

1. Your employee's *willingness* should be nurtured.
2. Isolate the *personal effectiveness* component of low work performance, as this is the basis for coaching.
3. Understand fully what the employee is *currently doing* before thinking about improvement—many times the problem is that they are not doing what was originally agreed or planned.
4. Maintain focus on *one improvement at a time*, even though performance pressures and your own time availability urge you to take a 'shotgun' rather than a 'rifle-shot' approach to the problem.
5. Stay with the steps of the *Action Learning cycle* because they keep you from leaping into 'what if?' before fully understanding 'what is?'—the same principle as in the performance feedback model.
6. *Be specific* about behaviours and actions—intended, acted and observed.
7. The cause of *failure to act as intended* is very important and often uncovers the real barrier to personal effectiveness, which may be a lack of understanding, fear, uncertainty, lack of self-confidence, etc.
8. The coach requires a lot of *patience* (your 'pull' energy) to encourage self-discovery in the employee.
9. The employee is '*learning to learn*'.

Skills development—a coaching perspective

It is a fairly orderly process when skills development is a planned event that arises out of Work Assignment and Planning. Managers generally find it more difficult when skills development needs arise on the job and are to be addressed by coaching. We look at how to identify and prioritise the skills that need attention and how to ensure that development takes place amid the pressures of daily work.

Identifying specific skills for development

For many managers the hardest part of getting started is identifying which behaviour or activity to work on first. The following ideas start with how to diagnose the skills that need attention, and then knowing where to start.

What to look for

First, check that employees are doing what they are supposed to because, if not, it is less likely to be a skill issue and more likely a procedural one. Next, check on the skills that were identified in Work Assignment and Planning. Finally, observe or ask what skills appear to be below requirement.

Observe or ask?

How employees currently work can be determined either by observation or by asking them. Whether you observe or ask depends on the nature and location of the work. Work that is well suited for observation includes short cycle time (e.g. call centre interactions), visible work (e.g. customer interactions) and work where the manager has regular access to the employee. Work more suited for asking the employee includes long cycle time (e.g. major client management), 'invisible' work (e.g. analysis), intermittent events (e.g. difficult customers) and situations where the employee is at a separate location.

If the employee is nervous of having you observe, a colleague of the employee can substitute. An alternative is to use a role demonstration, with you as either participant or observer.

Picking 'the one'

If only one action or behaviour seems to be deficient you have a starting point but, usually, you will find that a number of skills are involved and you have to choose where to start. Sometimes, you may elect to start with the one that is easiest to change (even though it may not have the biggest impact on personal effectiveness), giving the employee a quick win and getting the coaching relationship off to a good start.

Generally speaking, however, you look to identify the 'key'—the one thing the employee does that seems to be the main driver of ineffectiveness (using our various cause–effect performance models). Sometimes, it may be necessary to fix one skill before another because the former is a driver of the latter. For example, our customer service consultant should learn to key in accurately before learning how to soothe anxious customers (because miskeying leads to rekeying and an increased wait for the customer).

Ensuring skill development takes place

We all know that when employees (including ourselves!) go back to the job, inertia often causes them to 'forget' the new behaviours they are supposed to be using. In addition, when new interpersonal behaviours (such as dealing with customers or colleagues) are involved, fear is a very strong factor in the new behaviours not being attempted. You need ways to ensure that these new behaviours will be put into practice. Such ways include a compelling reason, a reminder, monitoring them at work or by debriefs and role rehearsal.

A compelling reason
In many cases the employee's *internal* motivation to improve is sufficient, while others need to be provided with an additional, *external* compelling reason. The range of reasons is a local issue but can include such things as the impact on business performance, remuneration or benefits at risk, reputation or career at risk, and having to do it all again.

Reminder
It sounds too simple, but often all that is needed is some form of reminder—asking 'How's it going?', a sticky note on their customer files or a telephone call at the start of the day.

Monitoring
The greater the change, the more closely you need to monitor, particularly in the early stages. If you can't observe them at work, use one of their colleagues and, if observation can't be used at all, hold regular debriefs.

Role rehearsal

This method is underused and misused. Employees who have made a few attempts at new skills in a role rehearsal are far more likely to adopt the new skills back on the job. A rehearsal helps to conquer inertia and the fear of trying something new. Despite some protests to the contrary, what people do in a role rehearsal is a mirror of what they do in their work—if not always literally so, at least it displays their underlying assumptions and behaviours. The further advantage of a role rehearsal is that you can observe the new behaviours at close quarters and you can debrief (Observe, Reflect, Hypothesise) immediately. Remember, in a role rehearsal the content is not important but the behaviour is—unless, of course, the low effectiveness is an issue of knowledge.

Many people fear a role rehearsal with their manager more than they do the real thing. Develop your people's trust in you so that you can make use of this very effective tool. When you have an idea (a 'what if'), be prepared to demonstrate it to them. This will boost their trust in you. In a role rehearsal you don't need to be at peak level with the new skill, you simply have to be able to *do it*.

Activity 9.1

Select one of your tasks or goals where you are not fully meeting your objectives and where you know that your *personal effectiveness* is at least part of the cause. Either when the task is due, or in a role rehearsal, apply yourself to the Action Learning cycle with the intention of diagnosing exactly what you are doing that is depressing your personal effectiveness.

1. Before you commence, what do you **Intend** to do?
2. Perform the task **(Act)**.
3. What did you actually do **(Observe)**? Looking more closely at the actions or decisions that were not effective, how finely can you dissect them?
4. **Reflect** on possible reasons for why you acted or decided as you did.
5. **Hypothesise** alternative ways you might do these things next time.

A business reality check

Having got personal effectiveness development under way, check that improvements are creating the desired work outcomes; if not, review your original planning assumptions. Also review your planning assumptions where the converse applies—that is, where you begin to get good work results independently of personal effectiveness. You should also be aware that improvements in an employee's personal effectiveness may alter the work system balance, requiring an adjustment elsewhere—for example, an employee becomes so effective that she creates more work for others, uses more resources or puts more pressure on suppliers.

Coaching and managing good performers

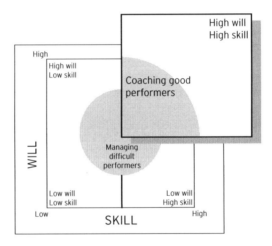

When you have an employee who is exceeding personal effectiveness requirements, two questions often arise: 'How do I add value as a manager?' and 'How do I maintain their interest and motivation?' While some managers say 'if only' in relation to good performers, other managers find them to be a problem, reporting the following challenges.

- I don't know how to keep them motivated.
- In the end there's nothing about the work I can teach them.
- It's hard to keep giving them stretch goals.
- There's always the worry that they might get my job (because they are technically superior).

- You can't always find a promotion for them.
- In the end you just can't pay them any more.
- It causes some resentment among the plodders.
- It's personally harder to keep recognising an exceptional performer than it is to keep pushing a poor performer.

Expanding the will–skill definition of 'good performers', we have three situations:

1. employees whose personal performance consistently meets requirements;
2. employees whose performance intermittently exceeds requirements; and
3. employees whose performance consistently exceeds requirements.

Experience shows that each of these groups is at risk of being under-managed in the workplace, particularly with respect to coaching support.

Defining and identifying good performance

We start with a basic concept of what we mean by good 'performance' as far as the coaching approach is concerned. If we have an employee who is meeting or exceeding their work performance requirements, can we assume that we have a person with high will and high skill? Possibly, but not necessarily. Since we coach the person, not the business, our first step to coaching must be to isolate the level of *personal effectiveness* as distinct from actual *work performance*.

When 'good' is not

Staff are sometimes recognised for good performance, which they know (as do their colleagues, very often) was the result of factors outside their own personal effectiveness. (As employees, we are often quick to acknowledge this phenomenon when our results are poor!). The common classes of these errors, as identified via the performance data model and the performance feedback model, are discussed below.

- *Work performance result is low but personal effectiveness is above expectations.* What normally leads you to identify a good level of personal effectiveness is good work performance. However, there are times when an employee's work results are below expectations but their personal effectiveness is above, indicating either faulty planning assumptions or underperformance of another part of the work system. For example, a trainer's course evaluations are poor but participants are protesting against the underlying business changes.

- *Work performance result is high but personal effectiveness is normal.* With many employees, their work performance is more visible than their personal effectiveness. The management trap is to respond personally to the former before knowing the extent of the latter. For example, an employee is tasked to change a cabinet minister's views and the manager subsequently focuses on the favourable outcome more than the employee's contribution.
- *Work performance result is high but personal effectiveness is lower than planned.* This situation is similar to that above except that, in this case, you are also dealing with personal underperformance.
- *Personal effectiveness is high but within the expected range.* We saw in Chapter 7 that a peak in business performance may be within the normal range and thus require no special response. The same can apply to personal effectiveness: for example, within a normal range of four out of five proposals requiring no rework, no one perfect proposal deserves special attention.

Three forms of good performance

Assuming that you have established that personal effectiveness exceeds or consistently meets agreed levels, your management and coaching responses will differ according to whether the personal effectiveness *meets* or *exceeds* requirements and whether it is *intermittent* or *sustained*.

Sustained good performance (Figure 9.2) describes an employee consistently meeting their performance targets. This means that the achievement of our work unit business goals is assured (assuming valid planning assumptions) and our business is predictable, which means it costs less to operate. We assume that these employees demonstrate consistent application of both will and skill.

Intermittent high performance describes personal effectiveness that occasionally exceeds plan or expectations (Figure 9.2). This peak in personal performance results from the application of additional will or skill by the employee. As an example of additional will, an employee may put extra time or energy into a particular work period, task or project and, as a result, generate higher activity and/or be more effective. Intermittent exercise of higher skill manifests when an employee is more

Figure 9.2 Three forms of good performance

diligent or persistent in applying existing skills. In both cases it requires a conscious and deliberate effort to work above the person's current 'natural' level.

Sustained high performance differs from intermittent in that the person's 'natural' level is now higher than that required for the current work (role, task or goal). It is seen as a shift or upward trend in personal effectiveness and comes as the result of a change in the person, either a sustained shift from low to high will or a sustained shift in the level of skill.

Responding to good performance

Coaching is part of the spectrum of management responses to good performers but, for the sake of better understanding, we will discuss separately both a *management* response and a *coaching* response. The management response includes feedback and considerations of recognition, reward, motivation and career. The coaching response involves further skill development in relation to the current role and ongoing development of the employee's ability to learn.

Responding to the three types of good performers involves some common approaches and some specific to one or the other, as illustrated in Table 9.1. In some organisations, particularly in the public sector, it is not possible to lift the performance requirements within the current role, nor can additional remuneration or benefits be offered. Many employees in such situations are fulfilled by their own sense of achievement, reinforced by manager feedback. Generally, employees in this situation consistently exceed the requirements of the role.

Table 9.1 Management and coaching responses to intermittent and sustained good performance

	Examples of responses		
	Sustained good performance	Intermittent high performance	Sustained high performance
Performance requirements	Performance requirements unchanged	Performance requirements unchanged	Higher level requirements within current role, or promotion
Feedback	Yes	Yes	Yes
Recognition	Acknowledge for meeting requirement	Appropriate for all employees, e.g. monthly award	Structural, e.g. new office/car/title/additional responsibilities
Remuneration	Normal	Bonus payment	Increase in base salary or benefits
Coaching	Build upon potential; work towards specific areas of potential high performance	Build upon potential; build more sustained high performance	Support to consistently meet new, higher level of requirement

All good performers suffer the risk that their further development needs may be overlooked. Employees who consistently meet their performance requirements frequently miss out on feedback and recognition, a situation that also often applies to those who consistently exceed. When managers are questioned about this, the underlying reason appears to be they manage exceptions to the normal—that is, underperformers and intermittent high performers. The inclusion of consistent high performers in the 'normal' group occurs when they have received some structural recognition of their contribution, such as increased salary or benefits, which tends to normalise their performance.

Management response

Common management approaches to both intermittent and sustained performance include giving feedback, recognition, reward—financial and non-financial—and role change. The first two of these approaches are essential to good management, while the others are used according to circumstances such as the need for motivation, career decisions or business needs.

Good performers also need feedback

We have seen feedback as a necessary tool for understanding and influencing performance. It is also a personally valued response, in that employees like to know that they have done well. Very often, good feedback for good performance is the most satisfying response an employee can receive. It is the most basic form of recognition.

Recognition

Recognition can exist in its own right or be implied in other responses, such as a promotion or pay rise. It is helpful to see your direct recognition choices as falling into two groups—personal recognition and symbolic recognition.

Personal recognition is discussed in Chapter 7 as part of positive manager-to-employee feedback. One additional piece of advice in giving recognition is to recognise the person, not the act. Just think what a difference it would make to you if someone said 'You must have really cranked up the brain cells on this proposal—we wouldn't have been successful without your analysis' rather than simply 'A great result, congratulations'. Your people, like you, want to be appreciated for what was special about them that created the good result. This means that, in the process of feedback, you explore what it is that the employee regards as special about their performance, and then acknowledge and recognise those things, as in this example, which is part of a feedback discussion.

Situation   *How did you manage to finally finish the report on time?*
               (Manager probes for what the employee had to *do* and *be* in order to achieve the result)
               (Discussion and agreement)

Implication   *So you decided to chase up the other contributors. What was it like having to do that?* (Probes for the personal implication)
               (Interaction and agreement)

Resolution   *I want to acknowledge you for the initiative in chasing up the other contributors so that you could finish the report on time. I also know you find it personally difficult to have to confront others.* (Manager recognises two specific aspects of the employee)

The second form of recognition, *symbolic*, uses symbols or rituals, such as trophies, awards ('employee of the month') and 'occasions' (award made at a staff meeting). Symbolic recognition of sustained high performance may also include being awarded higher-level or 'prestige' tasks, such as leading sessions at staff meetings, mentor roles, special projects or greater input into business unit planning. Be aware that symbolic recognition without personal recognition is hollow and counterproductive.

As you are aware, some people like public recognition, others don't. This may be a personal choice or determined by the dominant work culture. You should ultimately go with what the employee wants, which is not to say that you shouldn't attempt to sway them if public acknowledgment would be good for the employee or for the general work community.

Reward

Remuneration reward strategies are outside the scope of this book but we can identify some considerations, in line with the management principles already discussed.

- *Reward overachievement.* The basic principle is not to provide additional remuneration for employees who meet the agreed require-ments of their assigned work. To provide additional reward for peaks that are within the agreed requirement may create a culture that says it is okay to underachieve.
- *Intermittent or sustained high performance.* The type of reward will vary according to whether the high performance is intermittent or sustained. Reward for intermittent performance will be one-off events, such as a bonus, paid attendance at a conference or elective training course. Reward for sustained performance is more likely to be in the form of a permanent event, such as a pay rise, rise in benefits or upgraded motor vehicle.
- *Link to personal acknowledgment.* Personal acknowledgment must underpin all non-personal recognition or reward. In one example, staff one year received acknowledgment and a bonus and were very happy; the following year they received the same bonus but

without the acknowledgment, which lead to widespread and lasting dissatisfaction.

Role change

In the context of managing high performers, role change is used for the purpose of recognition, career development and deriving the best business use from the employee's ability. Role changes include enhancement of current role, special assignment, promotion and transfer with or without promotion, and are more appropriate to employees demonstrating sustained high performance.

- *Enhancement of current role.* Role enhancement can include the opportunity to undertake a higher level of the same work or to be a specialist in the same work. Supporting others is another form of enhancement and includes being a technical expert, a mentor or learning to be a coach of others. Another form of enhancement may be to stand in for the manager when absent.
- *Special assignment* generally refers to taking employees off their regular role, full-time or part-time, to work on another role. This can include such things as working on a project team or filling a temporary vacancy at a higher level or in a different area of the business. Special assignment should be relevant to employees' development, either within their current role or as part of a structured career plan, which should include associated development goals.
- *Promotion.* Sustained high performers attract attention to their potential for promotion. There are two obvious cautions here. One is that the employee actually wants promotion—some high performers are motivated by their current work and don't want to change. The second caution relates to employees moving up to their first management role—good technical performance does not necessarily mean good management performance.
- *Transfer.* Sometimes the nature of an employee's personal effectiveness suggests that they might do well in another type of role, in other words, not a direct line promotion. I can illustrate this with a personal example. In my late twenties my role was to call on medical practitioners and present the virtues of my company's prescription drugs. I didn't have the highest call rate but I was good at forming professional relationships with some of my client base and I was

very much on top of the published clinical research on our products. This didn't lead me to 'salesman of the year' award or even immediately to a sales manager role, but it did lead me to a Head Office position, networking professionally with key medical and scientific researchers.

Activity 9.2 Responding

Most employees desire or expect some recognition when they produce a good job, yet, as we have just seen, 'good' is not always what it seems. What implications would you face if you did not give recognition to an employee whose work perform-ance showed a good result, but whose personal effectiveness contribution was less than required?

1. Think about the impact of your actions (which includes 'no action') on:
    *   your employee;
    *   your relationship with the employee; and
    *   the business.
2. How would you handle such a situation with such an employee who was clearly looking for some form of recognition?

Coaching response

The coaching response will depend largely on whether the good per-formance is intermittent or sustained. In the case of performance that consistently exceeds the requirement, there may be additional coaching considerations.

The Action Learning cycle of the performance coaching model is the approach for all good performers whom you want to move towards better performance. Have them look back at their work system (open system of work model) and their key performance drivers and identify where their performance strengths lie—that is, help them to discover the specifics of what they are doing well. For example, they may intermittently predict and pre-empt external forces, or they may intermittently use questions more effectively in meetings with key stakeholders. If you coach them through the steps of Observe, Reflect and Hypothesise, they should then be able to create more consistent, high-level results. Sometimes the observation step may be based on previous experiences, whereas at other times you may need either to observe the employees at work or have them be more aware of what they do on future occasions when they achieve good performance.

In the following, we look at the specific coaching considerations associated with sustained good performance, intermittent high performance and sustained high performance. Before beginning, you will need to establish your employee's willingness to pursue the coaching path and particularly to ensure that they don't see your approach as indicating that they are underperforming in any way.

Sustained good performance

When coaching employees who consistently meet their performance requirements your aim will be either to build up weaker areas in their methods or to build towards intermittent high performance.

Building up their weaker areas amounts to strengthening their fundamentals, leading to more consistent and predictable performance. These fundamentals need to be sound before you attempt to coach them towards an overall higher level of performance—otherwise it's as if you are adding a second floor to a building with weak foundations.

The coaching focus of developing intermittent rather than high performance is chosen because it provides a sharper focus than that of trying to lift performance across the board. It can take the form of either excelling in one particular area of work or excelling under certain conditions. An example of the former would be taking a supervisor's ability to create a sense of trust in the team, developing a better understanding of that ability and then applying the strengths to excelling in, say, directing a team that responds quickly and flexibly to competitive changes in the marketplace. An example of excelling under certain conditions would be building on an order clerk's understanding of the retail trade to coach him towards being able to negotiate split orders during times of unpredicted demand or warehouse stock shortages.

Intermittent high performance

With intermittent events of exceeding performance requirements, your coaching aim will generally be to create more sustained high performance.

The coaching approach is to help the employee to discover what it takes to generate their high performance peaks more frequently and consistently. The application of the Action Learning cycle of coaching should be used to learn specifically of the differences in the employee's approach between normal and high performance events. The open system of work model will enable the employee to look separately at any differences in external performance drivers.

Sustained high performance

When responding to sustained high performance your coaching development aims will include:

- refining current performance;
- further improving current performance; and/or
- developing skills for future roles.

An early step would be to establish whether this employee wishes to continue to develop her skills. If she doesn't, the coaching approach would be to ensure that she stays up to date or ahead of developments in her field of work. In these cases, management responses to maintain her interest and motivation are described above. Once the employee decides that she wants to develop further, the next step is to consider her reasons or goals and which of the above aims meets her needs.

For employees at this level, their motivation to improve is probably more important to the coaching process than it is with other types of good performers. Some reasons for continuing development include recognition, ongoing satisfaction or fulfilment, higher rewards and career possibilities. Table 9.2, while not definitive, is a guide to the motivators most likely to be addressed by the three types of development aims.

Refining current performance

Refinement of performance refers to improving the quality of the results being achieved. The areas for refinement might be arrived at mutually or employees may already have their own ideas. Refinement might include these aspects.

- If achieving high quantity, look at improving quality or resource utilisation.
- Rather than looking at overall performance, microanalyse each goal to segment areas for improvement, for example. If planning exceeds

requirements, look for gains to be made in any of the components of planning, such as market analysis or risk analysis.

- Look for opportunities to improve consistency or predictability of results.

You can coach sustained high performance towards refinement in much the same way as described above, by use of the open system of work model, key performance drivers and the Action Learning cycle of coaching.

Table 9.2 Motivators for sustained high performers

Employee motivation	Coaching/development aims		
	Refining	Further improving	Future skills
Recognition	+	+++	+
Satisfaction or fulfillment	+++	+++	+++
Higher rewards*	+	+++	
Career possibilities	+	+	+++

* within this role

Further improving current performance

When we talk about improving current performance, we mean being better at the same thing—selling more, processing more, making better decisions. On the principle of building on a sound foundation, before coaching towards higher-level performance you should complete *performance refinement*, as described above. The coaching approach should include clear personal and business goals and should have a defined focus.

- *Personal goals*. For a high performer to lift performance even further, clear personal goals should be discussed because the next step up in personal effectiveness, from this high level, may demand a lot of the employee.
- *Business goals*. Set clear work performance targets so that there is a business focus, a level of demand and a sense of satisfaction when achieving.
- *Defined focus*. The coaching approach here is analogous to that used with sustained good performance, which is to focus on one skill or one circumstance at a time for improvement.

In relation to the Action Learning steps, an established high performer may lose focus on new skills (Act) and on self-awareness (Observe) so you should monitor closely and remind employees of their own motivation for taking this path.

Future skills
Rather than continuous improvement, the focus is one of leaping ahead to the future needs of this role or to the needs of a new role. Whereas each focus is of value to the employee, the former is particularly important to the business when significant changes are known to be ahead—for example, changes in technology, market structure or government regulation.

In some cases, the exact skills may not be known (e.g. specific technology) but you are aware of similar ones.

In other cases of future unknowns, you may both need to apply the open system of work model to identify possible drivers of the skills or performance needed. For example, your employee is a mid-level manager in charge of a market that is predicted to undergo significant amalgamations and acquisitions. Using the model you might identify that the employee will need to manage change and deal with staff whose world is changing and whose jobs are at risk. It may be possible to develop these skills in-house in analogous situations (same role or different role) or they may need to be developed externally (e.g. in voluntary community work).

10 Managing difficult performers

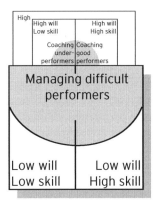

We use the term 'difficult performers' to describe those who lack the degree of will, or intention, to perform at the required level. To describe them as difficult is a reflection both of their unwillingness to fulfil their basic employment obligations and of the complexity that often surrounds the management of these employees. The overall aim of managing difficult performers is to restore their will to the point that their performance ability can be ascertained. At this point they will fall into one of the other two quadrants in the will–skill dynamic and can be coached appropriately from there. If an employee is ultimately unwilling to perform, your pathways will include your organisation's *performance management system and practices* and its policies and procedures on *formal discipline* and termination.

If the problem proves to be difficult to resolve in the first instance, you must maintain the quality of your management and not descend to a power game (the most common response) or an avoidance of the issue (the next most common response). Keep your outcomes always at the top of your mind—to achieve the best outcome for the enterprise as well as justice and dignity for the employee. You already have the *power*; situations like these demand the best of your *management*.

This chapter is called 'managing' rather than 'coaching' for the reason that the management aspects of the role lead the way, particularly as certain non-negotiables have to be spelled out in many of these cases. Having said this, since one of your outcomes should be to develop difficult performers rather than discipline or dismiss them, coaching forms an integral part of the process. Coaching is relevant to the low-will stage because an employee may agree to management support in overcoming the barriers to their wanting to perform.

In this chapter we work with issues of work performance—that is, not meeting agreed performance levels (which includes failing to agree to appropriate performance levels)—and not difficult behaviour such as absenteeism, poor teamwork or unethical behaviour. These difficult behaviours may be dealt with in the context of their impact on work performance but not as the primary focus of intervention. The reason for focusing on work performance is that the latter group of issues is overlaid with company policies and procedures, which vary from organisation to organisation. This is not to say that the approaches described are not appropriate to behaviour problems as well.

Understanding difficult performers

We need to understand something of the nature of difficult performers before we can look at ways of dealing with them. Often it is not what we do but how we do it that makes a difference to the outcome of difficult performance situations, and it is our background knowledge and assumptions that drive the 'how'. Part of our understanding includes the different dimensions of low-will performance, how difficult performance manifests and its common causes.

Four difficult performers

To characterise such difficult performers we present four example cases, which are fictitious composites based on a range of situations encountered in the workplace. They are therefore quite realistic. These four characters will be used throughout the chapter to illustrate points being made.

Case 1 Business line manager (female)

- *Role*: Responsible for managing the performance of a discrete area of the business, such as a specific product or service or a business line.
- *Situation*: Professionally qualified; intelligent; makes intuitive decisions; mostly correct but not necessarily optimum solutions.
    —Spends less than a full day working on business because of a very social life at work; arrives and leaves on time.
    —Does not fully analyse situations or data; reaches cursory conclusions based on intelligence and intuition. This same 'winging it' also applies to execution of new or changed processes, practices or systems.
- *Performance problems*: Being very intelligent, the employee achieves good results most of the time.
    —Some decisions and strategies are clearly not supported by the full information available. In some cases a more thorough analysis would have prevented bad decisions and, in other cases, decisions and strategies could have been better.
    —Some opportunities have been missed because of an inadequate grasp of the full scope and complexity of the particular issue.
    —Incorrect use of new systems causes rework for the employee and additional work for other employees.
    —Previous management attempts to change behaviour have not been successful.

Case 2 Technical expert on environmental sciences (male)

- *Role*: As a member of a project team of technical experts, review and make recommendations on a specific natural environment issue. Contribute to the whole team effort and work on specific aspects, as directed.
- *Situation*: Well qualified, passionate and enthusiastic about the project.
    —Participates in meetings; has many good ideas; has very strong views on many issues associated with the project and argues frequently with others in the team.
    —Believes that the others are not as competent as he is; openly critical of some of the work of the others.

—Will not work with ideas or decisions with which he does not agree; when forced to, may do so without applying himself fully to the task, or do it in his own way despite the instruction.

- *Performance problems*: Disharmony in the team; some others becoming less sure of their own capabilities.

  —Some work produced by this person does not meet the required content or style—he blames this on the fact that the requirement is flawed. Resistant to any feedback that requires change.

Case 3 Customer service officer (female)

- *Role*: Handle customer telephone inquiries and process customer transactions.
- *Situation*: Used to be full-time on customer inquiries, now split with processing.

  —Transaction rates are below the lower level of the normal range for this type of work—occurs for about 20 per cent of time; accuracy rate is within the standard.

  —Receives positive feedback from telephone customers; demonstrates good skills and provides appropriate and correct information; telephone inquiries last far longer than those of other staff.

  —High rate of absenteeism.

- *Performance problems*: Higher cost per transaction because of low transaction rates and high absenteeism rate.

  —Affects staff cohesion as others resent this employee's 'getting away with it'.

Case 4 Materials supervisor (male)

- *Role*: Manage a newly established outpost of the main materials supply store, to serve a particular production line in the factory.
- *Situation*: Employee has the greatest knowledge of materials supply to this production line.

  —Objected to splitting of new outpost from main supply store; was a good employee until the change. Since then will not cooperate with requests from stores manager; publicly criticises the company and the manager.

  —Will not control stock holdings; impolite to customers from the line; dress and appearance very shabby.

- *Performance problems*: Frequent stock outs delay the production line; production costs increase.
  —Line customers complain of poor personal service.
  —Manager feels a failure.
  —Low team morale.

Different dimensions of low will

From these four cases we can draw out four distinct dimensions of employee low will that are useful to their management. When faced with a low-will performance situation, four questions to ask are:

- How long? (*length*)—long time established or recent onset
- How much? (*breadth*)—all of work or part of work
- How often? (*consistency*)—sustained or occasional
- How deep? (*motivation*)—intrinsic or extrinsic

How long? (length)

One indicator of the size of the problem is the length of time the problem has existed. Long established patterns will be harder to change than those of recent onset. In some cases the employee has been through several managers, none of whom has been able to correct the problem. Case 1 is an example of a long-term issue—it has been present throughout the life of this role and is a style that is intrinsic to the employee. Given the length of time and previous experience of defending herself against previous managers, it is most likely that the behaviour and the underlying beliefs and values have become strongly entrenched. As a corollary, it is usually found that recent onset problems are easier to resolve, strengthening the argument for good quality investigative feedback and for dealing with issues at the time.

How much? (breadth)

Difficult performers may present with problems in just certain aspects of their work or it may affect all their work, including their work-based relationships. Aspects of work that may show up as low-will issues include specific goals or tasks, organisational values or behaviours and dealing with people (customers, suppliers or colleagues). Cases 1 and 4 exhibit problems across all areas of work with 2 and 3 only in some areas.

It is generally held that a problem affecting just one aspect of an employee's work is not as deeply entrenched and therefore easier to change. This may be so, if it is the particular aspect of the work that triggers the low will (situational). On the other hand, the cause may be intrinsic low will but the employee happens to enjoy other aspects of their work, in which they may perform to standard or even excel.

How often? (consistency)

Poor performance as a result of low will may be either occasional or sustained. Occasional low will describes performance that sometimes meets the requirement and sometimes doesn't, as exemplified in Case 3. It may affect all an employee's work or just some aspect of it (breadth), such as a particular task or goal or perhaps some behaviours. Managers will sometimes talk about 'occasional' poor performance but on questioning it turns out that they are referring to the same problem occurring occasionally, which in terms of management is sustained poor performance (Case 3). Thus, true occasional poor performance (i.e. different problems occurring) is probably uncommon.

Poor performance that is truly occasional receives less attention than when the problem is sustained; the usual reasoning is that 'on average' the employee comes in on target. Because it is not the dominant expression of employees' work or of their nature, occasional low-will performance is generally amenable to intervention. Here are some situations where you should take action.

- The consequences are significant when they do occur or, if not significant so far, they could be.
- You suspect or know of an underlying significant problem—work or personal.
- You believe that your employee is likely to be concerned about their bouts of low will.

Sustained low will describes continuous poor performance over a period of time, as in Cases 1, 2 and 4. If you have been dealing with issues as they arise, a sustained problem is one that is either on the mend or is already into, or about to progress to, formal disciplinary processes. If, for some reason, you are confronted with a longstanding situation for the first time (e.g. acquiring someone else's problem), you are most likely to have a slow and exacting task on your hands.

How deep? (motivation)

What is it that drives some people to put into their work what we consider to be reasonable effort, while others seem to do everything they can to avoid doing what we require of them? This is one of those really big questions that is beyond the scope of this book, but we can make some sense of parts of it.

In Case 4 the employee began to exhibit anti-work behaviour only after the reorganisation of the materials supply department. The low will was therefore most probably motivated by his work situation— an external cause, or extrinsic motivation. Case 3 presents a similar extrinsic motivation. By contrast, Cases 1 and 2 display low-will characteristics that are most likely motivated by something from within the employee (intrinsic) rather than the specific work environment. An employee displaying occasional low-will performance—either a different problem each time or a recurrence of the same problem—would probably have some extrinsic motivation.

Extrinsic low-will motivators are more visible, more discussable and more manageable than intrinsic motivators and are therefore usually easier cases to resolve.

How low will shows up

When low will is the cause of poor performance it should show up in the process of performance feedback, particularly if the work system model is used to support an examination of both personal and non-personal contributors to the employee's work performance. Some other common indicators of low-will work performance are:

- repeated failure to implement behaviours or practices that are designed to bring performance up to the agreed level (Case 1);
- low level of participation in the process of Work Assignment, planning or performance agreement (Case 2);
- wide fluctuations in performance, with no obvious external cause (Case 3); and
- failure to act within the full scope of authority (Case 4).

Poor performance through lack of will doesn't always show up through failure to meet performance objectives; in fact, some employees who are acting out of a deep sense of resentment will take care to ensure that their observed commitments are met or, at least, close enough to being met. In these cases a lack of intention can show up in a number of other ways, such as:

- poor quality of work;
- poor maintenance of equipment or systems;
- low personal flexibility, innovation, resourcefulness, or cooperation with others;
- behaving as a victim, whingeing or blaming others; and
- spreading rumours, disharmony or anti-company talk.

Some employees are labelled as low-will on the basis of manager bias or assumptions or because of the reputation they bring from other managers or work colleagues. As a warning against being duped by taking on someone else's opinions, there are many cases where one manager's problem employee has been a star in another environment.

Common reasons for low will

Once low will has been agreed as a problem, you should seek to understand the reasons so as to be able to support your employee's turnaround. Following are some of the more common reasons for low will that are encountered. In some cases there is a single reason for low-will performance but in most cases it is a composite of more than one. This means that you need to examine more deeply, beyond what seems to be the most obvious reason, otherwise you may achieve only temporary improvement.

The work
In some cases the reasons are specific to the actual work itself and have a clear logic for the employee. They include:

- Employee disagrees with the goals or methods of the work assigned and thus works to alternative goals or methods.
- Employee is unclear about or misunderstands the Work Assignment and is therefore very tentative in what she does.
- The work itself is not seen as stimulating, fulfilling or important.
- Employee does not have, or thinks he does not have, the requisite skill for the work assigned and either does not recognise the fact or is hesitant about raising it with his manager.

The workplace

Workplace causes include relationships (with co-workers and with own manager), pay and conditions, morale or climate, and work culture. Interpersonal difficulties plague a large number of employees and sap their work effort. One point of view is that these difficulties are part of the background social 'noise' and therefore not able to be modified. Another point of view is that some people handle this 'noise' less well than others and intervention to help them to cope better may free more energy and will to put into their work.

Pay and conditions and morale are determined on a whole-of-organisation basis, but individual responses vary. To the extent that these factors cause low-will performance you can deal with them on a whole-of-organisation, work-group or individual basis.

Organisational culture is worth considering separately as it is a deeply ingrained influence and one that is not quickly or easily modified. The culture of the whole organisation or of the subgroup to which an employee belongs has written and unwritten 'rules' (values and norms) about what kind of behaviour is rewarded. When that culture or sub-culture runs counter to what the work requires, the culture may win. The paradox is that some of these countercultural elements are actually created by management, as a result of their actions (as distinct from their words). As an example: in a culture where management won't listen to employees, the workforce is unlikely to take the risk of questioning lack of resources, inadequate systems or competing work priorities, or of challenging unrealistic targets.

Personal beliefs and values

Employees bring into the workplace their own set of beliefs about right, wrong and what gets results. In most cases these beliefs are reflected in the values and norms of the organisation. It is when employees perceive a conflict they can't resolve (whether or not it is real) that they may opt to work to their own values, at the expense of their work performance. Some examples include:

- personal values about morality and ethics;
- personal values about the most effective ways to achieve results;
- personal values about the relative importance of work and personal life;
- professional values and standards of one's profession, craft or trade; and
- trade union beliefs, values and rules.

Justice

The notion of justice is closely aligned with personal values and group values and largely manifests as the response to perceived 'wrongs'. These 'wrongs' may have been perpetrated by the manager, by management at large or by colleagues in the work group or in other work groups.

Low-will performance may manifest as follows:

- The employee resists performance requirements as a way of standing up for what is 'right'.
- The employee is motivated by payback of an unjust manager/management.
- The employee believes that management and/or owners exploit the staff and therefore it is a duty, or fair game, to exploit the enterprise.

Personal problems

Personal problems—that is, problems arising outside the workplace—are a common cause of low-will performance. Some social commentators say that we are going through a cycle of increasing social tension and that this is manifesting as work inefficiency. The increase in the number of organisations subscribing to Employee Assistance Programs may support this view. The scope of personal problems is wide and encompasses issues outside the general intervention of a manager, although one personal factor that may be within a manager's influence is self-esteem where, for example, an employee believes that their personal contribution is not important.

Managing difficult performers

We have just seen that in order to manage difficult performers you must understand them as individuals. When responding, the first principles include a non-judgmental and positive approach to difficult performers and their management. On this basis the processes and skills we have already discussed in relation to other performance situations will also be effective with difficult performers.

First principles

Difficult performers may not always be what they seem and there are some overarching principles that are worth considering before going into the management process. These principles begin with the mindset that you take into the performance interaction and end with the action you might take in implementing them.

Difficult can mean dedicated

I have been involved in, or encountered, many cases where the most 'troublesome' employees have been the brightest and most values-driven in the work group. Those who argue the most about the nature of their work, its purpose and its social contribution can be your fiercest opponent or your staunchest ally. Their commitment to 'right' (moral or practical) makes them very dedicated to their cause. When they see alignment between their own ideals and those of the rest of the organisation they become highly dedicated employees. We have witnessed some startling turnarounds.

Different does not equal 'wrong'

Don't put your employee in the wrong for a different point of view, and don't force agreement with your point of view simply because you are the boss. If you must back your own judgment, even though you can't get agreement on your case, be honest and admit that is the reason rather than implying that you are right and your employee is wrong. It's a case of 'I can't establish that your approach is wrong and mine is right but, please, I'm carrying responsibility for this, so how about you do it this way until there is evidence that indicates otherwise?'

Personal challenge

Difficult performers will challenge your biases and assumptions. When faced with 'difficult' employees you will constantly be tempted to *attribute* motives to them that make them wrong and you right. You have to guard constantly against 'knee-jerk' responses (silent or expressed), such as 'You just want to avoid work' or 'You are rorting the system', and stay with what is objective.

Shared responsibility

Put equal responsibility on your employee to solve the problem. This is only possible once you have both agreed the implications of not solving the problem and have moved into the Resolution step of the performance feedback model.

Creative opportunity

Different ideas are important because they are the foundations of the technical and social innovation that is critical for most enterprises. At the point when difficult performers turn around they often gain a fresh perspective on the work, and so to attempt to solve low-will performance by way of 'command and control' stifles creative solutions. This is another good reason to engage, rather than direct, the employee in the process of recovery.

The process

While some difficult performance issues will go all the way through to formal procedures and possibly dismissal, our aim should always be to recover difficult performers. With a focus on 'recovery' we need to complement our understanding of difficult performers with an effective and manageable process, because simply coercing employees to change their behaviour has limited, if any, benefit. 'Stick and carrot' sanctions, while sometimes effective, suffer limitations—there may be industrial/legal implications and worsening relationships; employees will mostly find a way around sanctions; they require too much management enforcement; and even with good intentions the employee may lapse.

Fortunately, the process for managing difficult performers is deceptively simple, since it is based substantially on the performance feedback model. You get to the point of agreeing that low will is the problem and that it will be resolved, and then you bring in the performance coaching model to support the improvement.

Phase 1 Performance feedback

The process of using the performance feedback model to identify low will is summarised in Table 10.1. Following the table is an illustration of how the process is applied, using Case 2 as an example, and taking into account the dimensions of low will and its possible causes, as described earlier.

Illustration of applying performance feedback to low-will performance, using Case 2 as an example

A. Complete the cycle of feedback
By using the three feedback steps you uncover and agree low will as the cause of underperformance.

Table 10.1 The performance feedback process for low-will performance

A. **Complete the cycle of feedback leading to agreement on low will as the cause of underachievement**	• Underperformance is agreed
	• Agreement that low will is the cause
	• Resolution is either:
	  (a) employee complies—exit the process
	  (b) performance requirement is amended— exit the process
	  (c) employee does not comply—continue the process

	If employee does not comply, a personal 'problem' has occurred:
B. **Embrace the problem**	• Empathise • Explore • Export

C. **Resume the performance feedback process, leading to an agreed performance resolution**	• Low will is confirmed
	• Present the options
	• Present the consequences of failing to meet peformance requirements
	• Resolution is either:
	  (a) employee agrees to perform as required
	  (b) employee agrees to being coached to perform as required (will and/or skill)
	  (c) employee enters a formal disciplinary process

- *Situation.* The employee's draft chapter of a report was required to be structured in a particular way and is not. The employee (a) agrees but (b) argues that his way is better. (Option (b) is an 'Implication'; don't debate it until the entire Situation is explored and agreed.)
- *Implication.* You explain that (a) the employee's structure makes the chapter difficult to understand and (b) its structure will be inconsistent with other chapters in the report. Your employee argues against the implications in that (a) the chapter will be far better understood his way and (b) consistency in structure is relatively less important. After a full discussion that exhausts all the arguments, you can't reach agreement on the nature of the Implication so you have to move to Resolution on that basis.
- *Resolution.* You explore options for Resolution—the choices are: (a) You accept the employee's work as it is;

(b) The employee rewrites it as per your original Work Assignment; or

(c) You mutually arrive at a third way that meets the needs of both.

Ultimately, you choose to stay with your original reasons and request your employee to do the rewrite (option b). Your employee is not willing to comply, so you clarify and confirm that he is not willing to structure the chapter as requested. This last step is critical to the ongoing process.

B. Embrace the problem

The employee now has a personal 'problem' that will need to be resolved before the performance issue can be addressed. You use the feedback 'recovery' model from Chapter 7.

- *Empathise.* You empathise with the employee's dilemma of being asked to do something that he considers to be less than his best.
- *Explore.* You confirm the reasons why he is not willing to comply. You keep exploring until you are sure that you have all the true reasons and that they are valid (use your 'pull' energy). You check willingness to be on the team and willingness to work with you.
- *Export.* These issues are all directly relevant to the current perform-ance so you 'Relate' the issues back to the feedback process. (If the issues had been valid but not related to the performance, you would have 'Reassigned' for consideration at another time.)

C. Resume and complete the performance feedback process

You resume the feedback process, now based on a new Situation.

- *Situation.* You establish or confirm that the situation is (a) that the performance does not meet the requirement and (b) that the employee is not willing to address the situation. You reaffirm that the require-ment must be met and that you will do whatever is needed to support the employee in complying.
- *Implication.* First, you explain the implications if the employee *is willing to comply* with the requirement. This might include how the quality of work will be ensured, how his self-esteem will be main-tained and the support he will get.

  If your first approach doesn't lead to a favourable resolution, you then explain what the implications are if the employee *does not comply with* this performance requirement. These implications might include removal from the team, adverse assessment, remuneration and career impact or disciplinary action. Your employee might want to debate whether these are the only options and you should support him in expressing himself in the best way that he can and *actively listen* to what he says. In your discussions, the one thing that is not negotiable is that performance must be at an acceptable level, as ultimately determined by you.

- *Resolution*. The sort of resolution that might come out of this includes:
  - (a) your employee agrees to correct the work;
  - (b) your employee agrees to work on his personal difficulty, supported by you; or
  - (c) you formally require him to comply.

If the outcome is (c) you will proceed in accordance with relevant company policies. Outcome (a) or (b) leads you into a *coaching role* with this employee.

Although outcome (a) looks like the end of the matter, two problems may arise.

1. The employee's ability to change may not match his intention.
2. There may be resentment, which will undermine this and future work.

To head off these possible problems you should explore further, using the feedback model, with the Implication step dealing with how he feels, how difficult the change might be, etc. In this case, you are dealing with entrenched beliefs and behaviours.

Phase 2 Performance coaching

When a low-will performer agrees to change, the aims of performance coaching are to ensure that they:

- do what they say;
- are supported in making the change; and
- learn to deal more effectively with similar situations in the future.

When a recovered employee agrees to work to the required level the response may be management or coaching. The former includes setting incremental targets and monitoring closely. The coaching response would follow that for underperformers but with greater emphasis on compliance with the coaching process.

When employees agree to work on their low-will difficulty, the coaching role is not to develop their work skills in the first instance but to enable them to understand their motivation and align it with the work requirements. This means that the performance coaching model needs to be reinterpreted from its work performance focus, as described in Table 10.2.

An illustration follows of how the coaching process might be applied, continuing with the Case 2 example.

If an employee fails to keep the commitments made during this coaching process, you deal with it using the performance feedback model, which essentially takes you back to the beginning. The outcome may be a renewal of this current coaching process or it may lead to an appropriate disciplinary path.

Illustration of applying performance coaching (Case 2 continued)

A. Set up the coaching agreement
(As per Table 10.2)

B. Understand the current work method
The principal focus is on the employee's motivation for resisting the required chapter format.

- *Observe.* With the employee, you examine (a) what he did in his version of the chapter and how it differed from the report requirement, and (b) his internal logic for non-compliance.
- *Reflect.* You help the employee to think about what caused this difference. Some of the thoughts might be a need to follow his own ideas, the need to be right, the belief that he knows better, etc.
- *Hypothesise.* Because you are dealing with his beliefs, you might begin by asking how it would be to accept that there could be ways to act within his professional beliefs while meeting the organisation's reporting needs. Other ideas might include his talking to colleagues—do they have the same issues? If so how do they handle it,

Table 10.2 Applying the performance coaching process to a low-will performer

By the time you get to this point the first two components of the Performance Coaching process, Analysis and Communication, will have already been handled. Coaching guidelines for the third component, Action, are as follows.

A. **Set up the coaching agreement**	• Trust will be a bigger issue than for a low-skill situation. • Be honest at all times. • Keep your non-negotiables in the open. • Commit to supporting the employee's personal change. • Clearly state required commitment from the employee. • Emphasise that only commitments they can keep should be made.
B. **Understand the current work method**	Adapt the model to a low-will issue. 3. **Observe** (a) the employee's work response to the assignment and (b) the employee's internal response. 4. **Reflect** upon the possible reasons for the employee's internal responses. 5. **Hypothesise** what the employee will need to do in order to change.
C. **Action Learning cycle**	The focus is on personal change in belief or behaviour. 1. **Intend** • Identify *one specific personal change* that the employee will make. • Set performance requirements at increasing levels over an agreed period, to provide realistic, attainable targets. • Set observation at short intervals, matching the performance increments, depending on the risk of non-compliance—intentional or unintentional. Thereafter, the coaching process follows the remaining four steps in the action learning cycle.

Note: The first two components of the performance coaching process, Analysis and Communication, are dealt with in Chapter 8 (see Figure 8.2 on page 138). The table shows coaching guidelines for the third component, Action.

etc? You might also hypothesise that if he provisionally restructured his work in the required style he may find that the differences are not as great as he currently envisages. Once you have agreed some worthwhile possibilities, you can move towards repeating the Action Learning cycle with a new focus.

C. *Action Learning cycle*

- *Intend.* From your hypotheses (above), select *one specific thing* for action. For example, talking to his colleagues, expressing his concerns and gaining their views, after which you will resume discussion. (As an aside, working with his colleagues is a good start because it helps him to reach his own conclusions and it may improve his collegiate relationships (see page 178), but he may also reject this choice for the same reason.)

    The cycle thus continues until the low-will issue is resolved.

Other aspects of the process

Two overarching responses are also worth considering:

- What do you do when the problem is bigger than one employee?
- What happens when an employee starts to improve and then reverts to their previous behaviour?

Broader approaches to broad problems. Some problems are bigger than the individual and, rather than just demanding compliance, it may be better to attempt to solve the cause if it is at a local level. Here are some guidelines for tackling broader issues.

- **Open**—be willing to see the employee as just one part of a bigger system.
- **Personal**—be open, be investigative, and be prepared to be part of the problem yourself.
- **Methods**—involve all concerned, ask questions, allow discussion and support the truth.

These principles are now illustrated by showing how Case 4 was brought to a successful outcome.

Illustration: taking a broad approach, using Case 4 as an example

The manager discussed the performance issues with the materials supervisor, using the performance feedback model. The outcome was that they agreed (a) that the issue was low will, and (b) that the restructure had put pressure on all the team, that the supervisor had been one of the worst affected and that the manager had not always handled the whole situation in the best way. As a starting point, the manager offered to meet with the whole team to discuss these issues. This was relevant because the whole team, at least indirectly, felt the influence of the disaffected supervisor.

At the meeting, the team, including the manager:

- worked on a reinterpretation of the company values as they applied to this group;
- discussed all the problems being experienced since the restructure, the manager taking responsibility where appropriate; and
- went through possible solutions for each problem; the manager undertook to solve certain problems, the team, others.

In the light of the outcomes of the team process, the manager re-engaged the supervisor in discussion, using the performance feedback model, the team's values and the undertaking to resolve certain problems. As a result, the supervisor finally felt that the negative effects of the restructure and the manager's behaviour had at last been recognised. The turnaround was complete and almost instantaneous.

One step forward and one step back. It is a common experience for poor performers to pick up their game for a while and then return to old habits. How do you handle that? The best answer seems to be: set up very specific requirements once the employee has agreed to comply. Thus, at the Resolution step of the performance feedback, when you deal with the low-will issue, you

- set *incremental targets* and dates, usually closely spaced at the start;
- include a *maintenance objective*, which requires the employee to maintain at least the required level of will once it has been reached; and

- specify the consequences if the employee defaults on their *intent* (as distinct from their achievement).

If the employee defaults, you go through the performance feedback process with your previously notified consequence already on the table as an option at the Resolution stage. Depending on the overall circumstances, you may elect to give the employee another chance, to modify your requirements or you may call upon your option.

Applying people management skills

The understanding and the processes presented above will enable all managers to deal with poor performers. The ease with which it is done and the time it takes to get a good outcome will vary according to the degree of skill possessed and applied by individual managers. The process is a matter of following the steps—skill has to be acquired and practised.

Being prepared is a good way of lifting your skill level and this can include revising the principles of managing people (Chapter 2) and knowing yourself. In addition, some practice with a colleague is invaluable.

The following activity, for which you should use Chapter 2 as a reference, may help to guide your preparation. Some of the jogger questions may be more relevant to you than others, depending on the occasion.

Activity 10.1 Personal preparation for managing difficult performance situations

The focus for these questions is to envisage the discussion with your employee.

Self-awareness

1. What is the greatest strength you will bring to managing the personal aspects of this discussion?
2. What do you most fear? What is your greatest vulnerability?
3. What will most challenge, and what will reinforce:
   - your confidence?
   - your self-esteem?
   - your communication?
4. What will make you defensive?
5. What will trigger you to act in negative ways towards the employee—harshly, unfairly, punitively, etc?

Relationship with the employee

6. What biases do you have about the employee and their likely handling of the discussion?
7. What opinions do you have of the employee that may be assumptions?

Questioning

8. Whereabouts in this discussion:
   - will open questions be most critical?
   - will closed questions be most critical?

Active listening

9. What can you do to strengthen your ability to listen actively?
10. What could the employee do that would weaken your ability to listen actively?

Part IV

'Crunch time'— the Formal Review Process

The annual performance review, sometimes referred to as 'appraisal', is a significant event in many large organisations. This is the time when employees, individually, sit down with their manager and, following a formal process, the whole of their performance over the whole of the year is reviewed and they come out of the meeting with some form of evaluation. The title, 'Crunch time', chosen for Part IV, is a reflection of how the process is regarded by both employees and managers, not how it should be.

The annual performance review is not a highly regarded process and against this background it requires skill and integrity for a manager to make it successful. Chapter 11 begins by exploring the nature and purpose of the formal review process in most organisations, and then provides some background to the process by presenting the basic principles of evaluation. Chapter 12 turns to the practicalities and realities of the evaluation process and outlines how you can manage the formal review process for the best outcome.

As a manager, your organisation may have a formal review system or you may simply wish to review your employees formally on a regular basis. Part IV will guide you effectively through either situation.

11 Principles of performance evaluation

Probably no organisational system or process generates so much cynicism, fear and resentment as does the process of formal performance evaluation (also referred to as 'assessment' or 'appraisal'). Staff concerns include lack of relevance, accuracy and justice and the intimidating nature of the experience. In a similar vein, managers' concerns include lack of relevance, the time commitment required and the difficulty of the process itself. While some line managers may concede benefits in the assessment process, the predominant view is that it does not contribute significantly to performance improvement and simply represents an administrative impost.

In many organisations and in the minds of many people, the evaluation process dominates the whole of the system, to the point that it is common for performance *management* systems to be referred to as performance *appraisal* systems. All of this should say two things to us, as managers: (1) we must not treat formal evaluation as the whole system, or even the principal driver of the system, and (2) there are many negative views that must be taken into account in its execution.

Many managers reading this book will work in an organisation with an established form of review and evaluation, including guidelines on how to conduct the exercise. The purpose of Chapters 11 and 12 is to provide ideas, principles and processes to enable you to produce a better result from formal review, with greater ease. The first step in using formal review better is to understand its nature.

The nature of formal review and evaluation

A normal part of managing employees' performance is to review their performance against their performance plan or agreement. The formal performance review has a number of essential differences, defined partly by its purpose and partly by its form.

Purpose

Given the concerns of both staff and line managers, why do organisations move beyond good day-to-day management of performance and institutionalise formal review and evaluation? To address this question we come at it from two perspectives—the organisational view and the user view.

The organisational view

The organisational view might be called the 'official view' and describes the motives of those who promote, introduce and maintain formal performance review and evaluation as a tool within the framework of performance management. They are represented by HR practitioners, the senior management (who are influenced by the HR position), consultants to the organisation and academics. Common reasons given for the value of performance evaluation are summarised in Table 11.1, where reasons have been clustered into four groups according to similarity of intention.

What the users say

There is a fair body of field research that expresses the views of those who are affected by the process—employees and their managers. These are summarised in Table 11.2 where like comments have been clustered and employee and manager comments matched as much as possible.

   While not apparent in the table, line managers express many of the same 'employee' needs as do all employees, in addition to their views in relation to their management role. Employee-only perspectives are mostly reactive responses to a process not of their choosing.

Form

The form, structure or components of the formal review and evaluation process are defined by its intended purpose (Table 11.1). Common defining characteristics of form are discussed on the basis that a better understanding of the underlying principles will help produce better outcomes.

Table 11.1 The value of performance evaluation—the organisational view

Individual performance	• Evaluate performance • Improve performance • Motivate employees to perform (positive and negative sanctions)
Business and team management	• Ensure that the sum of individual achievements is meeting group and/or enterprise goals • Check that required competencies match work performance requirements • Know where an individual's performance sits within the group
Communication	• Provide a formalised basis for feedback to employees
Training and development	• Identify an employee's strengths and weaknesses • Determine development needs for the current work
Organisational management	• Inform remuneration decisions • Evaluate an employee's overall suitability for the job/to know whether to terminate an employee • Provide an objective basis for termination

Table 11.2 Field research—what users want from formal review and evaluation

Issues common to both employees and line managers

	What employees want	What line managers want (in their manager role)
Performance-based	• Used to develop individual performance	• That it actually makes a difference to performance • A means to gain a comprehensive view of employee performance, individually and as a group • That it is more than just a personnel/HR administration exercise
Developmental focus	• Outcome is to help person's development • Helps career development	• Identifies employee developmental requirements • Identifies employee career issues

Table 11.2 (continued)

Issues common to both employees and line managers

	What employees want	What line managers want (in their manager role)
Feedback and recognition	• Manager gives feedback • Feedback is honest and complete • Provides recognition for good performance	• A structured way to give feedback and seek improvement and/or development • A means to formally acknowledge employees
Manager effectiveness	• Manager accountable for quality of performance evaluation • A senior manager oversees the process to prevent bias	• User-friendly method • Own manager will support them in their implementation of the evaluation process • To make them look as if they are managing well • A system without ratings

Issues expressed by employees only

Fair—based on good business practice	• Based on clear goals and clear work assignment • Based on sound performance information, objectively used • Takes account of all contributing factors • Based on previous regular feedback and guidance/coaching
Fair and just	• Consistency in application, across time, across people • Recognises effort as well as results • Fair, just, nil or minimal manager bias • Two-way communication
A positive process	• Used in a positive way, not critical, not used as a judgment • Not punitive • Dignifying, respectful
Team-building	• Fosters and rewards cooperation between employees, not competition

Characteristics common to most organisations

- *Evaluates the person.* The primary concept to grasp is that a formal performance review is an evaluation of the *person*, not of the work. This means that a whole range of types of achievements—task, goal and behaviour—are reduced to a single overall measure.
- *Uses attribute measures.* An employee's actual performance is evaluated and then *some meaning is attributed* to it; for example, a rating or ranking.
- *Is universally applied.* Review and evaluation is applied to all staff in the same way, or at least to all staff within a group—for example, senior management, those on individual contracts, blue-collar staff.
- *Is 'offline'.* Management of performance takes place on the job ('online') and is triggered by work results and employee performance. Formal review takes place independently of the work ('offline'), triggered by predetermined review periods and methods (Figure 11.1).

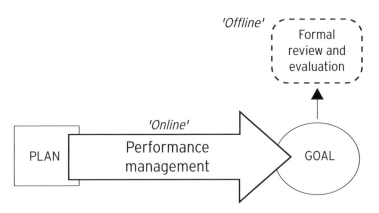

Figure 11.1 Online and offline management

- *Has mandatory timing or frequency.* All formal reviews are conducted at least annually, linked to the enterprise planning cycle, and reviewing the preceding 12 months' performance. Many organisations also mandate more frequent formal reviews.
- *Structured and documented evaluation.* Whereas day-to-day performance management is largely personalised in its approach, formal review and evaluation methods are generally quite prescribed and include formal documentation and filing requirements.

- *Links to other organisational systems.* Formal evaluation is widely used to link to other organisational systems, such as training and development, career development, workforce planning, remuneration planning, equity and fair treatment, discipline and termination.
- *Links to a performance discipline system.* Most organisations have a system for what we might call 'performance discipline', which is for the recovery or dismissal of difficult performers. Formal performance review and evaluation is often used to provide a fair and objective platform on which to enter this system.

Less common characteristics
The following are linked to review and evaluation in some organisations, but less frequently than those described above.

- *Direct link to contracts or industrial agreements.* The performance management system may be incorporated into individual employee contracts or into a contract with a firm providing contract staff. Individual Workplace Agreements or Enterprise Agreements may also incorporate whole or part of a performance management system.
- *Direct link to base remuneration or bonus payments.* A certain level of rating, ranking or score can mean an increase in base remuneration or a bonus (one-off) payment.
- *Evaluations are moderated.* In some cases management has a preconceived idea that certain proportions of employees should fit into certain rating or ranking categories. Moderation is the process where actual evaluations are 'normalised' to fit the predetermined pattern.

How effective is performance evaluation?

Generally, the process of performance review and evaluation ('performance appraisal') fails to live up to the expectations of its proponents and users, as evidenced by a large amount of field research. The reasons associated with failure are many and relate to the needs and expectations expressed in Table 11.2. They include:

- **Flaws in intent:** for example, espoused aims cannot be met by the process as designed.

- **Flaws inherent in the process:** for example, evaluation involves judgments and therefore the manager–employee relationship is part of the result.
- **Flaws inherent in the manager:** for example, lack of relevant abilities.
- **Flaws inherent in the employee:** for example, employee antagonism or fatalism towards the process.

The evaluation process is already prescribed in those organisations where it is a part of the system, but a high proportion of managers follow the process without understanding its underlying principles, the consequence often being outcomes contaminated by subjectivity and opinion, poor relationships and bad decisions. Our aim is to explore the theory behind the idea of evaluation and to understand some principles and guidelines about how to do it effectively.

By means of a better understanding of the principles, it should be possible for managers to improve the way in which they use their system and the consequent outcomes.

The basic concepts of converting performance into evaluation

Evaluation is the process of taking an employee's actual performance and *attributing some meaning* to it. In this process, comparability is a requirement. Thus, it is necessary to be able to take all the various measures of personal effectiveness that exist in the organisation or in a work group and make them comparable with each other. In this way, you hope to be able to compare the evaluation of a cost accountant with that of a production manager and with that of a field salesperson.

Types of evaluations
All evaluative measures fall into one of three pairs of methods— comparative or non-comparative, descriptive or numerical, and rating or ranking. The first basic pair is that of non-comparative and comparative measures (also known as absolute or relative measures). *Non-comparative measures* relate only to the individual—for example, 'met all work objectives'. In this case, each employee's evaluation is independent of others in the team. *Comparative measures* relate the individual to others— for example, 'ranked 3rd in the team'. Comparative measures mean that

each employee's evaluation is dependent on the evaluation of others in the team.

The next pair is concerned with whether the evaluation measure is descriptive or numerical. An example of a *descriptive evaluation* is 'highly satisfactory' while that of a *numerical evaluation* would be 'a score of 3.5 for customer service'.

The final pair of evaluative measures comprises two broad methods known as rating or ranking. *Rating* involves a scale, essentially with the best level of evaluation at one end and the worst at the other. *Ranking* also involves a scale but it refers to the best employee at one end and the worst at the other (comparative evaluation). Examples of rating and ranking measures are listed, together with examples, in Table 11.3. Within these measures, the descriptors are not mutually exclusive and may appear in various combinations with each other.

Bottom-up or top-down

One of two fundamental approaches is to evaluate achievement of each element (task, goal or attribute) and to use a formula to *convert* that into an overall evaluation ('bottom-up'). Alternatively, evaluation of the employee may be based on a *judgment* of overall work performance achievement ('top-down'). Table 11.4 illustrates these approaches.

The bottom-up evaluation method is more robust and more transparent because there is a clearer link between the achievement level against each element and the overall evaluation. In principle, top-down is based on the same logical process but it is a larger leap and leaves a lot more room for personal bias.

Interpretation issues

Subjective evaluations risk being more opinion than evaluation. Different interpretations of 'satisfactory' and 'outstanding', and the preconceptions of different individuals give this approach low reliability and validity. Thus, if you have to use a symbol, it is far better to avoid judgmental terms and use a numerical or alphabetical scale (1–2–3 or A–B–C), or a calculated mean value that relates directly to performance.

If you are required to use subjective evaluations as a component of your organisation's system, you need to develop, with your employees, some specific performance descriptors that relate to the subjective rating scale, as in the following example.

When an employee is rated as 'Satisfactory' it means that they have achieved plus or minus 5 per cent against their work objectives.

Table 11.3 Rating and ranking methods of evaluation

A. Rating—descriptive, objective

Types of ratings	Examples of a scale
Degree to which requirement achieved	Exceeded ← → Met ← → Not met
How consistently it was achieved	Always ← → Mostly ← → Never

B. Rating—descriptive, subjective

Types of ratings	Examples of a scale
Degree to which requirement achieved	Outstanding ← → Fully Effective ← → Poor
Summary/comprehensive	Highly Satisfactory ← → Satisfactory ← → Unsatisfactory

C. Rating—descriptive, scored

Personal attribute descriptor	Examples of a scale
Personalises customer service	Always 5 4 3 2 1 Never
Solves customer inquiries or problems	5 4 3 2 1
On-sells	5 4 3 2 1
Total customer service	(Calculated mean score)

Achievement descriptor	Score
Met all and exceeded most requirements	5
Met all and exceeded some requirements	4
Met all requirements	3
Met most requirements	2
Met few or no requirements	1

D. Ranking—position and points-allocation method

Employee	Position method	Points-allocation method
A	#1	35
B	#2	25
C	Equal #3	15
D	Equal #3	15
E	#4	10
		(Total points 100)

Table 11.4 Illustration of top-down and bottom-up evaluation

Employee work performance	(A) Top-down	(B) Bottom-up	
Achievement, relative to target	Overall evaluation	Evaluation	Overall evaluation
Work objectives			
1 100%		MET	
2 110%		EXCEEDED	
3 98%	SATISFACTORY	MET	MET MOST
Attribute objectives			
A 100%		MET	
B 90%		NOT MET	

Some poorly written evaluation templates draw managers into making assumptions about the *motivations* of an employee (as in the example below, where the assumptions are shown in italics). Beware, and stay with what is objective—for example, by exploring what actual behaviours would convey 'resentment'.

Behaviour	Score
Resents requests from other team members; does not participate in meetings; has a *poor attitude* towards other team members	0.5–1.4

The right measures

We dealt with measures in Chapters 3 and 5 and all the ideas expressed there apply to the evaluation process, although we may need to look at some of them through different eyes, with a focus not of monitoring the work but of evaluating the employee. A case in point applies to the 'Right measures' in the performance data model.

For evaluation, rather than 'start with Outcomes then the Drivers', confirm whether employees' performance agreements hold them accountable for outcomes or accountable for drivers and then evaluate the appropriate one.

Ensure also that you are working with the latest agreed requirement. The two cautions that are worth considering are that a time lapse could lead to uncertainty about the measures being used in the evaluation or to a manager's bias in selective weighting of certain measures over others.

Guidelines for applying evaluation principles

Having looked at the underlying principles of converting performance into evaluation, we now progress to the more practical application, as it might apply to any manager using an organisation's evaluation process. Before we get to the detail, one overarching principle to hold at the forefront of your mind is always to manage evaluation towards outcomes that are:

- fair for the *person*; and
- fair for the *business*.

For the sake of simplicity in demonstrating the guidelines, we work with only one form of evaluation, the attribute rating scale displayed in Table 11.3A and reproduced below. The same principles apply to other evaluation scales.

Degree to which requirement achieved	Exceeded ← → Met ← → Not met

One measure at a time, one goal/task at a time

Some goals or tasks in employee performance agreements will have more than one associated measure, and so we have to evaluate each measure before we can assess the goal or task. Figure 11.2 is a facsimile of what a completed evaluation might look like, showing a mix in the number of measures for each goal or task.

To evaluate each measure, we take into account the actual *performance* against each; to evaluate the goal or task, we need to take into account not only the performance but also the *nature and mix* of measures within that goal or task.

Figure 11.3 is a map summarising the principles of evaluating a performance agreement. The topic of performance data and monitoring was discussed in Chapter 5 and the principles relating to measures and goals or tasks are explored in the topics that follow.

Business unit, work group or key process goals	Individual goals and/or tasks	Measures		Achievement and evaluation
		Description	Target or Standard	
1. Xxxxxx xxxxxx xxx xxxx xx xxxxxxxxxxx xxxxx xx	Xxxxxx xxxxx xxxxxx xx xxx xxxxxxxxx xxxxx xx	1. Xxx xxxxx xxxx	999 xxxx	999 xxxxx (Met)
2. Xx xxxxxxx xxx xxxxxx xxxxxxx xxxx xx xxxxxxx x xxx xxxxxxxx xx xxxxx	Xxxxxx xxxxx xxxxxxx Xxxxxx xxxxx xxxx xxx	1. Xxxxxxx xxxxx 2. Xxxx xxxxxx xx	Xxxxx 999 xxxxxxx Xxxxx xxx xxxxxxx xxx	1. 99 xxxxxxx, xxxxx (Not met) 2. (Refer attached) (Met)
3. Xxxxx xxxxxxxx xxxx xx xxxxxxx xxxxxx xxxxxxx	Xxx xxx xxxxxx xxxxx xxxxxxxxxxxxxx	1. Xxx xxxx xxxxx 2. Xxxxxx xx xxx xxxx xxxxxxx 3. Xxxxxx	Xxxxxxxxxxx xxxxx Xxxxxxxxxxxxx xxx Xxx xxxxxxxxxxxx	1. Xx xxxxxx xxxxxxxxxxxx xxx (Met) 2. (Refer attached) (Not met) 3. (Refer attached) (Exceeded)
4. Xx xxxxxxxx xxxxxxxxxx xxxxxxx xx xxx xxxxxxx xxxxxxx xxxx xxxxxxxx xxx xxx	Xxxxx xxxxxx xxxxxxx xxxxxx xxxxxx xx xxx xxxxxxx xxxx xxxxxxxx xxx xxx	Xxxxxxxxxx xxxx	999 xxxxxxx xxxxxxxxxx xxxx	9999 xxxxxxx (Exceeded)

Figure 11.2 Facsimile of an evaluated performance agreement

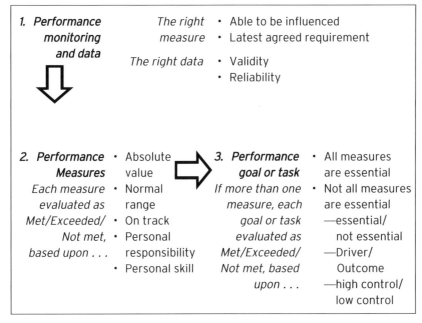

Figure 11.3 A map of evaluation principles

Evaluating measures

The process of evaluating measures begins with having a convention that links our rating or ranking scale to actual achievement. The process continues with an understanding of five dimensions in evaluating measures (Figure 11.3), which apply whatever rating or ranking is used. The five dimensions are Absolute value, Normal range, On track, Personal responsibility and Personal skill.

Met/Not met/Exceeded

Using our chosen rating descriptors, Table 11.5 outlines a convention as to what constitutes 'Met/Not met/Exceeded' for each measure. This same convention should be followed if you have a different set of evaluation descriptors, such as a 'satisfactory' or a scoring scale.

Absolute value, Normal range, On track, Personal responsibility and Personal skill are now explored in detail, dealing with the 'Met', 'Not met' and 'Exceeded' implications for each.

Table 11.5 A convention for what constitutes 'Met/Not met/Exceeded' for each measure

The measure is 'Not met'	The measure is 'Met'	The measure is 'Exceeded'
Achievement below what was planned and agreed	Achievement equal to that planned and agreed	Achiever greater than planned and agreed
• Worse than absolute value, or	• Equal to absolute value, or	• Better than absolute value, or
• Outside normal range	• Within the agreed normal range	• Outside normal range
	Achievement 'on track'	
	• Started slowly but now up to required level, or	
Performance may be improving but not 'on track'	• Made significant achievement towards target and *will achieve*	
		Achievement equal to or less than that planned and agreed, *plus*
Target technically achieved, but not as a result of the employee	Achievement below target, but	
• Personal responsibility requirement not met	• Factors beyond employee's influence, *plus*	• Factors beyond employee's influence *plus*
	• Personal requirement met	• Personal responsibility requirement exceeded

Absolute value or normal range

When performance management was set up during Work Assignment, the target level of performance will have been agreed as either an absolute value or as a value with 'normal range' limits.

• *Absolute value.* Where the target is an absolute objective, standard or limit ('exactly', 'no more than', 'no less than', etc.), actual performance needs to be on or better than target to be evaluated as having met the requirement, as illustrated in Table 11.6.

In some absolute target cases it may be difficult to define an 'Exceed' situation when setting up the performance agreement. Example (a) in Table 11.6 is one such case. Example (b) shows scope for an 'Exceed', by achieving better than 95.0 per cent. Example (d) is a case where the measure is qualitative and the manager and employee have previously agreed to some qualitative scope for exceeding the requirement. Examples (c) and (d) together illustrate combined quantitative and qualitative measures for the one task.

Table 11.6 Examples of evaluation of achievement against absolute target values

Measure	Met	The measure is Not met	Exceeded
a) All participants informed no later than 6 weeks before the event	All conditions achieved exactly	Any time greater than 6 weeks, for any less than 100% of participants	Probably not relevant
b) 100% processing accuracy in no less than 95.0% of transactions	All conditions achieved exactly	Any achievement less than 95.0%	Any achievement greater than 95.0%
c) Consult with all nominated clients, by the end of each quarter; submit report within 4 weeks	All conditions achieved exactly	Failure to meet any of the agreed timings	Any agreed early delivery
d) Consult with all nominated clients, using the standard questionnaire; produce a report in the agreed format	All conditions achieved exactly	Failure to meet any of the agreed format	Any agreed over-achievement in qualitative aspects, such as depth of inter-viewing or analysis

- *Normal range.* For some measures, a normal range (Chapter 5) may have been included in the performance agreement. Table 11.7 displays some examples of the evaluation of normal-range targets.

Table 11.7 Examples of evaluation of achievement against normal-range values

| Measure | The measure is | | |
	Met	Not met	Exceeded
a) Expenditure budget $3.450m (±5%)	Achievement between $3.280m and $3.620m	Achievement greater than $3.620m	Achievement less than $3.280m
b) Project complete within first 3 weeks of March	All conditions achieved exactly	Completed later than 3rd week of March	Completed prior to 1st week of March
c) Standard for press release turnaround, 75% between 8 and 10 hrs from briefing	All conditions achieved exactly	Less than 75% within 8–10 hrs	More than 75% within 8–10 hrs or 75% at (say) 6-10 hrs
d) Responses to market changes are timely, 80–90% of occasions	All conditions achieved exactly	Conditions met less than 80% of occasions	Conditions met more than 90% of occasions
e) Responses to market changes are appropriate, relevant strategies	Market share retention strategies	Loss minimisation strategies	Market share growth strategies

Where a 'normal range' has previously been agreed, actual performance falling within that range will have 'Met' the requirement. Performance below the range will have 'Not met' the requirement and performance above the range will 'Exceed' it. In Table 11.7 all the ranges are quantitative, except for one. Examples d and e list 'responsiveness' as the measure and use both a quantitative measure, 'timeliness' and a qualitative measure, 'appropriateness', for which a normal range has been defined.

Some targets set as absolute values are really arbitrarily set even when the actual behaviour of the work performance is one of natural variation. If normal range is ignored, two problems arise. First, employees manage the process or the outcome to meet the management target rather than the performance of the business. Second, there is an evaluation problem, as illustrated in Table 11.8. The first two evaluations, based on an absolute requirement, are not true, whereas those based on the real picture (normal range) are true.

Table 11.8 Influence of normal range on evaluation

	Absolute requirement		Normal range requirement	
	Employee A	**Employee B**	**Employee A**	**Employee B**
Plan	100	100	90–110	90–110
Result	110	90	110	90
Evaluation	Exceeded	Not met	Met	Met

Performance is 'on track'

The principle of 'on track' is similar to the concept of the 'normal range', where it may be reasonable to evaluate an employee as having met the requirements of the measure although it has not been fully achieved by the time of the review (Table 11.5). It deals more with a level of achievement that is *dynamic* or *moving* (Figure 11.4). For example:

a) An employee may have started off slowly but, by the time of the review, is performing at the required level (example A).
b) An objective that is cumulative is not achieved by the time of review but *will be reached shortly after* (example B).
c) An employee's ultimate target measure spans beyond an interim or annual assessment period so the 'work in progress' is assessed as to whether it is on track at that point (example C).

The principle underpinning examples A and B is that of 'fair for the person', on the assumption that the business is not affected adversely by the delayed achievement. Example C is not, strictly speaking, an 'on-track' issue because a long-term task or project should have milestone targets. This same principle of incremental targets should be built into the performance agreement when it is known that an employee's

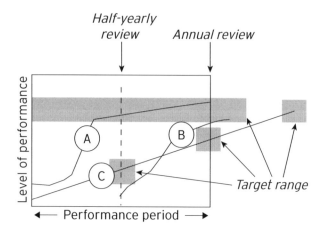

Figure 11.4 An illustration of three types of 'on-track' performance

performance level will grow over the period. This means your employees are always being managed against a level that is relevant to them and it also removes the need to consider the 'on-track' principle.

Personal effectiveness

Evaluating an employee requires us to differentiate between *personal effectiveness* and *work performance*. Chapter 8 (Coaching) introduced *will* and *skill* as basic components of personal effectiveness, which, for the purpose of evaluation, we will summarise as follows:

- *Personal responsibility (will)* refers to the extent to which the employee has applied themselves to achieve agreed objectives.
- *Personal skill* refers to the level of ability in relation to the agreed objectives.

Definition of the required level of will and skill will have been agreed at the time of Work Assignment and during any subsequent coaching. We now look at the impact of these elements of personal effectiveness on the evaluation.

Personal responsibility (will)

Employees who have failed to meet a particular goal quite often claim that it was for reasons 'out of my control' or for something that was 'not my fault'. Since the enterprise's goals have to be met, even when the unforeseen happens, we need an evaluation process that is fair to the business while still being fair to the person.

In Chapters 3 and 4 we present the notion of *personal responsibility* as an overall accountability requirement for all assigned work. Based on this accountability, you will be looking for an indication that the employee has met their personal responsibility requirement in relation to each measure, as follows.

The employee has pursued their performance targets at all times by employing:

- their fullest energy;
- their available skill; and
- their delegated authority;

and their manager has been kept informed of any performance targets at risk.

In cases where achievement was below target, but where the employee has met this requirement, they are evaluated as 'Met' for the measure. This is clearly 'fair for the person'; but consider, also, when an employee has met this requirement it means that responsibility for achieving the target has been passed on to someone with greater authority or resources (the manager) to pursue it—'fair to the business'.

A situation similar in principle, but different in scale, occurs when an employee has gone the extra mile—physically, intellectually or person-ally—to overcome significant unforeseen obstacles. Such an employee might be evaluated as 'Exceeded', on the principle of exceeding their personal responsibility requirement, irrespective of achievement to target.

As an example of the converse of this, how do you evaluate an employee whose work target was achieved but not as a result of the exercise of his responsibility, which has been less than agreed? This is a tougher one, but the *work achievement* should be celebrated for the good luck it is and you evaluate the *employee* as 'Not met'.

From a performance management perspective, any situation of 'achievement despite the employee' is something you would want to investigate on the job, first to intervene and, second, to determine whether it represents a challenge to your planning assumptions.

Personal skill

Sometimes an employee will fail to achieve a performance target and the reason is judged to be inadequate skill. The evaluation decision is whether the employee has Met or Not met the requirement. The evaluation principles that should be considered are:

1. 'Fair for the business'—planned enterprise/work group goals have to be met and therefore a personal skill issue should not get as far as an annual review before having been solved; and
2. 'Fair for the person'—evaluation is of the person, not the work achievement.

Both manager and employee are accountable for certain actions that prevent a low-skill situation from persisting. The following is a list of these respective accountabilities.

Manager's accountability
*   Know skill level required for the work (planning assumptions);
*   Know the skill level of the employee; if skill can't be acquired, the employee is wrong for the role, goal or task;
*   Set employee's performance targets, or appoint to roles, within their level of skill—current, or to be acquired; set incremental targets, allowing for skills development;
*   Manage employee's acquisition of requisite level of skill;
*   Monitor employee's acquisition of skill; and
*   Monitor employee's performance.

Employee's accountability
*   Know the skill level required for the work (planning assumptions);
*   Know own skills in relation to the role, goal or task;
*   Advise their manager when their skill is inadequate for the work;
*   Undertake requisite skill development; and
*   Advise their manager if a lift in skill is not followed by a lift in work performance.

In the case of a missed work target, the degree to which each party has met its own accountabilities will determine whether the evaluation is 'Met' or 'Not met'. An employee might be evaluated as 'Met' if she had met all her accountabilities (personal responsibility requirement). If a manager has met all his accountabilities but the employee has not, we have a low-*will*, not low-skill situation—that is, the employee would be evaluated as 'Not met' on the basis of the personal responsibility requirement not met.

Because evaluation is of the person, not of the work performance, the employee should not be penalised on the basis of low skill alone. The employee has the will but is limited, or 'capped', in terms of their ability.

Summary
Figure 11.5 is an illustration of how the application of the principles might appear on employees' evaluation forms. The illustration covers most of the principles discussed.

Evaluating each goal or task

Most organisations with an evaluation process require some overall evaluation of each employee. Depending on your own evaluation system, this may involve either forming an overall evaluation based directly on all individual measures or the intermediate step of evaluating each goal or task in the performance agreement. This topic deals specifically with the latter approach but the principles will assist you in overall evaluation methods.

When there is only a single measure for a goal or task, the evaluation of the measure is that of the goal. However, many employees will have more than one measure for each goal or task in their performance agreement. In this case, some principles are needed to convert multiple measure evaluations into one goal evaluation. Figure 11.6 is an example of single and multiple measures. The employee is a project manager who is managing several projects that are contracted to outside suppliers on behalf of internal stakeholders.

In the case of Goal 1, there is only one measure so a 'Met' for the measure is a 'Met' for the Goal. Goal 2, however, has five measures and the achievement is a mix of Met, Not met and Exceeded. To reach an overall assessment of the goal, we need some agreement on the relative importance of the measures; our initial approach to this is to consider which of two sets of conditions applies:

1. All measures are essential.
2. Not all measures are essential.

Measures	Achievement	Evaluation
Exenditure budget $3.450m (±5%)	Final expenditure $3.55m (+2.9%)	*Met—achievement as planned*
Project complete within first 3 weeks of March	Project ran late (problems in 5th month) Completed 1st week April	*Met—achievement 'on track'*
Responses to market changes are timely, 80-90% of occasions	Timely on 70% of events New product launch took time away from existing range Advised and kept manager informed–no other resources to spare Did everything she possibly could with limited resources	*Met—personal responsibility met*
All participants informed, no later than 6 weeks before the event	5 events conducted; advice sent out late (1–3 wks late) in 4 of them; consider this affected enrolments	*Not met—below plan*
Annual sales $30.0m (±5%)	Sales $30.5m Did not fully participate in programs Failed to follow up many leads Target achieved as a result of competitor's stock shortages in Nov–Dec	*Not met—personal responsibility not met*
Consult with all nominated clients: 1. By the end of each quarter	1) All on time	*Met—achievement as planned*
2. Using the standard questionnaire	2) Used questionnaire and probed for greater depth and future requirements	*Exceeded—achievement greater than target*
3. Document findings within 4 weeks	3) Progressively improved on the 4 wks—down to 2 weeks—by developing templates and links to previous reports	*Exceeded—achievement greater than target*
Shaft diameter no greater/less than 25.50mm–25.40mm, for 99.9% of production	Maintained for the Qtr, which included 2 weeks of machine problems where he trained the team to monitor on the job and to adjust the machine as it was running	*Exceeded—personal responsibility exceeded*

Figure 11.5 Illustration of applying the principles of evaluating measures

Goal/task	Description	Measures	Target or standard	Achievement	Evaluation
1.	Project stakeholders are kept up to date with information on regular reviews and variances		All stakeholders, all required events	Achievement as planned—all stakeholders, all required events	Met—achievement as planned **GOAL MET**
2.	• Project contracts reflect project goals and timelines		All	All contracts met the requirement	Met—achievement as planned
	• Systems established for monitoring contractor performance		On time	Completed but later than agreed deadline	Not met—less than planned
	• Monitoring of contracts, including scheduled reviews		On time	(Refer note below)*	Met—met personal responsibility requirement
	• Critical timelines		Meet as planned, all projects	All achieved within agreed variance	Met—within normal range
	• Expenditure		Meet budget, all projects	Unplanned project savings achieved	Exceeded—achievement greater than target **GOAL____**

Most requirements achieved as planned; some were delayed despite employee's effort; manager kept informed

Figure 11.6 Goal evaluation for single and multiple measures

All measures are essential

Under this condition, all measures must be met for the goal or task to be evaluated as 'Met'. The logic is quite clearly based on the essential nature of each measure, thus:

Met + Met + Met = **Met** the goal
Met + Met + Not met = **Not met** the goal

We advocate that only essential measures be included in performance agreements. These may be drivers, outcomes or both, depending on the employee's degree of influence over achievement. As an example of both, there are times when an outcome-accountable employee's performance agreement includes driver measures because their manager also wants them to focus on the 'how'. Thus, if all measures in Goal 2 of Figure 11.6 had been agreed to be essential, the goal would not have been met.

When it comes to exceeding a goal or task, a consistent approach is needed across the organisation. Two methods commonly used are *incremental* and *proportional*. The logic of the incremental method is that anything better than 'Met' is an 'Exceeded', thus:

Met + Met + Met + Exceeded = **Exceeded** the goal

The proportional method works on the basis of 50 per cent or better is an 'Exceeded', thus:

Met + Met + Exceeded = **Met** the goal
Met + Exceeded + Exceeded = **Exceeded** the goal
Met + Met + Exceeded + Exceeded = **Exceeded** the goal

In the context of simplicity and of evaluating the employee (and not the work), the incremental method is preferable.

If a scored rating scale is used, the goal or task evaluation is a number (Table 11.9).

Not all measures are essential

The first principle is: if a measure is not essential, leave it out of the performance agreement. However, there may be times, for reasons of focusing on the 'how', when you wish to include drivers in the performance agreement of an outcome-accountable employee, but where those

Measure for Goal 1	Employee A		Employee B		Employee C	
	Achievement to target	Rating score	Achievement to target	Rating score	Achievement to target	Rating score
1	Met		Met		Met	
2	Met		Met		Met	
3	Met	3	Met	4	Met	2
4	Met		Exceeded		Not met	

Table 11.9 Score rating of each goal or task

drivers are agreed to be non-essential. In such cases it would have been agreed that you would *review* them but not include them in the evaluation. Table 11.10 displays some examples of these scenarios.

The criteria for evaluation of 'Exceeded' are the same as in the condition of all measures being essential.

Measures		Employee A		Employee B	
		Measure	Goal	Measure	Goal
Not essential	1. Driver	na		na	
	2. Driver	na		na	
	3. Driver	na	**MET**	na	**NOT MET**
Essential	4. Outcome	Met		Met	
	5. Outcome	Met		Not met	

Measures		Employee A		Employee B	
		Measure	Goal	Measure	Goal
Essential	**1. Driver**	Met		Not met	
	2. Driver	Met		Met	
	3. Driver	Met	**MET**	Met	**NOT MET**
Not essential	4. Outcome	na		na	
	5. Outcome	na		na	

Table 11.10 Rating goals with a mix of essential and non-essential measures

Reaching an overall evaluation

Whenever we attempt to reduce the whole year's work of an individual into a single evaluation—descriptive or score—it is fraught with dangers. How could we truly evaluate the art of Michelangelo or the achievements of Ghandi in a single 'Outstanding' or 'Needs improvement'? Each employee brings a unique set of attributes and skills to their work and as soon as we try to portray that in a single evaluative form, whether 'good' or 'bad', we inevitably sell the employee short in some way. Nevertheless, large numbers of managers are required to undertake such a task and so our aim should be that the result is a worthwhile one, for the employee and for the organisation.

Three ways you can achieve the best result are to (1) know your own system, (2) understand some principles behind overall evaluation and (3) have a clear purpose for the exercise.

Methods of overall evaluation

Although the vast majority of managers undertaking overall evaluation will be doing so within a prescribed framework, it is worth understanding something of the principles behind their construction.

The first point to be made about overall evaluation is that it should be an objective process and a direct consequence of the evaluation of each measure and/or goal. The 'top-down approach' described earlier, where you throw away all objectivity and finally give your opinion, is a dangerous approach because, first, it realises employees' most dominant fears and, second, it is sinister because it lures employees along an objective path and then throws all this aside for the manager's sub-jectivity! The caution is worth making because some systems foster this approach and some managers take this approach, in spite of their systems. Some systems even encourage managers not to use an objective approach in this final stage but to make an 'informed judgment'.

The methods that come closest to any reasonable overall evaluation are those that reflect actual achievement in relation to planning targets. The reason for this choice is because planning targets are, at least in theory, the drivers of enterprise performance and so achievement in relation to these targets is a measure of organisational capability. In addition, it is the form of evaluation that allows comparability of (a) mixed types of measures (e.g. work performance and personal attributes or quantitative and qualitative) and (b) performance capability across all employees and all business units.

Attribute rating scale

This rating method is based on an attribute scale that reflects the *number* of requirements and the *degree* to which they were met. The 'Met/Not met/exceeded' scale is the form most commonly used. A form of this scale is displayed in Table 11.11.

Overall evaluation (rating)	Examples of optional rating symbols		
	(a)	(b)	(c)
Met all goals and exceeded most	5	A	Outstanding
Met all goals and exceeded some	4	B	Superior
Met all goals	3	C	Satisfactory
Met most goals	2	D	Needs improvement
Met none or some goals	1	E	Unsatisfactory

Table 11.11 Attribute rating scale used for overall evaluation

The reduction of the evaluation to a symbol worries some people because the substance of the achievement is obscured—for example, '4' is not as descriptive as 'Met all goals and exceeded some'. In particular, the value-laden terms in column (c) are both non-specific and open to a variety of interpretations, beyond the facts on which they are based.

Scored rating scale

If you use a method that rates each goal or task and represents the rating as a score the overall rating is the mean of the individual scores (Table 11.12). Being mathematical, this looks very precise, but it too suffers from moving away from the substance of the achievement on which it is based—for example, it doesn't tell us that Goal scores ranged from a high of five to a low of two.

Goals or Tasks	Rating	Overall rating
1.	3	
2.	2	
3.	3	3.2
4.	5	

Table 11.12 Scored rating scale used for overall evaluation

In some organisations, goals or tasks will have been weighted or ranked according to their importance. For example, if the customer service goal is regarded as twice as important as the productivity goal, the score for the former will be multiplied by 2 in arriving at the sum or total average score.

Link to the purpose of overall evaluation

Although you will be following a prescribed formula to reach an overall evaluation, you should keep in mind a purpose, or bigger picture, for the exercise. Doing this may help you to make better judgments—either in a complex evaluation or in the setting up of performance agreements in the first instance.

If we are to look for a worthwhile purpose we should base it on (a) the purpose expressed by your own organisation, as illustrated in Table 11.1, and (b) the needs of managers and employees, presented in Table 11.2. By way of illustration, Table 11.13 abstracts some needs from the earlier tables and presents the implications for overall evaluation.

Table 11.13 Approaches to evaluation based on its purpose

Purpose	Which means ...
Improve performance	It's not a substitute for on-the-job management of work performance so you need an evaluation perspective that is directed towards the future, not the past.
Feedback and recognition	It is far better that you are doing this on the job, but if the employee is relying on the end-of-year evaluation, focus on the detail. A 'Satisfactory' or a 3.2 is not effective feedback.
Individual development	Evaluation needs to identify: • their current capability against goals; • how they have changed; • how they are equipped for the future; and • where they fit within the team.
Provide input to work unit/business unit/ enterprise analysis and planning	Evaluation needs to identify: • capability of planning assumptions; and • how well the team is equipped for the future.
Provide input to whole of organisation analysis and planning	(Requirements are identified by your own organisation.)

If the evaluation is to be used as input into individual remuneration decisions (which it often is) this means that, apart from your organisational requirements, you should make sure that your evaluation is as representative as possible of the individual's *worth*, within the system that you have.

Summary

This technical approach to evaluation has been adopted deliberately to emphasise objectivity in the often non-objective process that is forced upon us. If you take the principles of objectivity from this chapter, combine them with management of the process (Chapter 12) and the requirements of your own system, you can make a worthwhile contribution to each of your employees and to the development of organisational performance.

12 Managing the review and evaluation process

Chapter 11 introduced the principles of evaluation and we now turn to the practicalities of implementing and managing the process.

The on-the-job processes and skills discussed in earlier chapters provide a strong foundation for managing formal reviews but some notable differences occur in the formal evaluation situation, leading to a greater demand on your management abilities. The differences that do occur are a result of the increased formality, the focus on formal evaluation, a greater likelihood of debate or disagreement, and the future implications of the evaluation.

Most organisations have their own formal review system so our approach is to help you to work better within the system you have. We will work with a sample system, based on a hybrid of good examples from a range of organisations. If you have no system and you wish to undertake formal reviews yourself, this chapter will provide you with the processes and skills and also implied design features.

A structural view of review and evaluation

A structural view helps introduce all the steps that are important and their most effective order and relationships. Producing effective evaluation has as much to do with good process as it does with good skill.

Figure 12.1 is a structural view of a typical evaluation process. The *evaluation* phase is preceded by a *preparatory* phase and the whole process has *inputs* and *outputs*. The inclusion of four discrete elements highlights

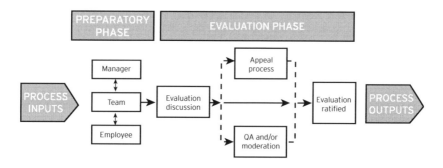

Figure 12.1 Four phases of performance review and evaluation

that there is more to an effective evaluation than just the evaluation discussion itself. The *process inputs* represent the givens upon which the evaluation is built and the *process outputs* describe what must come out of the evaluation, indicating the process has a purpose. The *preparatory phase* is a reminder that this is a process of importance and must be approached deliberately and skilfully.

Our discussion begins with the inputs and outputs. The type of inputs will be mostly the same for all organisations but the outputs will vary, depending on the aims of the review in your own organisation.

Inputs

The following are inputs that feed into the review and evaluation process. They need to be considered because the nature and quality of inputs will determine the quality of the ultimate output of the process.

- **Employee's performance plan or agreement**. Agreed, understood by both parties, and current.
- **Employee performance data**. The 'right data' accurate, complete, objective.
- **Work system compared to plan**. Work design, quality of upstream inputs, resource availability, manager support, operating environment.
- **Intrinsic nature of the employee**. Discussion skills, experiences, beliefs, values, biases, personal empowerment.
- **Intrinsic nature of the manager**. Bias, discussion and review capability.
- **Manager–employee relationship history**. Past experiences, intrinsic individual natures.

- **Culture of the organisation and the work group.** What gets rewarded, trust/distrust, individual/team, etc.
- **Formal review system and methods.** Your own system will be a significant determinant of your process and required outputs.

Outputs

Review and evaluation outputs effectively describe the purpose of the process, so what you do should not only follow the process but also be directed towards the purpose. Outputs can be divided into two basic groups, those that are required by your own system and those that were presented as components of the ideal purpose in Chapter 11 (Table 11.13).

Commonly required process outputs
- Item by item and overall evaluation (score, rating, ranking).
- A record of the formal review.
- A link to remuneration decisions.
- Development needs determined (by default).
- Information for career planning.

Outputs that support organisation development
The outputs should be the means to turn the evaluation into a product of value for the organisation. Products of worthwhile purpose were proposed in Chapter 11 (Table 11.13).

Process of review and evaluation

We made the point earlier that effective evaluation has as much to do with good process as it does with good skill. Figure 12.2 outlines a step-by-step process that is typical of those used by effective managers. This process also forms the framework for a later discussion on 'how'.

Inclusions/exclusions in the formal review process
Some activities that are commonly included in the formal review process could be more usefully dealt with outside the process. The major problems common to most are that (a) they are more relevant on the job and (b) they sidetrack from the evaluation process. These activities, and other reservations, are as follows:

- **Work assignment.** Important enough to do it separately.
- **Work system development.** Needs a bigger perspective than one individual.
- **Performance development plan.** When based on correcting past underachievement it is too late; forward-looking development thinking is okay, but not at this meeting.
- **Performance discipline.** This activity should not be associated directly with scheduled reviews because (a) it must be directly linked to the specific work and time and (b) it puts a punitive cloud over all formal reviews.

PREPARATORY PHASE

1. **Logistics**
   1. Plan
   2. Advise employees
   3. Arrange logistics

2. **Preparation**

   - Team   • Employee   • Manager

EVALUATION PHASE

3. **Review and evaluation meeting**

   - Meet and discuss
   - Complete the business

4. **QA and/or moderation of evaluations (as applicable)**

   Senior manager review

5. **Appeal process (as applicable)**

6. **Ratification of evaluations**

   Manager ratifies evaluation with employee

Figure 12.2 A typical process for formal review and evaluation

Preparatory phase of review

Good preparation improves the chances of successful outcomes and results in less costly disruption to your people's work, including your own. Preparation includes logistics, and personal preparation for both employee and manager.

Logistics

Often, little thought goes into the logistics because managers are passive or antagonistic towards the whole process. Whatever your views, good logistics smooth the way. The following three points are very brief but include some of the more important practices.

1. *Plan as a project*. The review process involves many steps, many people and a lot of time so if you approach it proactively, rather than reactively, it will go more smoothly and cost less. One strategy is to treat it as a project, planning it as a whole rather than fitting in each separate piece on demand.
2. *Communication*. What is communicated to employees and how the communication is made can affect how they approach the process. Tips are to allow employees enough lead-time, use some face-to-face group briefing, and beware that your non-verbal communication doesn't say that this process is adversarial or not important.
3. *Arrange logistics*. Schedule enough down-time for you and your employees; don't just 'squeeze it in'. The physical setting can make a difference so consider such issues as privacy, seating and arrangements to remain undisturbed.

Team preparation

Apart from employee and manager preparation there is also an important role for *team preparation*. A team briefing and preparation session presents a number of benefits, as shown in Table 12.1. In addition to these points, a team briefing is a good opportunity to deal with questions and concerns.

Personal preparation—employee

Two issues that we cover here are your role in the process and a set of guidelines for employees.

Your role
For many managers, their role extends only to sending out the advice and the materials, but we think that you can achieve a lot more by applying your management and coaching abilities to this part of the process as well.

Table 12.1 Benefits of a team briefing

Topic	What to discuss	Use in evaluation or planning
Work unit/team performance	Performance to date, in relation to the work unit's business plan or work plan	Provides manager and individuals with a general view of where each person's performance fits into the whole work unit performance
Current operating environment	Changes to planning assumptions during the period that have affected individual performance, e.g. resources, deadlines, standards, customers, community, government	Highlights issues that may have affected team and individual performance (good and bad) over the period being reviewed

Briefing your staff is a useful preparatory step. Many managers meet formally with their employees, individually and/or in groups, to discuss their preparation process, including agreeing issues to include/exclude. Miscommunications, unknowns and concerns are dealt with in a more collaborative, less adversarial manner than might occur at the formal review.

Coaching need not stop. When the preparation process begins, many managers go into a 'hands-off' with their employees—the contest has begun! However, an employee's preparation is important to a good discussion and there is no reason why you can't coach them without fear of favouritism or compromising your own reviewer role. Coaching also includes simply checking that employees are preparing and managing the task.

Guidelines for employee preparation

The following guidelines reflect common ideas on preparation and should be communicated to employees. They answer the employee question: 'Why should I prepare?'

- *Information*—ensures you have the right measures, performance data and understanding.
- *Confidence and comfort*—the better you are prepared, the more confident and comfortable you will be during the review meeting.

- *Your best presentation*—if there are important things you know you want to say, they will be communicated more effectively if you prepare well.
- *A broader view*—a time to step back from day to day work and gain an overall view of your personal effectiveness.

The preparation guidelines below are clustered around key headings. There will be other things you can do that are not listed here, but the headings may help you to think of them.

1. *The process*
   - ☑ Know the review process.
   - ☑ Know the implications of the process.
   - ☑ Know the meeting process.
2. *Your performance plan/agreement*
   - ☑ Review you performance plan/agreement; confirm the detail with your manager.
   - ☑ Review the extent of your accountabilities in relation to these assignments.
3. *Information on your work performance*
   - ☑ Record your performance against each assignment/goal/task/measure.
   - ☑ Review the results or notes from any interim formal reviews.
   - ☑ Refer to any previous notes or recall information relating to on-the-job performance interactions with your manager or supervisor, including coaching sessions.
4. *Your work system*
   - ☑ Note any variation in the work system that may have affected your performance, such as manager support, resources, upstream input, market.
5. *Information on your personal skills and abilities*
   - ☑ Your current skill level in relation to the work.
   - ☑ Skills development you have undertaken.
   - ☑ Lessons learned and actions taken either to correct or improve personal effectiveness.
   - ☑ What are your strengths and weaknesses?
6. *Information on exercise of your personal responsibility*
   - ☑ How have you exercised your personal responsibility?
   - ☑ How well have you monitored your work performance against objectives?

☑ How well have you kept up to date with work-unit performance?

☑ How have you responded to situations that placed your achievement at risk?

☑ Have you completed all agreed performance-dependent development activity, as planned?

7. *Information about you*

☑ How do you feel about your performance, your role, your work, your place in the team, etc.?

☑ What preferences do you have for next year?

8. *Ready yourself*

☑ Assemble all the above information and be familiar with it.

☑ Make sure you are able to present your information, opinions, ideas and needs; practise with a colleague if it helps.

☑ Review and revise whatever skills you use—questioning, listening, giving feedback, etc.

☑ Know yourself—review your interpersonal strengths and weaknesses, including biases you may have about your manager or work colleagues.

☑ Prepare any feedback for your manager.

☑ Consider what you need from your manager in the next period.

Manager preparation

Some managers do not prepare because they expect their employees to present and argue their case. In the extreme, some managers have said that their role is to be the 'judge'. This is wrong—the outcome of this process must be that you and your employee reach a *just and committed agreement* on the review evaluation. This means that you are both responsible for being prepared to present and discuss your views.

There are many reasons why you should prepare—here are some of the important but often overlooked reasons.

• Cost—it uses less time to get it right first time.
• Gain a complete view—a whole year is a long time to review.
• Gain a broader view—step back from day-to-day work to get an overall view of personal effectiveness.
• Confidence and comfort—the better you are prepared, the better you will facilitate the meeting.

- Relationship—the better prepared you are, the more skilfully you will be able to manage the relationship while also managing the process and content.
- Your self-awareness—knowing your own strengths and weaknesses will play a role in the outcome.

Manager preparation is addressed in five parts—(1) review the assignment or agreement, (2) review the operating environment, (3) review performance achievement, (4) draft workforce developmental ideas and (5) personal preparation. You could summarise the key headings of this topic and produce a check list for yourself, as we did for employees.

Review the assignment or agreement

Before you begin to review performance, ensure that you are working with the right Work Assignment or performance agreement and content. You also need to understand it.

Start by identifying the latest agreed assignments, goals or tasks that will be part of the review. This is particularly important when there have been significant changes during the year. The picture will be clearer if there have been interim formal reviews.

Review associated priorities, measures and personal accountabilities for each assignment or goal.

- **Priorities**
  First, identify those goals or measures agreed to be essential or non-essential and then any form of priorities assigned. Check for any unrecognised and competing priorities. A competing priority that may occur is one where additional work is added to existing performance requirements, without any relative prioritisation of the original work and the new work.
- **Measures**
  Check to see that you understand the measures, that they still seem to be appropriate and that they are the ones for which you have data. In checking they are appropriate, use the approach in the Performance Data Model. You should also know where the influence and accountability lies—Drivers or Outcomes.
  If you find any anomalies or faults, discuss them with your employee before you proceed because you need to know the assumptions your employee has been using.

- **Personal accountabilities**
  With each assignment or agreement the employee should have formed an understanding of their associated personal responsibility requirement. Therefore, you should review whether the expectations and limitations of the work defined and agreed between you and, if so, what were the expectations and limitations.

Review the operating environment

When the agreement was set up, assumptions would have included the expected and planned operating environment—for example, management support, resources and infrastructure. The four basic issues you need to review are:

- What was included in your planning assumptions?
- What was agreed with the employee?
- What variations in the operating environment, if any, have occurred?
- What was the likely performance impact of any variations?

Review performance achievement

Once you have a fix on the target goals, measures and accountabilities, the next steps are to source the performance data and then to determine work achievement and personal effectiveness.

Sources of data would have been agreed at the time of Work Assignment/performance agreement or at subsequent discussions. No new measures, data or data sources should be introduced at the time of review, unless agreed with your employee. As well as the performance data used to manage the work, you should also have data from interim formal reviews and notes from on-the-job performance discussions and observations.

- **Performance data from the employee**
  One important source that is often neglected in preparing for evaluation is the employee, particularly in relation to personal effectiveness (skill and will). Talk with your employee before the formal meeting so that you can separate data collection from evaluation, resulting in more honest and comprehensive information.
- **The 'Right Data'**
  The Performance Data Model specified three steps to ensuring you have the 'Right Data'. Two measures that are specific to *evaluation* are

employees' skills and abilities and their exercise of personal responsibility. Sourcing the Right Data in this case requires particular
caution with respect to Validity and Reliability.

Validity describes the extent to which the data relates to the
measure. The traps are: people give you what they want you to know;
or you select information that supports your opinion but which may
not be valid data for the chosen measure.

Reliability describes the quality of your data. Your choice of data
might be valid but the source or quantity may not support your conclusion. Reliability applies particularly in the use of three types of
data pairs where one in each pair is intrinsically more reliable than
the other.

Intrinsically more reliable	Intrinsically less reliable
Quantitative	Qualitative
Objective	Subjective
Primary	Secondary

The first two pairs were covered in Chapter 5. Primary data is information that is gathered first hand (e.g. by observing an employee's
behaviour) and secondary data is obtained from others (e.g. by
someone telling you about your employee's behaviour).

- **Performance data from third parties**
Third-party data requires a reliability check because it is not always
correct and certainly not always impartial. This sort of information
comes to us as either formal or informal feedback.

Formal feedback commonly comes from a questionnaire admin-
istered to colleagues, customers or suppliers and allows you to track
an employee's progress over time. Its validity depends a lot on respondents' interpretation of the questions so, if in doubt, double-check
with the source.

Conversations, prompted by you or another person, provide
informal feedback on your employee's performance. This method is
more unreliable but a few bits of structure can make a difference. For
example, structure some questions to focus the respondent on specific
areas, ask questions about consistency, specifics and examples. In
particular, probe for more information on short answers rather than
accepting at face value those views that support your own.

When it comes to determining achievement, the technical aspects of reviewing work performance are covered in Chapter 7. Three additional points are relevant during preparation.

- **Include lead measures**

  The performance data used in the evaluation process should include lead measures, even when the employee is accountable for lag measures. It is only in this way that you can fully understand *personal effectiveness*.

- **Avoid evaluation**

  Making evaluation decisions at this stage is a waste because your review still requires input from the employee. It's also unwise because it may bias your views and arguments in the formal discussion.

- **Special circumstances**

  If an employee's situation has changed during the review period and you didn't revise the measures or targets at the time, revise them now, rather than 'take the special circumstances into account'. The first reason for this is so that you don't set up an employee to fail, and the second reason is that, if one person's performance is expected to be down, you must pick up the work-unit performance in other ways.

In the process of determining achievement, you should be forming ideas for providing feedback for the employee. While specific-item feedback, good or bad, should be handled on the job, at the time, the formal review is an opportunity to reflect on the *whole* of the employee and to provide them with some form of overall acknowledgment. In your preparation, think about contributions that the employee has made to the work unit, to the business or to your work, and be specific.

Draft workforce developmental ideas

In this preparatory review phase you are looking at all your employees at more or less the same time. This is fertile ground for seeing potential for improvement in various aspects of the work system—structure, roles or employee skills. Beware the downside of going into the one-on-one review discussions with a vested interest in particular solutions.

Personal preparation

The following pointers on personal preparation address both your intrinsic capability and your technique.

- **Know your intentions**

  What you intend is what you are more likely to get so it is better to go into the process with some preferred intentions. There is a balance here though, between having an intention and being *attached to* a particular result, such as, 'There's no way that he'll get a "Met" for that one', which would bias the evaluation.

- **Know your capability**

  Review your interpersonal strengths and weaknesses, including biases you may have about this employee or the process. Review and revise your knowledge of the meeting structure, review and evaluation process and follow up procedures. Review and revise whatever skills you use—for example, questioning, listening, giving feedback.

- **Prepare and practise**

  Prepare to be able to present your information, opinions, ideas and needs; practise with a colleague often helps when you are nervous or if you have a particularly challenging review to conduct.

- **Develop 'prompt' questions**

  Prompts help to get your employee talking, either to get them involved or to encourage an expansive response to a question if your employee tends to give one-word answers. Open questions are important here, for example:

  'What in particular do you like about the way you handled that?'

  'That was a good result, what was the biggest challenge for you?'

  'For example?'

- **Develop guidepost phrases**

  Transitions in conversation are difficult for many people—closing off one topic and moving to another. Sometimes a topic doesn't come to a natural conclusion, so you have to bring it to one: 'Well, I think we've covered all we can on this, is there anything else before we move on?'

- **Consider risk management**

  When your preparation indicates difficulties that may arise in the discussion, think through beforehand the outcomes of your proposed direction so that you can *manage any risks*. For example, you may know that an employee expects a favourable evaluation but the information suggests otherwise. The risks may range from disappointment and upset through to subsequent withdrawal of full services or sabotage. Consider both the likely responses from the employee and how you will handle them in a way that protects the business and is empowering for the employee. The employee's responses are his own responsibility but you can help him to handle this responsibility by being empathetic and by listening to his concerns.

Evaluation phase

This phase includes the actual face-to-face meeting and discussion, as well as the necessary follow-up steps leading to ratification of the evaluation. Perhaps the greatest ability you need to bring to this particular task is that of being able to handle sensitive issues and make wise decisions. Because the outcomes of a formal evaluation include such personally important issues as sense of worth, reputation, career and remuneration, they are more far-reaching and more difficult to reverse than those of on-the-job decisions.

The review and evaluation meeting

Most managers experience at least some degree of apprehension when it comes to these discussions. It seems that no matter how well a manager and employee may discuss performance issues on a day-to-day basis, there is something about the formality and consequence of the formal review meeting that adds a dimension of anxiety for both parties. Our aim in this topic is to provide some processes to help the flow and some 'tips and traps' to aid the quality.

Principles

The principles of evaluation have already been discussed but it is worth reminding yourself of the intent of this process—that you and your employee reach an accurate and just agreement on the employee's personal performance and evaluation.

Three further principles, which relate to the discussion, need consideration.

- *Equity*. Employees who have a good grasp of performance concepts, are articulate and who get on well with people have a far greater probability of a favourable review than employees who lack any or all of these attributes. One way to achieve equity is for employees to take responsibility for presenting their achievements clearly and the other and most significant way is for you to support your people in presenting their performance as completely and honestly as possible. Adopt the mindset of *enabling your employees to be the best they can* in the meeting.

- *No surprises.* No employee should hear about a performance issue for the first time at the meeting; any problems should have been confronted on the job.
- *Accept your part.* When shortcomings in your management show up during the process, accept them, work with them as part of the facts, and then move on.

A meeting or discussion structure

One consistent factor in enabling managers to facilitate effective formal review meetings is (a) to have an effective structure and process, and (b) to stay with it. A structure helps you to keep on track and to free your mind to be able to deal with the content and the person.

The process we use is based on the practices of successful managers. Whether you follow the process literally or simply use the principles and logic you will find it useful. The process steps are shown below, followed by a detailed description of how you handle each step. .

SET-UP
  1. Create the environment
  2. Ensure employee is ready
  3. Confirm the meeting process

BUSINESS
  4. Review and confirm the performance plan or agreement
  5. Review and evaluate each goal or task
  6. Overall evaluation
  7. Personal review and acknowledgement

CLOSE
  8. Next steps
  9. Review the meeting

COMPLETING THE BUSINESS
  10. Complete outstanding issues

11. Reflection and reality check
12. Formally record the review and evaluation
13. Confirm with employee

In the discussion of each step of the meeting we cover the purpose of the step, the method and some 'tips and traps'.

Managing the set-up

1. Create the environment
The purpose of this step is to create an environment for informed and trusting participation.

Method
- Help the employee to feel comfortable.
- Outline the purpose of the meeting.
- Establish or reinforce up front a collaborative process.
- Assure the employee that you want to work with facts, not assumptions.
- Assure the employee that you intend to support them, that this is not adversarial.

Tips
- Allow some space for the employee to speak so they become more relaxed.
- If necessary, use open questions.

Traps
- Don't get drawn into specific performance issues at this time.
- If the employee indicates unwillingness in the process, attempt to confirm the purpose before you move to address the issue in Step 2.

2. Ensure employee is ready
The purpose of this step is to ensure that the employee has prepared and is willing to participate. If either of these conditions is not met, the outcome of the process is compromised.

Method
- Check how they feel about the meeting (willingness).
- Check what preparation they have done.
- If they've not prepared, decide whether to reconvene or proceed.

Tips
- If an employee is not willing, the reason may be disagreement with the idea of evaluation, lack of trust in the fairness of the process, premonition of a poor outcome or a feeling that you have already made up your mind.
- If an employee has not prepared, find out *why* before deciding on action.

Traps
- Assuming that all employees are participating willingly.
- Proceeding without taking account of an unwilling participant.

3. Confirm the meeting process

The purpose of this step is to create a greater sense of collaboration and the ability of the employee to take shared responsibility for the meeting.

Method

Discuss:
- structure/process/agenda of the meeting;
- meeting roles and responsibilities;
- time limits (and what action if out of time);
- your and employee's expectations;
- provision for note-taking; and
- what follow-up will occur.

Tips
- If you want time to reflect before making a final evaluation, advise employees up front.
- If the evaluation will be reviewed or moderated by your own manager, remind employees.

Traps
- You are so task-focused or nervous that you skip this step.
- You don't check that the employee actually understands before you move on.

Managing the business of the meeting

The order of play is very important here, particularly to ensure that the overall evaluation reflects the discussion.

4. Review and confirm the performance plan or agreement

The purpose of this step is to ensure that you are both working with the same information.

Method
- Confirm the detail of the assignment or agreement, including priorities and planning assumptions.
- Confirm any changes throughout the year or since the last formal review.
- Confirm any exceptions from the evaluation process.

Tips
- Prior to this meeting, work with each employee to ensure that their plan or agreement is correct and up to date.
- Resolve any discrepancies before engaging in the review.

Traps
- Ignoring or rushing this process and ultimately evaluating the wrong thing.

5. Review and evaluate each goal or task

Your purpose is to proceed in a logical way that enables you to reach an evaluation that is as objective as possible. Refer to Figure 11.2 (Chapter 11) for a reminder of how an evaluated performance agreement might look.

Method
- Agree the order of reviewing goals or tasks.
- Review achievement, using the methods from Chapter 5.
- Evaluate, using the methods in Chapter 11.
- Complete and agree one goal or task at a time.

Tips
- Do the 'hard yards' of logic and negotiation in this step, where you can exercise objectivity. Once you reach overall evaluation, the die is already cast.
- When you have an issue that you can't resolve, break the continuity in some way before resuming (but beware the associated 'trap', below).
- If certain elements are shared between goals, deal with each goal independently. The risk, otherwise, is a compromise in quality of evaluation.

Traps
- If you have to defer an issue, ensure that you have a system for coming back to it; deferment often leads to hard issues ultimately being skipped and to subsequent disagreements.

6. Overall evaluation

The purpose here is to bring together the evaluation of individual goals or tasks into one overall evaluation. Some organisations require that you agree the overall evaluation with your senior manager before agreeing it with your employees.

Method
- Explain and/or confirm the evaluation process and rationale.
- Confirm any exclusions from the overall evaluation.
- Determine the evaluation, based on your organisation's method.
- Seek and/or confirm agreement.
- If your evaluations will be reviewed or moderated by your own manager, remind your employees.

Tips
- Confirm that the employee is in agreement with the evaluation of *individual* goals, before you engage in overall evaluation.
- Maintain your objectivity and don't be lured back into subjectivity by any narrative that accompanies your final evaluation descriptions or guidelines.
- Ensure that the employee understands the underlying meaning of the particular evaluation.

Traps
- In some cases the final evaluation may challenge your preconceptions of the employee—that is, their evaluation may look better or worse than your preconception. You may be tempted to go back to individual goal evaluations and 'review' them to assure your preconceived overall rating.
- The employee has agreed with individual evaluations but disagrees with the overall one.
- In comparing period with period, you confuse the evaluation with actual performance.

7. Personal review and acknowledgment

The purpose of this step is to develop an overall view of the employee's strengths and weaknesses and to give acknowledgment.

Method
- Explore separately the employee's *role-related* strengths and weaknesses and those that are *intrinsic* (relate to the person).
- Acknowledge the employee's contribution over the year.

Tips
- Use the performance feedback model (S-I-R).
- Use open questions to uncover the employee's views.
- Acknowledge specifics about the person.

Traps
- You sound as if you are going through the motions.
- You find it hard to acknowledge the successes of an employee you don't like.

Managing the close

Many review meetings come to a sudden halt once the business is complete, with the problem that any misunderstandings may come back to haunt us. The 'close' stage involves clarifying the next steps in the process and confirming agreements and responsibilities.

8. Next steps

The purpose of this step is to make sure that the employee knows what to expect next.

Method
- Advise what happens next to complete the evaluation process.
- Advise what happens next with any associated processes, such as remuneration.
- Advise and agree respective action responsibilities for next steps.
- Advise expected timings.

9. Review the meeting

The purpose is to ensure that you and your employee go away with the same set of understandings.

Method
- Confirm the purpose of the evaluation process.
- Confirm what was covered at the meeting (optional).
- Confirm mutual understanding of decisions made.
- Confirm mutual understanding of actions agreed.

Completing the business

Once the meeting is over there is still important work before it is complete. Although completion activity takes place outside the meeting, we treat it as part of the meeting. The following four tasks cover the common completion issues.

10. Complete outstanding issues

Issues that could not be resolved at the meeting will require further work before you reconvene to complete them.

Tips
*   Make the next discussion soon so that you both retain an awareness of the overall picture.
*   Allow a certain amount of completions buffer time when you schedule the review process with your team.
*   Do what you undertake to do.

11. Reflection and reality check

Take time to step back and look at the whole picture, including any positive or negative bias you may have introduced into the evaluation.

Tips
*   Do it early, while your memory is fresh.
*   If, on reflection, something that was agreed doesn't look right, don't unilaterally change it but discuss it again with your employee.
*   Review from a whole team perspective to detect any flaws that you may have built into the work system.
*   Consider whether your evaluations reflect the business performance of your work or business unit. If they don't, investigate the reason.

12. Formally record the review and evaluation

In many cases, you will not complete the formal write-up of the review and evaluation during the meeting, but will do it afterwards The purpose of the formal record is to reflect what was agreed and to provide input into other organisational processes.

Tips
*   If there are gaps in your information from the meeting, check with your employee—don't guess it.

- Watch your language! Don't put any *assumptions* on the record—for example, 'Not committed to the team'—they have a way of later appearing to be *reality*.

13. Evaluation confirmed with employee

The purpose of this step is to ensure that the employee agrees your record of outcomes of the meeting. Depending on your own system, this may lead to your employee signing the record, or it may go to your own manager for review before employee ratification.

Tips
- If the employee disagrees, check first whether it's a misinterpretation of your words. Clarify before you defend because there may be no real disagreement.
- If there is disagreement with a fact, it may be a genuine misunderstanding of what was agreed, not necessarily a renegotiation by the employee.
- If the employee wants to renegotiate, first establish whether it is a disagreement supported by fact or simply a dislike of the outcome. Deal with each on its merits.
- Even if the evaluation is to be reviewed by a senior manager, the employee should confirm your notes and what was agreed beforehand.

It's not all plain sailing

Difficult situations often arise during the review meeting and include both technical and interpersonal difficulties. The general difficulties you might encounter (e.g. 'red herrings') are covered in Chapter 8 but there are several specific problems that managers commonly encounter. We list them briefly below and provide some ideas on how you might handle them.

Work Assignment issues
Includes
- Unclear assignment of work, measures, process, authority, etc.
- Conflicting or unclear priorities.
- 'That's not my job.'
- Negative performance influences, not predicted in the assignment or planning.

Responses
- Help the employee to explain what they understood in the first place and the logic of their understanding.
- Ask the employee to describe their subsequent actions and decisions and the work results they did achieve, based on their understanding.
- Test whether the employee fulfilled their personal responsibility requirement once they became aware of a problem with the assignment.

Achievement issues

Includes
- Can't agree the performance data or its interpretation.
- Employee claims that failure to achieve was not their fault or was out of their control.
- A personal problem has hindered achievement.

Responses
- Establish the reality of the situation.
- Review the original Work Assignment or performance agreement.
- Test whether the employee fulfilled their personal responsibility requirement once they became aware of a problem.
- Foster a collaborative approach to the discussion.

Employee difficulties

Includes
- Non-participative employee.
- Employee handles 'reviewee' role badly.

Responses
- Assure the employee of your support in the process.
- Use the performance feedback model to create discussion on the problem.
- Consider the feedback recovery model.

Manager difficulties

Issues
- You find yourself solving all performance problems with 'training'.
- You find yourself deferring difficult problems for later consideration at 'a meeting' or by 'a committee'.
- Employee claims that you're biased against them.

Responses
- Check your motives.
- Put energy and courage into uncovering the real problems for under-performance.
- Develop skills in confronting difficult intellectual or interpersonal issues.
- Consider the Feedback Recovery Model.

Ratification of evaluations

Once manager and employee have finally agreed the review and evaluation it has to be ratified—that is, they both sign the evaluation. In most cases, this is a straightforward step after the agreement has been documented. In other cases, the employee either appeals the evaluation, or the organisation requires moderation by a senior manager (Figure 12.1).

Our focus is on your role in the process of ratification, particularly once it moves 'out of your hands', where most managers hand over all responsibility.

Moderation of evaluations

One commendable form of moderation is for senior managers to exercise some quality control over the way their subordinate manager has conducted the process. The other form of moderation involves ensuring that the distribution of evaluations matches a predetermined pattern ('normalisation'), as discussed in Chapter 11.

In cases where the senior manager is performing quality control, you will automatically be involved, but when the aim is to normalise you *should* be involved to ensure that your employees are treated fairly in the process. Evaluations based on *ranking* logically fit better with normalisation, whereas to normalise a *rating* type of evaluation is to distort the facts by converting it into a ranking. Employee responses are generally in accord with whichever is the case.

Managing the outcome of moderation
The moderation process is dictated mostly by an organisation's procedures but if you are willing you should be able to influence a proper outcome. Here are some key points to get you started on your strategy.

- Have a clear preferred outcome.
- Know the process and prepare.
- Argue to be in on the deliberation.
- Be willing to argue the outcome, based on 'best for the person, best for the business'.

Managing an appeal process

Occasionally, you and your employee will fail to agree on some aspect of their evaluation and you will be faced with an appeal against your conclusions. You need to be prepared to handle such a contingency as well as you handle all other aspects of managing your employees.

Appeals are usually to a senior manager who will look at both views and then make a binding decision. In some organisations, the appeal may escalate upwards to a defined level of management.

The following ideas are directed towards appeals which are not vexatious and which are being handled internally—that is, not legally or industrially. They also apply only if you are not a vexatious manager.

- Go as far as you can to avoid going to appeal. A useful extension of this approach is to select a *mediator* whose role is to help you both to explore and explain your views, with the decision still up to the both of you.
- The appeal is against your decisions, not you, so don't make it personal.
- Maintain the relationship, team morale and the team's work output.
- Even within an appeal process, continue to be responsible for the performance, development and welfare of the employee concerned.
- Work towards 'win–win'; 'win–lose' is bad for business.
- Publicise your stance on appeals—for example, advise employees that genuine appeals are respected but vexatious claims are likely to place employees outside the team and organisational values.

Ratifying the evaluation with your employee

Finally, there comes a point when you sit down with each employee, you say that this is the completed review and you both ratify it. This may occur immediately the review discussion is formally written up, or it may occur after moderation or even after an appeal process.

When the evaluations have been moderated and all evaluations confirmed, remember to advise your employees promptly, as some may be anxious. For unfavourable changes, here are some tips:

- Make sure you discuss with employees the nature and logic of the changes.
- When you have to communicate a change that has had a corporate or 'political' motive, do what you can to be honest by presenting the real problem, so that your employees understand that this was not simply a thoughtless or uncaring decision. It might have been a bad decision, but it was an open decision. Also ask what you can do to moderate your employees' concerns.
- Be prepared to discuss implications and options with an affected employee.
- Don't 'cop out' of discussing bad news by blaming the senior manager—it doesn't help the employee and it makes you look weak.

Integration of the completed evaluation

Once the task of evaluation is over there is a risk that we breathe a sigh of relief and then promptly drop the ball on the immediate tasks of completing the business. Integration basically comprises three streams— (1) review the process, (2) complete what was agreed and (3) manage business and organisational integration.

Review the process

The conduct of formal review and evaluation can always be improved. When the process is complete, sit down with your team and discuss what went well, and what didn't, and ways to improve for next time.

Complete what was agreed

The need to complete what was agreed is self-evident but what is needed is some ways of ensuring that you do it. Here are some examples:

- A written schedule or action plan.
- A process for monitoring implementation.

- A schedule for regularly reporting to your manager, your team, or both.
- A process for evaluating the result.

Manage business and organisational integration

Many actions arising from the evaluations require changes to business and organisational systems for them to be effective. Set yourself up with a plan to address these changes, and also involve relevant employees, to keep you on track.

Part V

Workplace Renewal

Having made it thus far in the book, we assume you are serious about creating high performance in your own workplace. This book has followed the two most basic forms of approaching the task, which are to:

1. create a culture and practice of good on-the-job performance management; and
2. use your existing performance management systems wisely and skillfully.

In creating a high performance workplace there are some gains you can make in your own right, for example, development of your skills, while other gains will only come with the involvement of others. This concluding part of the book deals with the changes that will need to occur, the potential barriers and the action required by you to bring about the necessary changes in yourself and in your workplace.

13 Creating a high-performance workplace

Introducing and maintaining new performance management practices will involve some degree of *change*—in you, your people and your workplace. The scope of such change might include the following:

- change in your approach to performance management;
- development of your abilities;
- change in your employees' approach to performance management;
- development of your employees' performance management abilities;
- development of your employees' work abilities; and
- change in work practices, processes and systems.

To be successful in bringing about a change in your workplace, you need to know something about the management of change. Many changes fail, either because they were not well planned or they lacked staying power. The following information is to help you create a successful change.

Strategies for change

Probably more management books and articles have been written on 'change' and 'change management' than almost any other topic. We have gathered from the collective published wisdom a summary five-strategy guideline which can be applied to the specifics of changing to a high-performance workplace.

1. Identify a compelling reason to change.
2. Create a team.
3. Develop a plan.
4. Communicate the change.
5. Maintain the change.

Identify a compelling reason to change

You create a compelling reason to change so that you can enlist the support of others, such as your staff, your manager and the other people or functions on whom your changes will depend. Reasons commonly come from both an *urgent need* and a promise of *something better*.

Increase the level of urgency

The reason for change must come from an inadequacy in the current situation, for example:

- *For your staff*—people are not fully recognised for their work; they have to work twice as hard, etc.
- *For your manager*—staff are underutilised, work systems are inefficient and costing money, etc.

Create a vision of something better

While the compelling reason to change is designed to disturb the status quo by highlighting the downside of not changing, the vision should present the upside, a worthwhile outcome of the change. Such a vision might include a greater sense of achievement and the opportunity to influence the way work is done.

Create a team

Depending on the scope of the change, it is wise not to try it on your own. For example, you could enlist the active support of your own manager or of another manager whom you trust, to help you. There may be people among your own staff who are committed and willing to be part of the 'change team'.

Develop a plan

For the change to have the best chance of succeeding you need to know *where* you want to go, the best *way* to go and by *when*. This simple view gives rise to four basic change-planning tools:

- 'Goals and gap' analysis;
- 'Force field' analysis;
- 'Ability to act' plan; and
- Action plan.

Goals and gap analysis

A useful starting point is to be clear about what outcome you want, preferably in detail. Next, look realistically at your current situation and form some idea of how far you will have to travel to bridge the gap. Knowing the nature and extent of the gap gives a factual basis on which to base your strategies. Figure 13.1 displays an example.

Force field analysis

To help in your planning for the change, think about the forces that already support your future performance management picture and the

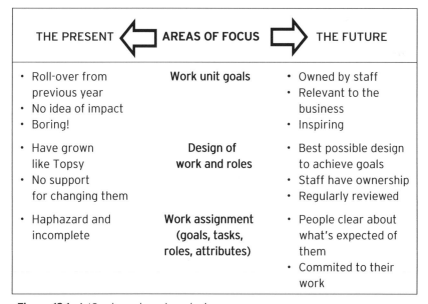

Figure 13.1 A 'Goals and gap' analysis

forces that might oppose it. With this insight you can look at your options more effectively. Gather all the information together first before looking at solutions, as many issues are common.

By way of example, a *supporting* factor might be that your employees have been asking for greater involvement in planning and work process improvement. Your *strategies* might include communicating to your staff the links between certain aspects of your new performance approach to greater employee involvement.

An *opposing* factor (a barrier) might be that most of your work practices are highly dependent on input from another function. Your *strategies* might include enlisting the manager of the other function to be part of your change team.

Ability to act plan

One of the most important steps in your strategy is to be clear on what you can change and what you can't. This reality check channels your effort into actions that have the greatest chance of success. The following is a very useful tool for sorting your options.

Sort your issues into groups 1, 2 or 3, as follows:
1. What you have the power to change *directly*;
2. What you can change by way of *influence*; and
3. What you can neither change nor influence (not ever or right now).
Within groups 1 and 2, set priorities. For group 3, put them aside or *let them go* totally.

Examples of group 1 might include: you, your people, work practices in your own area.

Examples of group 2 might include: senior management culture and practices, HR systems (such as performance management system, remuneration scheme), work practices in other areas that are integral to your own group's performance.

Examples of group 3 might include: industrial awards, shareholder expectations.

Action plan

As with any change, map out a timing schedule showing when key steps are to be achieved. You should also identify 'milestones', certain strategically important points along the way where you can stand back and check that you are on track. These are also the points where you can celebrate achievements (see below).

Introduce and bed down one change at a time. Many changes fall over because too much is attempted too soon and the expectations set up cannot be met. For example, you might start with Work Assignment basic practices for new assignments before even looking at planning or performance feedback.

Communicate the change

Quite clearly you need to communicate the change to your people so that you can influence their new thinking and behaviours. Here are some brief pointers on the 'what' and the 'how'.

What to communicate

These are some basic content areas, followed by comment on two of them:

- The urgency and the vision;
- The specific goals;
- The plan;
- The 'next steps';
- Achievements to date; and
- Whatever they want to know.

Sometimes, managers give their people the 'big picture' and gain their employees' commitment, but then fail to explain to them exactly what they have to do in order to realise the vision. You need to provide individuals with the specific 'next steps' required of them.

Check continually to find out what your people need to know—this may include reinforcement of existing communication or new issues that have arisen.

How to communicate

Communication is a book in itself but these points are particularly useful for managing change.

- Communicate personally, face to face, so that people take you seriously, they can get to trust you and you can determine what they understand. As well as yourself as the communicator, there is your 'team' and staff who take to the change early—'early adopters'.

- Information on change needs many exposures before it reaches everyone and has been understood by all. Remember that once is never enough and that you need to repeat the message, as many times and in as many ways as possible.
- Stay in touch with your people (a) to know what they understand about the change and your messages, and (b) to be informed of their experiences of the change, how it is working, how they are feeling and ideas for improvement.
- You and your change team will communicate more by what you do than by what you say. This means that you have to lead by example and that your example has to be visible.

Maintain the change

Apart from holding your own course, the most significant impact on the success of your change will be your people. This means that supporting your people is a paramount strategy. Following is a list of some key actions.

Remove barriers
Often people are willing but management has failed to detect organisational barriers, or actually unintentionally creates new barriers.

Support people
Change can be painful for some and change experts talk about the 'grief', the fear of actual or perceived loss associated with change and the fear of trying something new. Check how things are for your staff and show empathy.

In addition, let people be involved in planning their own journey; allow them to experiment, make mistakes and learn.

Focus on the converted
International change authority David Hutton[1] tells us that:

A. 20–30 per cent of employees commit early to the change.
B. 30–60 per cent wait and see and then go with the flow.
C. 20–30 per cent resist—actively or passively.

You should help and protect A and B, and use A as ambassadors. Don't try to convince C but, if they start to sabotage, neutralise their influence swiftly and effectively.

Celebrate wins
Recognise and celebrate short-term wins, to reward the followers and to let everybody know that you are on your way.

Strategies for you

The above strategies deal with managing the change and other people but you also have to consider the adjustment needed on your part and the support you may need.

Be willing to change first
Many managers see the need for change but point elsewhere for where the change should happen. The truth is most likely that some things 'out there' do need to change but the best place to start is where you have 100 per cent control, and that is with *you*. Here are the things you can change about yourself.

- Know yourself—your biases and assumptions about people, your knowledge and skill, strengths and weaknesses.
- Learn more about social and business changes and trends that affect your people and their work.
- Develop your own personal vision or view of the sort of performance manager you want to be.
- Follow through on the 'what you can do' sections of this chapter.

Allow time for change to occur
Change will occur at about one-tenth of the rate you would like, so be patient and don't interpret the slow pace as resistance. The advantage of setting milestones in your action plan is that you can reflect on what has already been achieved.

When you 'hit the wall'
We all know how marathon runners get to a point known as 'hitting the wall', the testing point where they are either made or broken. All leaders

who champion and relentlessly drive a change will at some time 'hit the wall', where the pain seems to outweigh the gain and everyone you trust tells you it was a bad idea, so just let it go! This is the point that will make or break you as a leader and your vision.

Remember, once you take a stand on something, you force others to take a stand as well—some will be with you and some will be against you.

Involve your own manager
You need your own manager's informed support; make it a Work Assignment so that it has importance and a priority in the scheme of things. Allow your manager to coach you and to hold you accountable for the results of the change.

Enlist peer support
This is a most important point. You shouldn't have to do it alone—there will be others who think as you do. Find and spend time with other managers of like mind. Even if you don't act as a team, at least support each other. You will get better support if you tell the truth about what you've tried, where you have succeeded and where you have failed. Often, because of the organisation's culture, many managers play 'tough' and don't disclose mistakes to their peers, thus forgoing the benefits of peer coaching, mentoring and support.

Take pride in becoming a better manager
Being a manager of the performance of other people is a privileged role. On the one hand it allows us to achieve greater results than we could alone and on the other we have the ability to affect the lives of others— our staff. Both aspects of the role should be taken seriously so as to provide best value for the enterprise and the best work fulfilment and reward for our people.

For this reason, the effort you put into becoming a better manager and the manager you become should be a source of pride to you.

Reference
1. D. Hutton, 'Survival skills for change agents—Part 5', *The Quality Magazine*, October 1995, 72–7.

Appendix 1 Examples of the environmental components of an open system of work

Environment and components	Examples
Individual work environment—where the employee has direct impact on the work	
Personal effectiveness	Task abilities, commitment, people abilities, ability to recognise exceptions, resourcefulness, initiative, relevant training and/or coaching provided, etc.
Work process	What happens between the start and the completion of the person's work
Management of resources	Materials, money, time, people, information, workload/competing priorities, etc.
Measures, measurement, feedback	Quality of performance measures, means of measurement, and quality of analysis and feedback
Effectiveness of own manager	Quality of the Work Assignment, role description, availability and approachability, feedback, coaching, etc.

Environment and components	Examples
Process environment—other parts of this work process, upstream or downstream; may include partnerships or alliances with outside organisations	
Upstream	Quantity, quality and timeliness of inputs to the work—from other staff, from suppliers, from partners or alliances
Downstream	Capability of the process; personal effectiveness of staff who have to further process the work
Systems capability	Capability of systems on which this process depends.
Quality of management support	Management's approach to this process—whether they are amenable to improvements, investment in the process, etc.
Enterprise environment—what happens in the rest of the organisation that has an impact on the work	
Culture, policies, strategies	Describes the overriding ideas or ideologies that influence decisions and behaviours
Enterprise systems	Refers to systems that affect more than just this work or this process; would include IT, communication, planning systems, etc.
Resources	Materials, money, time, people, information, access to people, priorities, etc. applied to this work and this process
Products or services	Performance, quality, price, range, availability, strength of brand name, etc.
External environment—outside the organisation or its alliances/partnerships	
Customers, the market, competitors	These are the factors that directly influence the enterprise's revenue stream

Community	Enterprises are increasingly subject to the influence of the communities in which they are allowed to operate (even the global community is catching up with global commerce)

Environment and components	Examples
Suppliers	Regularity of supply, reliability, stability of pricing, etc.
Government	Regulation, legislation, responsiveness to international or global events, policy, etc.
Globalisation	How wide do you have to extend your environmental scan?

Appendix 2 A tool for assessing performance management tensions

Managers are caught in the cross-fire between two dominant sets of opposing forces:

1. **Old assumptions versus the new reality**—the traditional assumptions about work, workers and management are out of sync with the new reality.
2. **Workplace versus corporate**—the requirements for actual on-the-job management of performance by employees and their managers are in conflict with performance management requirements by personnel/HR and executive management.

The degree to which these tensions exist will determine how easy or how hard it will be for you to adopt effective management practices and culture in your own work unit.

The following exercises are designed to help you understand the degree to which such tensions might exist in your organisation and the nature of such tensions. This is the starting point to your being able to take action to reduce the tensions.

Social and business assumptions versus reality

The decisions managers make about how to manage the enterprise business and the performance of their people are based on assumptions about the way things supposedly are. These assumptions are frequently based on a reality that existed once but now has ceased to exist in some industries and is in the process of disappearing in others.

Exercise A2.1 summarises some of the key differences between assumptions and reality that have the potential for tension. The chart is grouped under three headings—work itself, the workers and their management. The first two are obviously of relevance to managers as well.

To estimate the degree of assumption–reality tension, you are asked to work through the exercise, identifying both your assumptions and actual reality. This could be done at two levels—at the level of your own assumptions and the level of the assumptions of senior or executive management.

To complete the exercise yourself, you need to step out of your own assumptions and get a 'real' view of your workplace, but how do you do that? Imagine you are not an employee but an outsider—how would you view each of the listed issues then? Alternatively, or as well, ask other managers in your organisation, ask your employees or, if you are part of an industry group, ask other organisations. In doing this part of the exercise, you need to account not just for how things are now but in what direction they are moving.

Exercise A2.1

Tensions between managerial assumptions and reality—work, workers and management

Work through the chart, taking one line at a time

1. On a daily basis, do you operate more along the lines of A or B? Tick one. Continue until you have completed the 'Assumptions' questions.

2. Taking an 'outsider' view, what do you believe is the real situation in your workplace? Tick one of 'a' or 'b'. Continue until you have completed the 'Reality' questions.

	Assumptions: A or B			Emergent reality: a or b	
	A	B		a	b
WORK					
1 *Work environment*	stable, predictable	changing, less predictable	⇕	stable, predictable	changing, less predictable
2 *Planning focus*	mostly controllable outcomes; infrequent planning	mostly uncontrollable outcomes, continuous dynamic planning		mostly controllable outcomes; infrequent planning	mostly uncontrollable outcomes; continuous, dynamic planning
3 *Form of work*	activity-based, visible; fixed processes and structures	intellectual, invisible, relationships; dynamic processes and structures		activity-based, visible; fixed processes and structures	intellectual, invisible relationships; dynamic processes and structures

continues

4 Manageability	easy to manage; predictable responses to management actions	information overload; much trial and error management needed
WORKERS **5 Work contract**	company provides security and career in return for loyalty	low security; employees may have many careers—loyalty to self
6 Organisation	authority hierarchy, firm boundaries	matrix, teams, movable boundaries
7 Composition	permanent, full-time; mostly homogeneous (e.g. age, culture)	increasing part-time, casual; multicultural, transgenerational
MANAGEMENT **8 Role**	initiation and control	strategy and support
9 Value-added	task ability	situation and people management
10 Style	one style fits all	a range of styles—situational

continues

	Assumptions—A or B		Emergent reality—a or b	
	A	B	a	b
11 Means of control	authority, task knowledge	personal influence, management knowledge	authority, task knowledge	personal influence, management knowledge

Estimate the assumption–reality tension in your workplace

1. Go through your answers, one at a time and highlight the mismatches between assumptions and reality—that is, A-b or B-a paired responses. How many mismatches do you have?

2. The more mismatches you have, the greater will be the tension in your workplace as you attempt to manage your people's performance in the most effective way.

3. The lines that showed up as a mismatch are obviously the areas where you would need to take action.

4. If the mismatch is a result of your own assumptions, you need to get to know the reality better and to adjust your management practices or work systems to match the reality.

5. If the mismatch is in senior management assumptions, you need to use whatever channels are available to you (including in concert with other like-minded managers) to bring this mismatch to the attention of senior management.

Workplace priorities versus corporate priorities

When we look at what different groups want from a performance management system, we discover that there are often significant differences between the needs of the workplace, represented by *work groups and their direct managers*, on the one hand, and those of *personnel/HR and executive management*, on the other hand.

Exercise A2.2

Tension between performance management system priorities of two groups

For each work group priority in the following chart, estimate whether your own performance management system looks more like A or more like B. Mark the individual items that most closely represent your system.

WORK GROUP PRIORITIES	Our performance management system is more like: A or B	
	A	**B**
1 Has practical value	• practical perform-ance planning • skills development planning • clearly links to day-to-day realities • provides practical targets for daily work • provides data for on-the-job/day-to-day monitoring and management of performance • provides basis for on-the-job feedback for employees • enhances work satisfaction	• annual plan (only) • rigid system, not responsive to day-to-day realities of the work • looks at perform-ance retrospectively (fixed intervals—quarterly, annually, etc.) • judgmental (evaluates, asssesses, rates, ranks employees) • provides no management skills development for managing perform-ance

continues

WORK GROUP PRIORITIES	Our performance management system is more like: A or B	
	A	**B**
1 Has practical value	• positively motivates employees • positively motivates managers • develops management skills • develops employee skills in managing their own performance	• provides no employee skills development for managing performance • focus on the paperwork • time-consuming
2 Is manageable	• understandable • simple to use • links clearly to daily work • has supporting methods and tools • able to keep it up to date and relevant • provides employees and managers with the skills to use it	• complex, difficult to understand or use • weak or absent links to daily work • poorly described methods or principles; no tools • difficult to keep it up to date and relevant • doesn't provide employees or managers with the skills to use it
3 Is fair and equitable	• fosters cooperation as well as individual performance • targets are reasonably attainable • designed to minimise or control supervisor bias	• fosters internal competition, more than cooperation • targets may be set arbitrarily (at individual or work-group level) • allows supervisor bias

continues

WORK GROUP PRIORITIES	Our performance management system is more like: A or B	
	A	**B**
	• includes or links to a dispute or fair treatment system • promotes feedback for all • advocates skilled and fair feedback practices • advocates recognition • reward is based on personal effectiveness	• promotes management authority • does not include or has no links to a dispute or fair treatment system • no inbuilt provision for feedback or recognition • substantially influenced by concerns of short-term shareholder return • reward is based on other than personal effectiveness
4 Has integrity	• can trust management to apply the system, as promised • system exists to support people to do their best work	• management able to move the goal posts with respect to targets or rewards • a tool to penalise • sanctions-based motivation ('stick and carrot')

Estimate the workplace–corporate tension in your workplace
1. For any of the four priorities where you have said that your system is more like 'A', the system *coincides* with your work-group priorities and there is a *low tension* between your workplace and corporate.
2. For any priorities where you have said that your system is more like 'B', the system *conflicts* with your work-group priorities and there is a *high tension* between your workplace and corporate.

Appendix 3
Work templates

> ### *Work Assignment and Planning*–WORK TEMPLATE

PRE-MEETING CHECKLIST

Advise your employee:
☑ Purpose ☑ Intended outcomes
☑ Preparatory work ☑ What to bring

Your preparation:
☑ You understand the work assignment/know the content.
☑ What are any implications for the rest of the team?
☑ What are any implications for other parts of the business or organisation? e.g. Will the employee need the cooperation of another work group? How will the output affect downstream processes?
☑ What are any implications for other work of this employee? e.g. Will it take time from other work?
☑ What are the risks and consequences of non-achievement?
☑ Is there any potential role or goal ambiguity or conflict?

MEETING

SET-UP	Confirm purpose, agenda and timing, process, outcomes

BUSINESS
Process
Stay with the
process
Anchor milestones
Regular checks
Confirm outcomes
Agree to follow up
	PART A. **WORK ASSIGNMENT**
	Step 1. **Establish purpose and relevance of intended work assignment**
	Step 2. **Explore the current situation**
	Step 3. **Define the work**
	  ☑ Description
	  ☑ Dimensions–QQRT
	  ☑ Means

276

Skills	
Self-awareness *People are* *different* *Encourage* *self-discovery* *Question* *Listen* *Bias and* *assumptions* *Compassion +* *firmness*	Step **4.** Specify authority and accountability Step **5. Ensure system and personal capability** ☑ System ☑ Personal ☑ Planning implications Step **6. Agree performance management of the work** ☑ Measures ☑ Objectives `OUTPUTS ⇨ OUTCOMES` or standards ☑ Monitoring

PART B. *FACILITATED PLANNING*

Step **1. Review work assignment**
(If conducted at a separate meeting)
Step **2. Specify what planning is required and provide method and tools**
☑ Statement of work assignment
☑ Action plan
☑ Analysis-Strategy-Action plan
☑ Personal development plan
☑ Business plan
☑ Performance agreement
☑ Project plan
Date for plan to be reviewed/approved
Step **3. Ensure personal capability to plan**
☑ Assess
☑ Educate and train
☑ Coach
Step **4. Review and acknowledge the plan**
☑ Use questions to review
☑ Be specific with acknowledgment

CLOSE	☑ Confirm understanding and agreements ☑ Agree follow-up ☑ Review meeting effectiveness

Personal Development Plan
WORK TEMPLATE

Employee:

Manager:

Work unit:

Plan agreed
—date:

1. WORK OUTCOME SERVED

2. DEVELOPMENT OUTCOMES REQUIRED

3. DEVELOPMENT ACTIVITY

WORK OUTCOME	Priority	DEVELOPMENT OUTCOMES	Activity	Resources	By when

Performance Data Model — WORK TEMPLATE

THE RIGHT MEASURES

STEP 1 — Start with the Outcomes (*then* the Drivers)

STEP 2 — Confirm the agreed measures
- *Stay with what was agreed, or renegotiate*

THE RIGHT DATA

STEP 3 — Data supports the agreed measures (valid)
- *NO misattribution*
- *NO biased selection*

STEP 4 — Comparable ('apples with apples')
- *between People*
- *between Behaviours*
- *between Periods*

STEP 5 — Reliable
- *Sufficient and representative*
- *Unbiased*

THE RIGHT UNDERSTANDING

STEP 6 — Cause and effect

Outcomes on track (good performance)
- Drivers on track → PLANNING ASSUMPTIONS Okay
- Drivers not on track → TEST PLANNING ASSUMPTIONS REVISE PLAN

Outcomes not on track (performance problem)
- Drivers on track → FAULTY PLANNING ASSUMPTIONS REVISE PLAN
- Drivers not on track → GET DRIVER OUTPUT UP TO PLANNED LEVEL

NEW, UNKNOWN FACTOR EMERGED REVISE PLAN

– the Outcome-Driver Decision Tree

STEP 7 — Variation
- *between Periods* –'Normal Range' or case management
- *between People* – control and reduce variation
  – move the graph higher

STEP 8 — Capability
- *Accept as reality*
- *How 'wide' is Okay?*

and now, the Drivers . . .

Performance Feedback–MEETING TEMPLATE

PRE-MEETING CHECKLIST	**Advise your employee:** ☑ Consider impact of time and place

Your preparation:
☑ Performance data   ☑ Separate positive and negative (no 'buts')
☑ Likely difficult responses ☑ Don't overload

MEETING

SET-UP	*Confirm purpose, agenda and timing, process, outcomes*
BUSINESS	Agreement on:

Outcomes
• *Correction or consolidation*
• *System development*
• *Coaching*
• *Learning and development*
• *Recognition and reward*
• *Discipline*
• *Evaluation*
 	
⌘ ⌘ ⌘ ⌘
 	
Key elements
• *Motivation and mood*
• *Be honest*
• *Respect and dignity*
• *Prepare to receive*
• *Avoid 'but'*
• *Keep it manageable*
• *Facts, not assumptions*
• *Specific*
• *Involve employee*
 	
⌘ ⌘ ⌘ ⌘
	1 **P**articipation
	   –a committed partner in the process
	   ☑ Intention
	   ☑ Language
	
	2 **S**ituation
	   –understand aspect of the employee's performance that is the subject of feedback
	   ☑ Facts, not assumptions or opinions
	   ☑ Explore
	   ☑ Be honest
	   ☑ Don't leap ahead
	
	3 **I**mplications
	   –understand consequences of the employee's performance
	   ☑ Business Outcomes or Drivers, not personal
	   ☑ Motive for change
	   ☑ Context for change
	   ☑ No judgment

Self-awareness
People are
different
Questions
Active listening
Bias and
assumptions
Compassion +
firmness

4 Resolution
−bring issues to a completion
☑ *A response is not a resolution*
☑ *Resolution = verbal conclusion, immediate action or decision on future action*
☑ *Balance directing and discussing*
☑ *Avoid underreaction and overreaction*

5 Integration
−ensure that changes will be supported back in the workplace
☑ *Same wavelength*
☑ *System resources*
☑ *Conditional performance*

Recovery model
• red herring • road block • confusion
• swamp • new information
1. Stop and regroup
2. Stay with the process
3. Deal with the concern or emotion: Embrace, Empathise, Explore, Export (relate or re-assign)
4. Acknowledge employee's personal validity

CLOSE MEETING

Agree follow-up
Review meeting effectiveness

Performance Coaching–WORK TEMPLATE

PRE-SESSION CHECKLIST | **Advise your employee:** ☑ Consider impact of time and place

Your preparation:
☑ Review coaching qualities   ☑ Personal effectiveness issue
☑ Review coaching skills   ☑ High/low will and skill
☑ Review feedback session or previous coaching session

COACHING SESSION

SET-UP

A. Set up the coaching agreement
☑ Confirm the overall aim and purpose
☑ Coaching to (a) reach performance expectations, or (b) build on good performance, or (c) resolve a difficult performance issue
☑ Mutual commitment to the process
☑ Discuss and agree coaching method

COACH
   Your coaching capability

B. Begin with the current work method
☑ You can't improve what you don't understand
☑ Apply the five action learning steps to the current work

Coaching qualities
• *Self-awareness*
• *Trustworthy*
• *Desire to develop others*

C. Action learning cycle of coaching
   1. Intend
   A clear intention is essential for learning
☑ Be specific

Coaching skills
• *Feedback*
• *Communication*
• *A 'pull' energy*
• *Create a learning culture*

☑ Work on, or change, one thing at a time
☑ Talk through the new behaviours or practices
☑ Demonstrate

   2. Act
☑ Encourage to do as intended; avoid ad hoc 'improvements'

☑ Monitor
☑ Help to keep focus: *'Mind your feet!'*

The coaching process
ANALYSIS
COMMUNICATION
ACTION

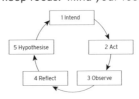

*Performance
capability*
WILL ⟷ SKILL

Learning ability
· *Experience*
· *Trust*
· *Awareness*
· *Follow plan*
· *Perseverance*
· *Risk*

**Employee's
capability**

3. Observe
☑ On-the-job observation or self-reporting
☑ Intention does not automatically translate into action
☑ Suspend judgment

4. Reflect
☑ When intention is not enacted
☑ Plan or execution?
☑ Confirm success and learning

5. Hypothesise
☑ What if we change the objective?
☑ What if we change the plan?
☑ What if we change the execution?

© 1997–2001. Amadeus Performance Systems

Action Learning Guide for Developing Personal Effectiveness

1 Intend

5 Hypothesise   2 Act

4 Reflect   3 Observe

A clear intention is essential for learning

*Focus on **one thing at a time***

What I intend to **do** is:

1. ....

2. ....

3. ....

. . . with the intention of creating the following **results**:

1. ....

2. ....

---

1 Intend

5 Hypothesise   **2 Act**

4 Reflect   3 Observe

Keep focus:
'Mind your feet!'

How do I ensure that I will do what I intend?
What on-the-job factors might inhibit me from carrying out my intention?

People..

Processes ....

Resources/time ....

(Other) ....

What personal factors might inhibit me from carrying out my intention?

My fear ....

My will ....

(Other) ....

---

1 Intend

5 Hypothesise   2 Act

4 Reflect   **3 Observe**

Suspend judgment

1. **What happened?**
What did I **do**? ....

What did others **do**? ....

2. **What was the result** in relation to my intended outcomes?

Objective # 1. ....

Objective # 2. ....

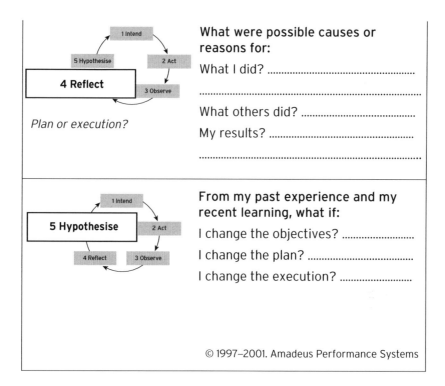

What were possible causes or reasons for:

What I did? ....

....

What others did? ....

My results? ....

....

From my past experience and my recent learning, what if:

I change the objectives? ....

I change the plan? ....

I change the execution? ....

Further reading

Part I

Callus, R. et al. 1991. *Industrial Relations at Work: the Australian Workplace Industrial Relations Survey*, AGPS, Canberra.

Conger, J. 1997. 'How generational shifts will transform organisational life', in F. Hesselbein et al. (eds) *The Organisation of the Future*, Jossey-Bass, San Francisco.

Dowling, P. & Fisher, C. 1999. 'Support for an HR approach in Australia: the perspective of senior HR managers', *Asia Pacific Journal of Human Resources*, 37(1): 1–19.

Grint, K. 1991. *The Sociology of Work*, Polity Press, Cambridge.

Hunter, J. 1991. *Supervision, The Australian Context*, McGraw-Hill, Sydney.

James, D. 'Nightmare on mahogany row: the unmanageable workforce', *Business Review Weekly*, 1 March 1999, pp. 58–9.

Kramar, R. 1999. 'Policies for managing people in Australia: what has changed in the 1990s?', *Asia Pacific Journal of Human Resources*, 37(2): 24–32.

Morehead, A. et al. 1997. *Changes at Work*, Longman, South Melbourne.

Nankervis, A. & Leece, P. 1997. 'Performance appraisal: two steps forward and one step back?', *Asia Pacific Journal of Human Resources*, 35(2): 80–92.

Robbins, S.P. 1986. *Managing Human Resources*, Prentice Hall, Sydney, p. 4.

Williams, T. 1997. 'The end of supervision? A case study and critique of the attempted conversion of supervisors into team leaders', *Asia Pacific Journal of Human Resources*, 35(3): 62–79.

Part II

Harrington, H.J. 1991. *Business Process Improvement*, McGraw-Hill, New York.

McConnell, J. 1991. *Safer Than A Known Way*, Delaware Books, Manly Vale.

Mink, O.G., Schultz, J.M. & Mink, B.P. 1991. *Developing and Managing Open Organisations*, Austin, Somerset.

Scholtes, P. 1995. 'Performance appraisal: obsolete and harmful', *The Quality Magazine*, October, 66–70.

Sinclair, D. 1995. 'The new year's resolution school of management', *Management*, February, 22–24.

Walsh, P. 1995. 'Measuring business as usual', *The Quality Magazine*, December, 16–24.

Part III

Argyris, C. 1992. *On Organisational Learning*, Blackwell, Massachusetts.

Bandura, A. 1977. *Self-efficacy: The Exercise of Control*, Freeman, New York.

Heslin, P.A. 1999. 'Boosting empowerment by developing self-efficacy', *Asia Pacific Journal of Human Resources*, 37(1).

Revans, R. 1985. *Action Learning: Its Origins and Nature*, Gower, Aldershot, UK.

Webb, N. & Webb, J. 1993. 'An active approach to personal empowerment', *Management*, September, 26–29.

Webb, N. & Webb, J. 1994. 'A new paradigm for personal empowerment', *HR Monthly*, October, 12–15.

Part IV

Bradley, L.M. & Ashkanasy, N.M. 2001. 'Formal performance appraisal interviews: can they really be objective and are they useful anyway?', *Asia Pacific Journal of Human Resources*, 39(2): 83–97.

Marshall, V. & Wood, R. 2000. 'The dynamics of effective performance appraisal: an integrated model', *Asia Pacific Journal of Human Resources*, 38(3): 62–90.

Nankervis, A. & Leece, P. 1997. 'Performance appraisal: two steps forward and one step back?', *Asia Pacific Journal of Human Resources*, 35(2): 80–92.

Webb, J. & Murray, K. 1999. *Performance Management—Culture and Counter-culture*. Presented at the Australian Human Resources Institute Human Resources Week Conference, Canberra, August.

Index